걸프 사태

유엔안전보장이사회 동향 1

걸프 사태

유엔안전보장이사회 동향 1

한국학술정보

| 머리말

걸프 전쟁은 미국의 주도하에 34개국 연합군 병력이 수행한 전쟁으로, 1990년 8월 이라크의 쿠웨이트 침공 및 합병에 반대하며 발발했다. 미국은 초기부터 파병 외교에 나섰고, 1990년 9월 서울 등에 고위 관리를 파견하며 한국의 동참을 요청했다. 88올림픽 이후 동구권 국교 수립과 유엔 가입 추진 등 적극적인 외교 활동을 펼치는 당시 한국에 있어 이는 미국과 국제 사회의 지지를 얻기 위해서라도 피할 수 없는 일이었다. 결국 정부는 91년 1월부터 약 3개월에 걸쳐 국군의료지원단과 공군수송단을 사우디아라비아 및 아랍 에미리트 연합 등에 파병하였고, 군·민간 의료 활동, 병력 수송 임무를 수행했다. 동시에 당시 걸프 지역 8개국에 살던 5천여 명의 교민에게 방독면 등 물자를 제공하고, 특별기 파견 등으로 비상시 대피할 수 있도록 지원했다. 비록 전쟁 부담금과 유가 상승 등 어려움도 있었지만, 걸프전 파병과 군사 외교를 통해 한국은 유엔 가입에 박차를 가할 수 있었고 미국 등 선진 우방국, 아랍권 국가 등과 밀접한 외교 관계를 유지하며 여러 국익을 창출할 수 있었다.

본 총서는 외교부에서 작성하여 30여 년간 유지한 걸프 사태 관련 자료를 담고 있다. 미국을 비롯한 여러 국가와의 군사 외교 과정, 일일 보고 자료와 기타 정부의 대응 및 조치, 재외동포 철수와 보호, 의료지원단과 수송단 파견 및 지원 과정, 유엔을 포함해 세계 각국에서 수집한 관련 동향 자료, 주변국 지원과 전후복구사업 참여 등 총 48권으로 구성되었다. 전체 분량은 약 2만 4천여 쪽에 이른다.

2024년 3월

한국학술정보(주)

| 일러두기

· 본 총서에 실린 자료는 2022년 4월과 2023년 4월에 각각 공개한 외교문서 4,827권, 76만
여 쪽 가운데 일부를 발췌한 것이다.

· 각 권의 제목과 순서는 공개된 원본을 최대한 반영하였으나, 주제에 따라 일부는 적절히
변경하였다.

· 원본 자료는 A4 판형에 맞게 축소하거나 원본 비율을 유지한 채 A4 페이지 안에 삽입
하였다. 또한 현재 시점에선 공개되지 않아 '공란'이란 표기만 있는 페이지 역시 그대로
실었다.

· 외교부가 공개한 문서 각 권의 첫 페이지에는 '정리 보존 문서 목록'이란 이름으로 기록물
종류, 일자, 명칭, 간단한 내용 등의 정보가 수록되어 있으며, 이를 기준으로 0001번부터
번호가 매겨져 있다. 이는 삭제하지 않고 총서에 그대로 수록하였다.

· 보고서 내용에 관한 더 자세한 정보가 필요하다면, 외교부가 온라인상에 제공하는『대한
민국 외교사료요약집』1991년과 1992년 자료를 참조할 수 있다.

| 차례

정 리 보 존 문 서 목 록

기록물종류	일반공문서철	등록번호	2017060003	등록일자	2017-06-05
분류번호	731.33	국가코드	XF	보존기간	30년
명 칭	걸프사태 관련 유엔안전보장이사회 동향, 1990-91. 전5권				
생 산 과	국제연합과/중동1과	생산년도	1990~1991	담당그룹	
권 차 명	V.1 1990.8월				
내용목차	* 1990.8.2 긴급 안보리 회의 　　　- 이라크의 쿠웨이트 침공 규탄 결의안 (안보리 결의 660호) 채택 　8.6 안보리 속개 회의 　　　- 이라크에 대한 포괄적 경제제재 조치 결의안 채택 (안보리 결의 661호) 　8.9 안보리 속개회의 　　　- 이라크의 쿠웨이트 합병 무효 결의안 (안보리 결의 662호) 채택 　8.18 안보리 속개회의 　　　- 걸프사태 관련 결의안 (안보리 결의 664호) 채택 　8.25 안보리 속개회의 　　　- 결의안 661호 위반 선박에 대한 조치 권한 부여 　　　결의안 (안보리 결의 665호) 채택				

0001

長 官 報 告 事 項

1990. 8 . 2 .
中東.아프리카局
中近東課(27)

題目 : 이라크, 쿠웨이트 침공

이라크와 쿠웨이트간의 산유 및 국경 분쟁 해결을 위한 양국 회담이 결렬된 후, 이라크가 쿠웨이트를 침공 하였는바, 관련사항을 다음과 같이 보고 드립니다.

1. 상 황

○ 90.8.2. 새벽2시(한국시간 상오 8시) 이라크군 2개 사단 병력, 쿠웨이트 국경지대 압달라 지역 침공 개시

○ 이라크군 쿠웨이트 국왕 왕궁 포위 및 쿠웨이트 정부 청사 완전 장악

○ 이라크 혁명위 성명 발표

- 이라크의 쿠웨이트 침공은 자유 쿠웨이트 임시 정부의 요청에 의한 것임

- 이라크군은 사태 정상화 여부에 따라 수일 또는 수주내에 철수할 예정

※ 아국 교민 피해 전무 (8.2. 현지공관 보고 및 통화)

2. 배 경

○ 양국간 산유 분쟁으로 상호 강경 비난 및 아랍언맹 중재 촉구(7.17)

- 쿠웨이트내 "루마일라" 유전 지역을 이라크 영토라고 주장

○ 이집트.사우디 중재로 양국 회담 개최, 이라크 요구에 대한 쿠웨이트측 수락 거부로 회담 결렬(8.1. 쨋다)

0002

o 이라크 국내 경제 피폐 빛 종신 대통령제에 대한 국민 삼반 고조

3. 주요 국가 반응

o 미 국 : - 이라크의 쿠웨이트 침공 비난 및 이라크 군대의 무조건 침수
요구

- UN 안보리 긴급 회의 소집 요구 (90.8.2.)

o 호 주 : - 이라크의 쿠웨이트 침공 비난 및 이라크군 철수 요구

4. 분석 및 전망

o 이라크의 금번 쿠웨이트 침공은 걸프 역내의 패권 장악 시도

o 이라크의 대 쿠웨이트 부채 탕감 및 일부 영토 요구를 관철
시킬 것으로 봄

o 국제 원유가 상승 예상

o 국제적 관심 고조로 군사 행동 사태 장기화 되지 않을 것임

o 아랍권 전체와 원유 공급선등 중요성에 비추어 본질문제 해결은 많은 난관이
예상됨

5. 당부 조치 사항

o 주 이라크 및 쿠웨이트 대사관에 아국 교민 안전 대책 강구 및 사태 진전
사항 보고 지시 (90.8.2.)

o 주요 국가의 반응 및 사태 판단 파악 지시 (주요 공관)

o 공관 조치 사항

- 쿠웨이트 건설현장 인원을 캠프로 침수 (시내 출입 제한)

- 비상 연락망 유지, 비상시 철수 계획 점검

0003

〈참 고 자 료〉

1. 대 이라크,쿠웨이트 아국 진출 현황

가 . 이라크

  1) 건설현황

    ○ 진출건설업체 : 현대, 삼성, 정우, 한양, 대림, 남광,

       동아 (7개 회사)

    ○ 총 건설 수주 누계(81-89) : 6,439 백만불

  2) 교역현황

    ○ 진출상사 : 현대, 삼성, 대우, 국제상사, 선경, 효성(6개상사)

    ○ 수출액(89) : 67 백만불(고무제품, 섬유류, 철강류등)

       수입액(89) : 63 백만불(원유 〈99%〉)

  3) 교   민 : 621 명 (근로자 포함)

나 . 쿠웨이트

  1) 건설현황

    ○ 진출건설업체 : 현대, 대림, 효성중공업(3개 회사)

    ○ 총 건설수주 누계 (81-89) : 2,110 백만불

  2) 교역 현황

    ○ 수출액 (89) : 210 백만불(선박, 견직물, 전기기기, 철강)

    ○ 수입액 (89) : 381 백만불(원유, 구리제품)

  3) 교   민 : 706명 (근로자 포함)

0004

2. 이라크, 쿠웨이트간 군사력 비교 (89.90)

군별 국가명	이 · 라 크	쿠 웨 이 트
총 병력	1,850,000 명 (예비군 85만명 포함)	40,000 명 (예비군 2만명 포함)
육 군 (전 차) (각종 포 및 미사일)	955,000 명 6,600 대 4,034 문	16,000 명 625 대 400 문
해 군 (군 함)	5,000 명 100 척	2,100 명 55 척 (잠수함 2척 포함)
공 군 (전투기)	40,000 명 597 대	22,000 명 115 대
인구 및 면적	1,780 만명 44,000 ㎢	203 만명 17,818 ㎢

0005

발 신 전 보

번 호 : WUN-0949   900802 1920 EZ   종별 :

수 신 : 주 유엔   대사. 총영사

발 신 : 장 관 (국연)

제 목 : 이라크-쿠웨이트 분쟁

8.2. 이라크-쿠웨이트 간의 무력분쟁 발발과 관련、안보리의

관련 토의등 동향을 수시 보고바람·   끝·

(국제기구조약국장 문동석)

1990.12.31에 예고문에
의거 인반문서로 재분됨

앙고재	90년8월2일 ?과	기안자	과 장	국 장	차 관	장 관	보안통제	외신과통제
		오름	홍대			~	홍대	

0006

외 무 부

종 별 : 지급

번 호 : UNW-1439   일 시 : 90 0802 1230

수 신 : 장관 (국연,중동,기정)

발 신 : 주 유엔대사

제 목 : 안보리 (이락-쿠웨이트 분쟁)

　　1. 쿠웨이트 및 미국의 요청에 따라 금 8.2. 오전 5시부터 1시간동안 긴급 안보리가 소집 되었음. (의장: 루마니아) 안보리는 이락의 쿠웨이트 침공을 규탄하는 아래 내용의 결의안을 만장일치로 채택함. (단, 예멘은 훈령 미접수를 이유로 표결에 불참)

　　2. 카나다, 콜롬비아, 코트디브와르, 이디오피아, 핀랜드, 말레이지아 및 미, 영, 불 등 9개국이 공동 제안한 결의안 (660호) 전문은 아래와 같음.

THE SECURITY COUNCIL

ALARMED BY THE INVASION OF KUWAIT ON 2 AUGUST 1990 BY THEMILITARY FORCES OFIRAQ, DETERMINING THAT THERE EXISTS ABREACH OF INTERNATIONAL PEACE AND SECURITY AS REGARDS THEIRAQI INVASION OF KUWAIT,

ACTING UNDER ARTICLES 39 AND 40 OF THE CHARTER OF THE UNITEDNATIONS.

1. CONDEMNS THE IRAQI INVASION OF KUWAIT

2. DEMANDS THAT IRAQ WITHDRAW IMMEDIATELY ANDUNCONDITIONALLY ALL ITS FORCESTO THE POSITIONS IN WHICHTHEY WERE LOCATED ON AUGUST 1, 1990

3. CALLS UPON IRAQ AND KUWAIT TO BEGIN IMMEDIATELY INTENSIVENEGOTIATIONS FOR THE RESOLUTION OF THEIR DIFFERENCES ANDSUPPORTS ALL EFFORTS IN THIS REGARD, AND ESPECIALLY THOSE OFTHE ARAB LEAGUE

4. DECIDES TO MEET AGAIN AS NECESSARY TO CONSIDER FURTHERSTEPS TO ENSURE COMPLIANCE WITH THIS RESOLUTION.

　　3. 금일 안보리 참석국의 발언 요지

　　0 쿠웨이트

　　이라크의 침공은 헌장위반임. 안보리는 쿠웨이트의 주권과 영토를 보호할 책임이 있음. 안보리는 이라크의 즉각적, 무조건 철수를 요청해야함.

국기국　　차관　　1차보　　2차보　　중아국　　정문국　　안기부

90.08.03　　05:22 DA

외신 1과 통제관

0007

0 이라크

금번 사태는 국내문제로 안보리가 관여할 문제가 아님. 쿠웨이트 임시정부가 국내 질서 회복을 위해 이라크의 지원을 요청하였음. 쿠웨이트내 질서가 회복되면 즉시 철수할 예정임. 쿠웨이트에 신정부가 수립 되었으므로 현 쿠웨이트 대사는 대표권이 없음.

0 미국

8.1.18:30 (뉴욕시간) 이라크가 쿠웨이트를 침공하였음. 이라크의 침공은 사전음모 되었음. 미국은 쿠웨이트를 지원하겠음. 이라크 침공을 규탄하고 즉각적인무조건적 철수를 촉구하고 지금의 시대는 평화와 외교의 시기이지 침공과 전쟁의때가 아님.

0 콜롬비아

어떤 이유로든 무력사용은 반대함.

0 카나다

이라크의 침공은 유엔헌장과 국제법 위반으로 전적으로 수락할수 없음. 이라크의 완전한 철수를 요구함.

0 프랑스

침공을 규탄함. 대화가 분쟁해결의 유일한 수단임.

0 말레이지아

국제관계에서 무력의 사용이나 위협에 반대함. 특히 이원칙은 소국들에게 중요한것임. 즉각적인 철수를 요청함.

0 영국

영국은 유엔헌장과 아랍연맹 헌장 위반조치를 강력히 규탄함. 안보리는 소국을보호해야함. 1990년에 이러한 침공이 발생한데 대해 분노와 경멸을 금하지 못함.

0 핀랜드

동 침공은 유엔헌장의 명백한 위반임. 이라크의 철수를 촉구함.

0 소련

안보리가 신속하고 단호하게 조치를 취할것을 촉구함.

0 중국

국가간 분쟁은 평화적으로 해결되어야함. 이라크의 행동에 유감을 표명함. 이라크 군대는 철수 되어야함.

PAGE 2

0008

ㅇ 루마니아

국제분쟁 해결을 위해 무력이 사용되어서는 안됨. 쌍방이 금후 유엔헌장의 원칙을 준수하기 바람.

ㅇ 예멘

분쟁의 평화적 해결을 촉구함. 본국 훈령을 접수하지 못하여 표결에 참석치 않겠음.

4.의장은 동건이 안보리에 계속 계류되어 있음을 선언함. 동건 진전사항 추보 예정임. 끝

(대사 현홍주-국장)

외 무 부

종 별 : 지 급

번 호 : UNW-1440　　　　　　　　　일 시 : 90 0802 1230

수 신 : 장관 (국연,중동,기정)

발 신 : 주 유엔대사

제 목 : 이라크-쿠웨이트 분쟁

　　금 8.2. 아침 표제건 안보리 결의안이 채택된 직후 안보리 회의장 밖에서 DE CUELLAR 유엔 사무총장이 발표한 성명문을 별첨 보고함.

　　(대사 현홍주-국장)

　　첨부: 상기성명 FAX (UNW(F)-0116) 끝.

이락 - 쿠웨이트 상황
육연 동향

○ 일반서
○ 사무총장

국기국　　1차보　　중아국　　정문국　　안기부　청와대

　　　　　　　　　　　　　90.08.03　　05:23 DA
　　　　　　　　　　　　　　　　　　　외신 1과 통제관

0010

United 🌐 Nations

Press Release

Department of Public Information ○ News Coverage Service ○ New York

UNW(F)-0116 · 00802 1230 총 1 PH

SG/SM/4474
SC/5200
2 August 1990

SECRETARY-GENERAL'S STATEMENT TO CORRESPONDENTS FOLLOWING SECURITY COUNCIL'S ADOPTION OF RESOLUTION CONDEMNING IRAQ'S INVASION OF KUWAIT

Following is the text of a statement by Secretary-General Javier Perez de Cuellar, delivered this morning to correspondents outside the Security Council chamber, following the adoption by the Council of resolution 660 (1990), condemning Iraq's invasion of Kuwait:

I am pleased to see that the Security Council has met promptly and taken an important decision on the problem between Iraq and Kuwait.

The events of the past hours are of the gravest consequence to the United Nations and, I am sure, to its Member States, who are obliged to honour its Charter.

As the Secretary-General of this Organization, whose duty it is to serve as custodian of that Charter, I can do no less than quote Article 2.3 and 2.4 of the Charter:

2.3 "All Members shall settle their international disputes by peaceful means in such a manner that international peace and security, and justice, are not endangered."

2.4 "All Members shall refrain in their international relations from the threat or use of force against the territorial integrity or political independence of any State, or in any other manner inconsistent with the Purposes of the United Nations."

(총영. 중동. 기정)

* *** *

0011

이라크, 쿠웨이트 사태 속 보
(8.3. 07:00)

1. 상 황

- 이라크, 쿠웨이트내 의회 해산, 친 이라크 괴뢰정권 "자유임시정부" 수립 발표
- 쿠웨이트 국왕 사우디 피신, GCC 국가와 대처 방안 모색중
- 쿠웨이트 국왕 형제중 1명 왕궁 사수중 피살
- 이라크군 쿠웨이트 전역 완전 장악 (이라크, 쿠웨이트군 교전중 200여명의 쿠웨이트 병사 사망)
- 이라크, 동 사태 관련 어떤 외세 개입도 용납치 않을 것임을 경고
- 쿠웨이트 국왕, 미국에 군사 지원 요청 및 아랍연맹 회원국의 지원을 호소
- ※ 미.소는 이라크군의 즉각적인 쿠웨이트 철수 요청의 공동 성명을 발표(8.3)

2. 유가 영향

- 유가 배럴당 20$(8.2) → 23.5$로 인상 (8.3) 〈현물가〉
- 단기간, 세계 오일시장 불안정 예상

〈각국 추가 반응〉

- 미　국 : - 쿠웨이트 요청에 의해 미국내 모든 쿠웨이트 자산 동결 조치 결정

- 영　국 : - 이라크의 쿠웨이트 침공 강력 비난
  - UN 안보리의 이라크 제재에 어떤 조치에 대하여도 지원할 용의 표명

- 이스라엘 : - 이라크의 쿠웨이트 침공은 후세인의 전쟁 위협 심각성에 대한 이스라엘측 경고를 확인해 주는 것임
  - 이라크는 이스라엘뿐만 아닌 전 세계에 위협이 되고 있으며, 또 다른 국가 침공을 노리고 있음

0012

U.N. Condemns the Invasion With Threat to Punish Iraq

By PAUL LEWIS
Special to The New York Times

UNITED NATIONS, Aug. 2 — The United Nations Security Council voted overwhelmingly early this morning to condemn Iraq's invasion of Kuwait, demanding the immediate, unconditional withdrawal of all of Baghdad's forces from the tiny Persian Gulf nation, and threatening to invoke mandatory sanctions if it does not promptly comply.

The Council called on Iraq and Kuwait to begin "immediate intensive negotiations" to resolve their differences and gave its backing to Arab League efforts to mediate in the crisis.

Citing Articles 39 and 40 of the United Nations Charter, which gives the Council the authority to impose such sanctions on aggressor nations and to intervene against them with military force, the Council resolved to meet again "as necessary to consider further steps to insure compliance with this resolution."

A Seldom-Issued Threat

This is the language the Security Council traditionally uses when it threatens Charter violators with punitive action. Today's move is believed to be only the fifth time in the organization's 45-year history that the Security Council has issued such a threat.

A failure to withdraw from Kuwait could draw sanctions.

The four previous occasions were the imposition of arms embargos against South Africa and Rhodesia, the threat of sanctions to obtain a cease fire ending the first Israeli-Arab war in 1948, and and the council's action ordering a cease-fire in the Iran-Iraq war in 1987.

The 1948 and 1987 actions preceded cease-fires, and the Rhodesian arms embargo lapsed after that country became Zimbabwe under majority rule in 1980. The South African embargo remains in effect.

Several Council members emphasized that they are deadly serious about the sanctions threat, arguing that at a moment when a more peaceful and cooperative world order is evolving, the United Nations must show itself ready to compel compliance with the principles of its Charter.

'The World Is Watching'

"It is a time for peace and diplomacy, not for war and aggression," the United States chief delegate, Thomas R. Pickering, told the Council. "The world is watching what we do and will not be satisfied with vacillation and procrastination."

Kuwait's United Nations representative, Mohammed A. Abulhassan, called the resolution "a test of the Council and its ability to preserve the peace and security of all small nations." After the vote, the delegate of one third world nation said, "We have threatened sanctions and we mean it. Our credibility is at stake."

The 15-member Security Council consists of five permanent members — Britain, China, France, the Soviet Union and the United States — and 10 rotating seats, currently held by Canada, Finland, Colombia, Ethiopia, Malaysia, Ivory Coast, Zaire, Romania, Cuba and Yemen.

Western members of the Council said they will probably delay the next meeting until Monday to give Iraq time to comply and allow the Arab League to pursue its mediation efforts. But if, as they anticipate, Iraqi forces are still occupying Kuwait, they expect to reconvene and start planning a worldwide program of mandatory economic sanctions against Baghdad.

Early-Morning Vote

After a night of frenzied negotiations, the Security Council voted just before 6:00 this morning to condemn Iraq's invasion. Fourteen of the Council's 15 members voted in favor of the resolution and none against. Yemen, the only Arab country on the Council, did not participate in the vote because its delegate said he had no instructions from his government.

Iraq's Deputy Representative, Sabah Talat Kadrat, accused the Council of illegally interfering in his country's internal affairs. He said Iraqi troops entered Kuwait at the invitation of a new provisional government to restore order and would withdraw as soon as that goal was achieved.

Diplomats said the five permanent members had ruled out military force in the situation but may start discussing economic moves informally over the weekend.

August 3, 199(
NYT

0013

이라크, 쿠웨이트 사태 속보
(8.3. 13:00) <2>

1. 상 황

o 미국, 항공모함 걸프만에 급파

o 이라크 평의회, 성명을 통해

- 쿠웨이트 혁명 세력의 사바하 쿠웨이트 정부 타도

- 사태 정상화시 및 쿠웨이트 정부 요청시, 이라크군 철수 예정임을 발표
(수일내지 수주내)

o 친 이라크 쿠웨이트 자유 임시정부, 방송을 통해 아래와 같이 발표

- 알 사바하 쿠웨이트 국왕 폐위 및 의회 해산

- 무기한 통행금지령 및 모든 공항과 항구 봉쇄, 출입금지 조치

- 사태 안정되면 선거를 실시할 것임 (성명)

o 쿠웨이트 총리, 이라크 배반자를 쿠웨이트로 부터 몰아내자고 호소(비밀장소 방송)

o 쿠웨이트 도심 내 차량 전화 모두 단절

2. 각국 조치사항

o 미.영.불, 자국내 모든 이라크 자산 동결 조치

o 미.영 : 사태 해결을 위한 UN 집단 행동에 대한 공동 지원 합의

o 미.소 : 사태 해결 관련, 양국 공동 협력 노력 합의

o 이라크, 대 미국 부채 상환 동결 결정

<각국 추가 반응>

미 국 : - 걸프역내 미국의 중요 이익 보호 위한 모든 필요조치 강구 예정

영 국 : - 동 사태 해결 위한 UN 회원국의 집단적이고, 효율적인 결의
필요성 피력

- 이라크의 즉각적 철수가 이루어지지 않을 경우, UN 헌장 7조
의거 안보리 조치가 고려될 것임을 시사

E C : - 이라크 침공 비난 및 즉각적인 무조건 철수 요구

G C C : - 회원국 정상들 젯다 회동, 사태 해결 방안 논의 예정 (8.3)

0014

분류기호 문서번호	국연 2031- **223**	(	)	협조문용지		결 재	담당	과장	국장
시행일자	1990. 8. 3.								(서명)
수 신	**각**.실국장, 외교안보연구원장			발 신		국제기구조약국장			
제 목	이락의 쿠웨이트 침공에 관한 안보리 결의안 송부								

이락의 쿠웨이트 침공에 대하여 쿠웨이트 및 미국의 요청에

따라 8.2. 오전 긴급 안보리가 소집되었는 바, 동 안보리에서 만장

일치로 채택한 결의(660호)을 별첨 송부하오니 업무에 참고하시기

바랍니다.

첨 부 : 표제결의안 1부.   끝.

0015

안보리 결의(660호) 전문

o 공동제안국 : 미.영.불.카나다.콜롬비아.코트디브와르.이디오피아
                핀랜드.말레이지아 (9개국)

o 결의내용 :

The Security Council,

Alarmed by the invasion of Kuwait on 2 August 1990 by the military forces of Iraq, determining that there exists a breach of international peace and security as regards the Iraqi invasion of Kuwait,

Acting under articles 39 and 40 of the Charter of the United Nations,

1. Condemns the Iraqi invasion of Kuwait

2. Demands that Iraq withdraw immediately and unconditionally all its forces to the positions in which they were located on August 1, 1990

3. Calls upon Iraq and Kuwait to begin immediately intensive negotiations for the resolution of their differences and supports all efforts in this regard, and especially those of the Arab League

4. Decides to meet again as necessary to consider further steps to ensure compliance with this resolution

0016

이락-쿠웨이트 분쟁

90. 8. 3.
국제연합과

1. 긴급안보리 소집 (8.2. 05:00-06:00)

가. 소집요청국 : 쿠웨이트·미국

나. 의 장 국 : 루마니아

다. 결의안 채택 : 이락의 쿠웨이트 침공을 규탄하는 하기내용의 결의안을
만장일치로 채택 (예멘, 표결에 불참)

ㅇ 결의안 제안국 : 카나다·콜롬비아·코트디봐르·이디오피아·핀랜드·
말련·미·영·불(9개국)

ㅇ 결의안 내용
- 8.2. 이락의 쿠웨이트 침공비난
- 8.1. 군사배치선으로의 이락군 즉각 철수
- 이락·쿠웨이트간 즉각적 협상 요청 및 이락·쿠웨이트 및 Arab
League 의 협상을 통한 분쟁해결노력 지지
- 본 결의안 이행을 위한 조치강구를 위하여 필요시 안보리 재소집

2. 각국 발언요지

ㅇ 쿠웨이트
- 이라크의 침공은 현장위반임.
- 안보리는 쿠웨이트의 주권과 영토를 보호할 책임이 있음.
- 안보리는 이라크의 즉각적. 무조건 철수를 요청해야 함.

0017

o 이라크

  -- 금번 사태는 국내문제로 안보리가 관여할 문제가 아님.

  - 쿠웨이트 임시정부가 국내질서 회복을 위해 이라크의 지원을 요청
    하였음.

  - 쿠웨이트내 질서가 회복되면 즉시 철수할 예정임.

  - 쿠웨이트에 신정부가 수립 되었으므로 현 쿠웨이트 대사는 대표권이
    없음.

o 미국

  - 8.1. 18:30(뉴욕시간) 이라크가 쿠웨이트를 침공하였음.

  - 이라크의 침공은 사전음모 되었음.

  - 미국은 쿠웨이트를 지원하겠음.

  - 이라크 침공을 규탄하고 즉각적인 무조건적 철수를 촉구하고 지금의
    시대는 평화와 외교의 시기이지 침공과 전쟁의 때가 아님.

o 콜롬비아

  - 어떤 이유로든 무력사용은 반대함.

o 카나다

  - 이라크의 침공은 유연헌장과 국제법 위반으로 전적으로 수락할 수 없음.

  - 이라크의 완전한 철수를 요구함.

o 프랑스

  - 침공을 규탄함.

  - 대화가 분쟁해결의 유일한 수단임.

o 말레이지아

  - 국제관계에서 무력의 사용이나 위협에 반대함. 특히 이 원칙은 소국들
    에게 중요한 것임.

  - 즉각적인 철수를 요청함.

0018

o 영 국

  - 영국은 유엔헌장과 아랍연맹 헌장 위반조치를 강력히 규탄함.

  - 안보리는 소국을 보호해야 함.

  - 1990년에 이러한 침공이 발생한데 대배 분노와 경멸을 급하지 못함.

o 핀랜드

  - 동 침공은 유엔헌장의 명백한 위반임. 이라크의 철수를 촉구함.

o 소 련

  - 안보리가 신속하고 단호한 조치를 취할 것을 촉구함.

o 중 국

  - 국가간 분쟁은 평화적으로 해결되어야 함.

  - 이라크의 행동에 유감을 표명함. 이라크 군대는 철수되어야 함.

o 루마니아

  - 국제분쟁 해결을 위해 무력이 사용되어서는 안됨.

  - 쌍방이 금후 유엔헌장의 원칙을 준수하기 바람.

o 예 멘

  - 분쟁의 평화적 해결을 촉구함.

  - 본국 훈령을 접수하지 못하여 표결에 참석치 않겠음.

o 의 장

  - 동건이 안보리에 계속 계류되어 있음을 선언함.

0019

3. 유엔사무총장 성명 발표 (8.2)

o 지난 수시간동안의 사태는 유연과 유연회원국들에게 중대한 영향을
   끼치고 있음.

o 유연헌장의 준수라는 의무를 지닌 본인은 헌장 2조 3항과 2조 4항을
   원용치 않을 수 없음.

┌─────┐
│ 참 고 │
└─────┘

   2조 3항 : 모든 회원국들은 국제평화와 안전, 정의가 위해받지 않도록
              평화적인 방법으로 국제분쟁을 해결한다.

   2조 4항 : 모든 회원국은 타국의 영토 및 정치적 독립을 침해하는
              유연헌장 규정에 반하는 모든 무력 사용 행위를 취하지
              아니한다.

이락-쿠웨이트 분쟁

(긴급안보리 소집)

90. 8. 3.
국제연합과

1. 긴급안보리 소집 (8.2. 05:00-06:00)

   가. 소집요청국: 쿠웨이트 · 미국

   나. 외 장 국: 루마니아

   다. 결의안 채택: 이락의 쿠웨이트 침공을 규탄하는 하기내용의 결의안을
      만장일치로 채택

   ○ 결의안 제안국: 카나다 · 콜롬비아 · 코트디봐르 · 이디오피아 · 핀랜드 ·
      말련 · 미 · 영 · 불(9개국)

   ○ 결의안 내용
      - 8.2. 이락의 쿠웨이트 침공비난
      - 8.1. 군사배치선으로의 이락군 즉각 천수
      - 이락 · 쿠웨이트간 즉각적 협상 요청 및 이락 · 쿠웨이트 및 Arab
        League 의 협상을 통한 분쟁해결노력 지지
      - 본 결의안 이행을 위한 조치강구를 위하여 필요시 안보리 재소집

2. 각국 발언요지

   ○ 쿠웨이트
      - 이라크의 침공은 현장위반임.
      - 안보리는 쿠웨이트의 주권과 영토를 보호한 책임이 있음.
      - 안보리는 이라크의 즉각적, 무조건 철수를 요청해야 함.

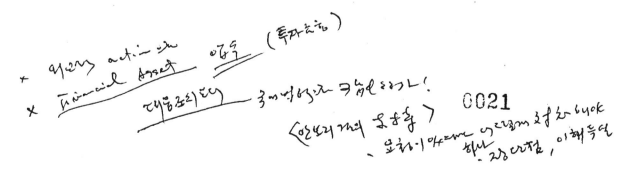

o 이라크

- 금번 사대는 국내문제로 안보리가 관여할 문제가 아님.
- 쿠웨이트 임시정부가 국내질서 회복을 위해 이라크의 지원을 요청
  하였음.
- 쿠웨이트내 질서가 회복되면 즉시 철수할 예정임.
- 쿠웨이트에 신정부가 수립 되었으므로 현 쿠웨이트 대사는 대표권이
  없음.

o 미국

- 8.1. 18:30(뉴욕시간) 이라크가 쿠웨이트를 침공하였음.
- 이라크의 침공은 사전음모 되었음.
- 미국은 쿠웨이트를 지원하겠음.
- 이라크 침공을 규탄하고 즉각적인 무조건적 철수를 촉구하고 지급의
  시대는 평화와 외교의 시기이지 침공과 전쟁의 때가 아님.

o 콜롬비아

- 어떤 이유로든 무력사용은 반대함.

o 카나다

- 이라크의 침공은 유엔헌장과 국제법 위반으로 전적으로 수락할 수 없음.
- 이라크의 완전한 철수를 요구함.

o 프랑스

- 침공을 규탄함.
- 대화가 분쟁해결의 유일한 수단임.

o 말레이지아

- 국제관계에서 무력의 사용이나 위협에 반대함. 특히 이 원칙은 소국들
  에게 중요한 것임.
- 즉각적인 철수를 요청함.

0022

o 영 국

- 영국은 유엔헌장과 아랍연맹 현장 위반조치를 강력히 규탄함.

- 안보리는 소국을 보호해야 함.

- 1990년에 이러한 침공이 발생한데 대배 분노와 경멸을 급하지 못함.

o 핀랜드

- 동 침공은 유엔헌장의 명백한 위반임. 이라크의 철수를 촉구함.

o 소 련

- 안보리가 신속하고 단호한 조치를 취할 것을 촉구함.

o 중 국

- 국가간 분쟁은 평화적으로 해결되어야 함.

- 이라크의 행동에 유감을 표명함. 이라크 군대는 철수되어야 함.

o 루마니아

- 국제분쟁 해결을 위해 무력이 사용되어서는 안됨.

- 쌍방이 금후 유엔헌장의 원칙을 준수하기 바람.

o 예 멘

- 분쟁의 평화적 해결을 촉구함.

- 본국 훈령을 접수하지 못하여 표결에 참석치 않겠음.

o 의 장

- 동건이 안보리에 계속 계류되어 있음을 선언함.

0023

3. 유엔사무총장 성명 발표 (8.2)

ㅇ 지난 수시간동안의 사태는 유엔과 유엔회원국들에게 중대한 영향을
   끼치고 있음.

ㅇ 유엔헌장의 준수라는 의무를 지닌 본인은 헌장 2조 3항과 2조 4항을
   원용치 않을 수 없음.

참 고

2조 3항 : 모든 회원국들은 국제평화와 안전, 정의가 위해받지 않도록
          평화적인 방법으로 국제분쟁을 해결한다.

2조 4항 : 모든 회원국은 다국의 영토 및 정치적 독립을 침해하는 유엔헌장
          규정에 반하는 모든 무력사용 행위를 취하지 아니한다.

0024

이라크, 쿠웨이트 침공 관련
관계부처 대책 회의 자료

1990. 8. 3.

외 무 부

0025

회 의 자 료

제 목 : 이라크, 쿠웨이트 침공

1. 경   위

o 90.7.17.   후세인 대통령, 쿠웨이트, UAE 원유 쿼타 초과 비난
o   7.18.   이라크, 쿠웨이트가 "루마일라" 유전에서 24억불
                       원유 도굴 주장
o   7.20.   쿠웨이트, 이라크가 채무 불이행 목적이라고 주장
o   7.25.   이집트.사우디 중재로 회담 개최 발표
o   7.26.   OPEC 유가 인상 합의
o   7.31.   쿠웨이트.이라크 젯다 회담
                       이라크 10만 병력 쿠웨이트 국경 집결
o   8. 1.   젯다 회담 결렬
o   8. 2.   이라크 새벽 2시 침공(한국시간 상오 8시)

2. 상   황

o 90.8.2. 새벽 2시 이라크, 쿠웨이트 침공
o 이라크군, 쿠웨이트 왕궁 및 정부청사 완전 장악
o 쿠웨이트 국왕 및 왕세자겸 총리 8.2. 헬기편 사우디로 피신
o 미 항공모함 "인디펜던스"호 걸프만 이동
o 유엔 안보리 긴급 회의 소집 (8.2)
   - 이라크군 즉각 철수 요구 결의

0026

3. 배 경

1) 이라크 요구사항
- 쿠웨이트 OPEC 쿼터 준수 요구
- 루마일라 유전 도굴 24억불 보상 요구
- 국경지역 일부 영토 "부비얀" 섬 99년 조차 요구
- 이.이 전비 250억불 외채를 쿠웨이트에 탕감 요구

2) 이라크 국내 경제 피폐 및 종신 대통령제에 대한 국민 불만 고조

4. 각국 반응

- 미 국 : - 이라크의 쿠웨이트 무력 침공 비난 및 이라크
군대 무조건 철수 요구
- UN 안보리 긴급 소집 요구
- 미 군함의 걸프만 파견
- 모든 선택 방안 검토중

- 소 련 : - 무조건 쿠웨이트 점령 이라크군 즉각 철수 요청

- 영국,불란서 : - 이라크 군사 행동 비난 및 이라크군 즉각적 철수
요구

- 일 본 : - 이라크의 쿠웨이트 침공에 유감 및 사태 진전에 깊은
관심 표명

- 이라크.쿠웨이트간 분쟁이 무력이 아닌 평화적 방법으로
해결 되길 희망

- 카 나 다 : 침략 행위 규탄, 전부 중지 및 전면 즉각 철수

- 호 주 : - 이라크의 쿠웨이트 침공 비난 및 이라크군 철수 요구

- 이스라엘 : - 이라크의 쿠웨이트 침공이 걸프만 지역내 위험
상태를 유발할 것임을 표명

0027

o 이 집 트 : - 이라크의 쿠웨이트 침공 사태 토의 위한 아랍연맹
　　　　　　　　긴급 소집 요구

o 인　　도 : - 사태 추이 관망후 논평 예정

o 사 우 디 : - 동 사태 토의 위한 GCC 6개 회원국 회의 소집

o 유　　고 : 이라크 규탄, 즉각 철수 및 협상 촉구 (비동맹 의장 자격)

o U　N : - 안보리 긴급 소집, 회의 개최

o 아랍연맹 : - 동 사태 토의 위한 회의 소집 예정

o O I C : - 이라크 침공 규탄 합의 실패

―――――――――――――――
| 5.　아국과의 관계 |
―――――――――――――――

가. 이 라 크
　o 건설현황
　　- 진출건설업체 : 현대, 삼성종합, 정우개발, 한양, 대림,
　　　　　　　　　　　남광토건, 동아건설
　　- 총 건설 수주 누계(81-89) : 6,439 백만불
　　　　　　　　　　　　　　(시공액 : 13건 22억 8천만불)

　o 교역현황
　　- 진출상사 : 현대, 삼성, 대우, 국제상사, 선경, 효성(6개상사)
　　- 수출액(89) : 67 백만불 (고무제품, 섬유류, 철강제품등)
　　　수입액(89) : 63 백만불 (원유)
　o 교　　민 : 621 명 (근로자 포함)

나. 쿠웨이트
　o 건설현황
　　- 진출건설업체(약 350명) : 현대, 대림, 효성중공업
　　- 총 건설 수주 누계(81-89) : 2,110 백만불
　　　　　　　　　　　　　(시공액 : 4건 2억 3천 2백만불)

0028

o 교역현황 :
  - 수출액(89) : 210 백만불 (선박, 견직물, 전기기기등)
  - 수입액(89) : 381 백만불 (원유)
o 교   민 : 648 명 (근로자 포함)

다. 유가에 미치는 영향

  1) 유가 급등

    o 7.27. OPEC 총회의 공시유가 3달러 인상으로 유가 상승
      - 브렌트 유가 ; 배럴당 16.49 (4월 평균) → 20.40 달러
    o 이라크의 쿠웨이트 침공으로 8.2 오전 하루만에 유가 급등
      - 북해 브렌트유 현물가격 : 배럴당 20.40 → 23.50 달러
      - 두바이유 현물가격 : 배럴당 17.30 → 18.80 달러

  2) 유가 전망

    o 단기전망
      분쟁 지속시 두바이 유가가 배럴당 20달러 정도로 유가 상승
      예상 (일본 석유회사)
    o 중장기 전망
      - 세계 재고량(약 135 천만배럴)과 이라크, 쿠웨이트 생산비중
        (OPEC 생산량중 약 1/5)에 비추어 유가 급등 문제는 사태 추이에
        좌우될 것임
      . 자유세계 일일 소비량 : 5,300만 배럴

  3) 대   책

    o 아국의 석유 수급 대책
      - 90.8월 현재 83일분 비축물량 확보로 유가 급등 및 단기 공급
        차질에 대처 가능 (일본 비축물량, 180일분)
    o 장기적인 유가 상승 대책 수립 필요
      - 원유 도입선 다변화
        (90.1-5월 이라크.쿠웨이트산 석유 도입 비중 12%)
      - 원유 및 가스 개발 도입 확대
      - 비축물량 확대

0029

- 대체 에너지 개발 통한 석유의존도 완화

  (89년 소비량 79.6천 B/D로 전년대비 13.9% 증가)

6. 조 치 사 항

o 사태 보고서 청와대 송부

o 주 이라크, 쿠웨이트 대사관에 아국 교민 안전 대책 강구 및 사태
  진전사항 보고 지시

  - 아국 교민 피해상황 접수

    . 미 귀환자 : 현대건설 소속 근로자 3명

                 (송전선로공사 현장, 조준택, 노재항 연락 불통,

                 이라크군 사령부 영내 김영호 억류)

o 주요 국가 반응 및 사태 파악 지시 (주요공관)

o 정부 공식 입장 성명 발표 (각국반응 종합후)

  - 주한 미 대사 : 이라크군의 무조건 즉각 철수 촉구, 한국내

                 쿠웨이트 자산 동결 협조 요청

o 공관 조치 사항

  - 쿠웨이트 건설 현장 인원을 캠프로 철수

  - 비상연락망 유지, 비상시 철수 계획 점검

7. 분 석

(이라크의 의도)

o 이라크는 소련의 후퇴를 기회로 걸프지역 패권 장악 시도

o 이라크의 새로운 걸프만으로의 진출 확보

  - 쿠웨이트령 부비얀섬 조차 요구

  - Shat Al Arab 수로 개통 전망 불투명

o 이라크와 쿠웨이트의 원유 매장량을 동시 장악하여 세계 유가 조작

  (세계 총매장량의 25% 이상)

o 이라크 국내 정치, 경제 문제 타개책

o 사우디의 지도력에 대한 도전

0030

8. 전   망

o 외교적 경제적 해결 방안 탐색
   - 아랍제국의 군사적 대처 능력 없음
   - 미국의 군사적 개입 난망
   - 미.소가 해결에 협조 예상
o 이라크군 점령 장기화 가능성
   - 쿠웨이트에 친이라크 정권 수립이 철수 관건
o 궁극적으로 이라크 요구 대폭 충족 예상
   - 후세인 대통령의 경직성으로 타협 난망
   - 장기화 경우 사태 해결을 위한 국제 압력 가중시
o 장기적으로는 미국등 강대국들의 이라크에 대한 압력으로 패권
   유지에 한계

9. 중동사태에 미치는 영향

o 이스라엘의 경계심 고조로 긴장 조성 예상
o 팔레스타인 문제 해결 노력 냉각
o 부비얀섬의 조차가 실현될 경우 이라크.이란간 화해 가능성 증대

0031

참 고 자 료 (쿠웨이트)

가. 통 상

(단위 : 백만불)

	84	85	86	87	88	89
수 출	256	205	211	188	341	210
수 입	482	523	215	159	205	381

- O 주요 수출품 : 선박, 견직물, 전기기기, 철강, 고무제품, 기계류
- O 주요 수입품 : 원유, 구리제품, 철강, 알미늄제품, 연제품(Lead)

나. 건설 수주 실적

(단위 : 백만불)

년도	76-82	83	84	85	86	87	88	89
액수	2110	130	214	340	15	49	95	90

- O 진출업체(약 350명) : 현대건설, 대림산업, 효성중공업
- O 시공잔액 : 2억 3천 2백만불 (4건)

다. 인력 진출 현황

(단위 : 명)

연도	82	83	84	85	86	87	88	89	90.7.
인원	10,409	5,577	4,227	3,817	4,229	2,505	707	706	648

라. 원유 도입 현황

(단위 : 천 Bbl, %)

년 도	82	83	84	85	86	87	88	89	90.7.
도입량	19,827	19,708	14,970	17,520	13,207	9,693	9,465	12,544	14,700
점유율	12.1	11.8	8.7	10.7	5.7	4.5	3.6	4.8	7.6

※ 내수기준(비축용 및 재수출용 원유 도입 제외)

0032

마. 교민 현황 (90.7.31. 현재)

 o 체류자 현황 : 648명

  - 체류자의 대부분이 근로자임

 o 단체 조직 현황

  - 한인회('75.5. 창립, 회장 : 이수영)

  - 건설지사 협의회('76.5. 창립, 회장 : 전재연)

  - 한인학교('81. 개교)

0033

이 라 크 . 쿠 웨 이 트 사 태 에 관 한
외 무 부 대 변 인 성 명

1. 대한민국 정부는 이라크 군대에 의한 쿠웨이트 영토내에서의 군사적
   행동과 관련한 걸프 지역내의 사태 진전에 깊은 우려를 표명한다.

2. 대한민국은 이라크 및 쿠웨이트와 다같이 우호적 관계를 유지하고
   있는바, 양국간의 분쟁이 무력이 아닌 평화적 방법으로 해결되기를
   강력히 희망한다.

3. 또한 대한민국 정부는 이라크군이 가능한 한 조속히 쿠웨이트 영토로
   부터 철수하기를 바란다.

0034

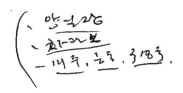

유엔의 경제제재조치

90. 8. 3
국제연합과

o 국제기구에 의한 잡단적 경제 제재조치는 국제연맹에 의하여
최초로 취하여 졌는 바 (1935년 이태리의 에디오피아 침공시),
성공적 효과를 가져오지는 못하였음.

o 유연은 국제연맹의 군사 및 경제 제재조치(military and ecnomic
sanctions)의 실패 경험에 비추어(국제연맹에서의 군사제제 조치는
강제적이 아닌 임의적 성격이었음), "제재조치(sanction)"라는
표현대신 "집단조치 (collective measures)" 또는 "강제조치
(enforcement measures)"라는 표현을 사용하고 있음.

o 유연헌장 41조는 안보리가 평화의 유지 또는 회복을 위하여 병력의
사용이외에 사용할 수 있는 조치로서 "경제관계 및 철도, 항해,
항공, 우편, 전신, 무전통신 기타의 운수통신 수단의 전부 또는
일부의 중단과 외교관계의 단절 "을 열거하고 있음.

  * 안보리외에 총회도 회원국들에 의한 특정 경제제재조치를 촉구
    하는 결의를 채택할 수 있으나, 이는 현장 7장에 의한 강제제재
    조치가 아닌 권고적 성격의 조치임.

0035

o   유엔이 경제제재 조치를 취한 예는

   1) 1951년 중공에 대한 교역금지 조치

   2) 1962년 로데지아에 대한 무기, 원유등의 운송금지 조치

   3) 1977년 남아공에 대한 무기 금수조치등이 있음.

   *   1980년 미국은 미대사관 인질사건과 관련, 이란에 대한
       경제제재조치를 위한 결의안을 안보리에 상정하였으나,
       소련의 거부권 행사로 부결됨.

유연의 경제제재조치

90. 8. 3
국제연합과

o 유연은 국제연맹의 군사 및 경제 제재조치(military and ecnomic
   sanctions)의 실패 경험에 비추어(국제연맹에서의 군사제재 조치는
   강제적이 아닌 임의적 성격이었음), "제재조치(sanction)"라는
   표현대신 "집단조치 (collective measures)" 또는 "강제조치
   (enforcement measures)"라는 표현을 사용하고 있음.

o 유연헌장 41조는 안보리가 평화의 유지 또는 회복을 위하여 병력의
   사용이외에 사용할 수 있는 조치로서 "경제관계 및 철도, 항해,
   항공, 우편, 전신, 무전통신 및 기타 운수통신 수단의 전부 또는
   일부의 중단과 외교관계의 단절"을 열거하고 있음.

   * 안보리외에 총회도 회원국들에 의한 특정 경제제재조치를 촉구
      하는 결의를 채택할 수 있으나, 이는 헌장 7장에 의한 강제제재
      조치가 아닌 권고적 성격의 조치임.

o 유연이 경제제재 조치를 취한 예는

   1) 1951년 중공에 대한 고역금지 조치

   2) 1966년 로데지아에 대한 무기. 원유등의 운송금지 조치

   3) 1977년 남아공에 대한 무기 금수조치등이 있음.

   * 1980년 미국은 미대사관 인질사건과 관련, 이란에 대한
      경제제재조치를 위한 결의안을 안보리에 상정하였으나,
      소련의 거부권 행사로 부결됨.

0037

대이락크 경제조치

일 본 (90.8.5)

1. 대이락크 연차관 제공 전면금지
2. 이락.쿠웨이트산 원유 도입금지
   (7.6억불 규모 일본 총수입의 0.4% 분량, 이락 수출분량의 8.6%)
3. 대이락 수출중지
4. 경제협력 중지

프랑스

EC 의 경제 제제조치(원유 수입금지)의 효과 별무시 이락 해안선
봉쇄 검토

카나다

1. 이락 및 쿠웨이트산 원유 수입금지
2. 이락을 수출통제 대상지역 리스트에 포함
3. 카.이락간 무역, 경제, 기술 협력 협정 효력 중단 및 최혜국
   대우 폐지
4. 대 이락수출 관련 지원활동 중단, 카 기업의 대이락, 쿠웨이트
   신규사업에 대한 수출개발공사(EDC)의 금융지원 중단
5. 카, 이락간 학술, 문화, 스포츠 교류 양해각서 효력 중단

0038

원 본

외 무 부

종 별 :

번 호 : UNW-1457

일 시 : 90 0803 1800

수 신 : 장관(국연,중동,아프일,기정)

발 신 : 주 유엔 대사

제 목 : 안보리내 동향

금 8.3 권참사관은 CHAN 안보리 담당관과 오찬, 이라크의 쿠웨이트 침공, 라이베리아 사태등과 관련 안보리 동향을 탐문한바 동인 주요 언급사항은 아래와같음.

1. 금일 현재 까지는 이라크-쿠웨이트 분쟁관련 안보리 회합이 예정되어 있지않음. 미국대표부로부터 이라크가 사우디와의 국경선에 군대를 집결중에 있다는 정보를 들었음. 중동내 상황이 유동적이므로 언제 안보리가 재소집될지 알수없음.

2. 라이베리아내 국내사태와 관련 라이베리아 주유엔대사는 유엔사무총장앞8.1 자 서한에서 라이베리아 문제가 더이상 내전으로 간주될수 없으며, 대규모의 난민이 인접국으로 유입하고 있어 서부아프리카지역의 안정을 해치고 있으므로 유엔이 헌장상 임무를 수행하기 위하여 개입하여 줄것을 요청하였음. 라이베리아는 특히 유엔사무총장이 중재역할을 담당, 즉각적인 휴전과 유엔평화유지군의 배치가 개시될수 있도록 요청하고 아울러 동건을 안보리에 제기하여 줄것을 당부하였음.

3. 금 8.3 오전 안보리 회원국간 비공식 협의회가 개최되었음. 이라크 사태와는 무관하며 사무총장이 엘살바돌 내전 관련 자신의 중재활동을 보고하였음. 사무총장은 7.27 자 엘살바돌 정부와 FMLN 간 인권 보호에 관한 합의 내용을 보고하고 동인 중재하에 엘살바돌 정부와 FMLN 간 차기 협상이 코스타리카에서 8.17-22 간 개최 예정임을 통보하였음. 끝

(대사 현홍주-국장)

예고:90.12.31 일반

1990.12.31. 에 예고문에
의거 일반문서로 재분류됨

국기국	장관	차관	1차보	2차보	중아국	정와대	안기부

90.08.04   10:25

외신 2과 통제관 FE

0039

외 무 부

종 별 :

번 호 : UNW-1459

수 신 : 장 관(국연,중동,기정)

발 신 : 주 유엔 대사

제 목 : 이락-쿠웨이트 분쟁

일 시 : 90 0803 1800

연: UNW-1439

1. 표제건, 주 유엔 미국대표부는 금 8.3 오후 유엔내 서구 국가, 카나다, 호주, 뉴질랜드, 일본대표를 미국대표부로 초청, 미국이 준비중인 별첨 안보리결의안 초안 내용을 설명하고 각국의 적극적인 지지와 협조를 요청하였음.

2. 금일의 모임에서 PICKERING 미국대사는 연호 안보리 결의에도 불구하고 이락의 쿠웨이트 침공이 계속되고 있어 광범위한 경제 제재를 중심으로한 안보리 결의안을 채택코자 하는것임을 설명하면서 안보리 상임이사국 및 기타 회원국들과 결의안 내용을 조속협의할 것이라고 말함. 동 대사는 국제평화를 위한 유엔의 역할이 재평가되고 있는 시점에서 유엔이 금번 사태에 효과적으로 대처하지 못한다면이는 유엔의 앞날과도 직결된 문제임을 강조함.끝

별첨:안보리의 결의안 UNW(F)-118

(대사 현홍주-국장)

국기국   1차보   중아국   정문국   안기부

PAGE 1

90.08.04   10:22 WG

외신 1과   통제관

0040

The Security Council

<u>Reaffirming</u> its Resolution 660 (1990)

<u>Deeply concerned</u> that this Resolution has not been implemented and that the aggression by Iraq against Kuwait continues with further loss of human life and material destruction,

<u>Determined</u> to bring the invasion and occupation of Kuwait by Iraq to an end,

Noting that Kuwait has expressed its readiness to comply with Resolution 660 (1990)),

Mindful of its responsibilities under the Charter for the maintenance of international peace and security,

Resolved to preserve the sovereignty, independence and territorial integrity of Kuwait,

Affirms the inherent right under Article 51 of the Charter of individual or collective self-defense in response to the armed attack by Iraq against Kuwait.

Acting under Chapter VII of the Charter of the United Nations,

1. <u>Determines</u> that Iraq has failed to comply with Resolution 660 (1990);

2. <u>Decides</u>, that, in furtherance of the objective of ending the aggression against Kuwait, all States shall prevent:

-   (a) The import into their territories of all commodities and products originating in Iraq or Kuwait exported therefrom after the date of this resolution;

-   (b) Any activities by their nationals or in their territories which would promote or are calculated to promote the export or transshipment of any commodities or products from Iraq or Kuwait; and any dealings by their nationals or in their territories in any commodities or products originating in Iraq or Kuwait and exported therefrom after the date of this resolution, including in particular any transfer of funds to Iraq or Kuwait for the purposes of such activities or dealings;

-   (c) The sale or supply by their nationals or from their territories of any commodities or products, including weapons or any other military equipment, (whether or not originating in their territories but not including supplies

3-1

0041

- 2 -

intended strictly for medical purposes, and, in special
humanitarian circumstances, foodstuffs) to any person or body
in Iraq or Kuwait or to any person or body for the purposes of
any business carried on in or operated from Iraq or Kuwait, and
any activities by their nationals or in their territories which
promote or are calculated to promote such sale, or supply or
use of such commodities or products;

3. Decides that all States shall not make available to the
government of Iraq or to any commercial, industrial or public·
utility undertaking in Iraq or Kuwait, any funds for investment
or any other financial or economic resources and shall prevent
their nationals and any persons within their territories from
making available to that government or to any such undertaking
any such funds or resources and from remitting any other funds
to persons or bodies within Iraq or occupied Kuwait, except
payments exclusively for strictly medical or humanitarian
purposes and in special humanitarian circumstances, foodstuffs;

4. Calls upon all States, including States non-members of the
United Nations, to act strictly in accordance with the
provisions of this resolution notwithstanding any contract
entered into or license granted before the date of this
resolution;

5. Decides to establish, in accordance with rule 28 of the
provisional rules of procedure of the security Council, a
Committee of the Security Council consisting of all the members
of the Council, to undertake the following tasks and to report
on its work to the Council with its observations and
recommendations:

-   (a) To examine the reports on the progress of the
implementation of this resolution which will be submitted by
the Secretary-General;

-   (b) To seek from all States, further information regarding
the action taken by them concerning the effective
implementation of the provisions laid down in this resolution;

6. Calls upon all States to cooperate fully with the Committee
in the fulfillment of its task, including supplying such
information as may be sought by the committee in pursuance of
this resolution;

7. Requests the Secretary-General to provide all necessary
assistance to the committee and to make the necessary
arrangements in the Secretariat for the purpose;

8. Decides that notwithstanding paragraphs 4 through 8,
nothing in this resolution shall prohibit assistance to the
legitimate government of Kuwait;

2

0042

9. Requests the Secretary-General to report to the Council on the progress ofthe implementation of this resolution, the first report to be submitted within thirty days;

10. Decides to keep this item on its agenda and to continue its efforts to put an early end to the invasion by Iraq.

3

0043

이락.쿠웨이트 분쟁에 관한 미측 안보리 결의안

90. 8. 4.
국제연합괴

1. 미측 견의안 작성

   ° 8.3. 오후 주유엔 미대사는 서구국가, 카나다, 호주,
     뉴질랜드, 일본대사에게 별첨 안보리 견의안 초안을 설명,
     지지 요청

2. 결의안 작성 경위 (미대사 설명내용)

   ° 쿠웨이트에서 이락군 철수 및 무력사용 중지를 요청하는
     안보리결의(660호)에도 불구 이락의 쿠웨이트 침공이 계속
     되고 있으므로 광범위한 경제 제재를 중심으로 한 견의안
     작성케 됨.

   ° 국제평화를 위한 유엔역할이 재평가되고 있는 현시점에서
     금번 사태에 대한 효과적 대처는 매우 중요함.

첨 부 : 미측 결의안 초안 1부.

0044

UNW(F)-118 UNW-1459 00803

The Security Council

__Reaffirming__ its Resolution 660 (1990)

__Deeply concerned__ that this Resolution has not been implemented and that the aggression by Iraq against Kuwait continues with further loss of human life and material destruction,

__Determined__ to bring the invasion and occupation of Kuwait by Iraq to an end,

Noting that Kuwait has expressed its readiness to comply with Resolution 660 (1990)),

Mindful of its responsibilities under the Charter for the maintenance of international peace and security,

Resolved to preserve the sovereignty, independence and territorial integrity of Kuwait,

Affirms the inherent right under Article 51 of the Charter of individual or collective self-defense in response to the armed attack by Iraq against Kuwait.

Acting under Chapter VII of the Charter of the United Nations,

1. __Determines__ that Iraq has failed to comply with Resolution 660 (1990);

2. __Decides__, that, in furtherance of the objective of ending the aggression against Kuwait, all States shall prevent:

- (a) The import into their territories of all commodities and products originating in Iraq or Kuwait exported therefrom after the date of this resolution;

- (b) Any activities by their nationals or in their territories which would promote or are calculated to promote the export or transshipment of any commodities or products from Iraq or Kuwait; and any dealings by their nationals or in their territories in any commodities or products originating in Iraq or Kuwait and exported therefrom after the date of this resolution, including in particular any transfer of funds to Iraq or Kuwait for the purposes of such activities or dealings;

- (c) The sale or supply by their nationals or from their territories of any commodities or products, including weapons or any other military equipment, (whether or not originating in their territories but not including supplies

3-1

0045

- 2 -

intended strictly for medical purposes, and, in special
humanitarian circumstances, foodstuffs) to any person or body
in Iraq or Kuwait or to any person or body for the purposes of
any business carried on in or operated from Iraq or Kuwait, and
any activities by their nationals or in their territories which
promote or are calculated to promote such sale, or supply or
use of such commodities or products;

3. Decides that all States shall not make available to the
government of Iraq or to any commercial, industrial or public·
utility undertaking in Iraq or Kuwait, any funds for investment
or any other financial or economic resources and shall prevent
their nationals and any persons within their territories from
making available to that government or to any such undertaking
any such funds or resources and from remitting any other funds
to persons or bodies within Iraq or occupied Kuwait, except
payments exclusively for strictly medical or humanitarian
purposes and in special humanitarian circumstances, foodstuffs;

4. Calls upon all States, including States non-members of the
United Nations, to act strictly in accordance with the
provisions of this resolution notwithstanding any contract
entered into or license granted before the date of this
resolution;

5. Decides to establish, in accordance with rule 28 of the
provisional rules of procedure of the security Council, a
Committee of the Security Council consisting of all the members
of the Council, to undertake the following tasks and to report
on its work to the Council with its observations and
recommendations:

- (a) To examine the reports on the progress of the
implementation of this resolution which will be submitted by
the Secretary-General;

- (b) To seek from all States, further information regarding
the action taken by them concerning the effective
implementation of the provisions laid down in this resolution;

6. Calls upon all States to cooperate fully with the Committee
in the fulfillment of its task, including supplying such
information as may be sought by the committee in pursuance of
this resolution;

7. Requests the Secretary-General to provide all necessary
assistance to the committee and to make the necessary
arrangements in the Secretariat for the purpose;

8. Decides that notwithstanding paragraphs 4 through 8,
nothing in this resolution shall prohibit assistance to the
legitimate government of Kuwait;

2

0046

9.   Requests the Secretary-General to report to the Council on the progress ofthe implementation of this resolution, the first report to be submitted within thirty days;

10.   Decides to keep this item on its agenda and to continue its efforts to put an early end to the invasion by Iraq.

3

0047

이라크의 쿠웨이트 침공 관련, 각국 반응

미 국 : - 이라크의 쿠웨이트 무력 침공 비난 및 이라크 군대 무조건
        철수 요구
      - UN 안보리 긴급 소집 요구
      - 미 군함의 걸프만 파견
      - 모든 선택 방안 검토중

소 련 : - 이라크의 쿠웨이트 침공 지역인 걸프역내 사태에 예의 주시

영 국 : - 이라크 군사 행동을 비난 및 이라크군 즉각적 철수 요구

일 본 : - 이라크의 쿠웨이트 침공에 유감 및 사태 진전에 깊은 관심
        표명
      - 이라크.쿠웨이트간 분쟁이 무력이 아닌 평화적으로 해결되길
        희망

호 주 : - 이라크의 쿠웨이트 침공 비난 및 이라크군 철수 요구

이스라엘 : - 이라크의 쿠웨이트 침입이 걸프만 지역내 극한 위험상태를
         유발할 것임을 표명

이 집 트 : - 이라크의 쿠웨이트 침공 사태 토의 위한 아랍연맹 긴급
         소집 요구

사 우 디 : 동 사태 토의 위한 GCC 6개 회원국 소집

U   N : 안보리 긴급 소집, 회의 개최 예정

아랍연맹 및 OIC : 동 사태 토의 위한 회의 소집 예정

0048

이라크, 쿠웨이트 사태 속보
(8.4. 08:00) <3>

1. 상   황

- o 8.3. 정오를 분수령으로 이라크군과 쿠웨이트 저항군간 교전 소강
  상태, 평온을 유지하고 있음
- o 미국무부, 이라크군이 쿠웨이트, 사우디 국경선 8-16 km 떨어진
  지점에 위치하고 있다고 밝히고 이에 대한 심각한 우려 표명
- o 이와 관련, 미국은 이라크가 사우디등 여타 중동국가를 공격할 경우
  무력 사용 입장을 NATO 맹방에 통보
- o 미.소 외무장관, 세계 각국에 이라크에 대한 무기 공급을 일체 중단
  하도록 촉구하는 내용의 양국 공동 성명 발표
- o 아랍 및 국제사회의 비난 및 제재조치가 확산되고 미.영.불의 걸프만
  내 군사력이 증강되는 가운데 8.3 이라크 혁명 평의회는 관영 INA 통신을
  통해 이라크 및 쿠웨이트 안보에 위협이 내재하지 않을 경우 8.5 부터
  쿠웨이트로 부터 군대를 철수 시킬것 이라고 발표
- ※ 참고사항 (걸프만 주둔 군사력)
- - 미   국 : 항공모함 및 전함 14척
- - 영   국 : 전함 2척 파견 결정
- - 프 랑 스 : 전함 1척 추가 배치 (총2척)

2. 각국 반응 및 제재 조치

- o 미   국
  - - 8.2. 이라크 및 쿠웨이트 자산 동결 및 교역 금지
  - - 안보리에 경제 및 군사 제재 조치 요청 계획(이라크군의 조속 철수
    불이행시)
  - - 사우디 및 터어키에 자국 통과 이라크 송유관 폐쇄 요구(원유 수출로
    차단 목표)

0049

o 소   련
  - 대 이라크 무기 금수 조치 (중공에도 동참 요청)
  - 동 사태 해결을 위한 미국과의 긴밀한 협력 제공 의사 표명
o 중   국
  - 이라크군의 쿠웨이트 조속 철수 촉구
  - 미국의 함대 걸프만 주둔 및 이라크 자산 동결 조치로 중동지역 긴장을
    고조시키고 있다고 비난
o 이란, 이집트, 뷔니지, 모로코, 알제리, 이디오피아, 쿠바 :
  - 이라크의 쿠웨이트 침공 비난 및 조속 철군 촉구
o 일본, 서독, 이태리, 벨지움, 룩셈부르크 :· 8.3. 쿠웨이트 자산 동결 발표
  ※ 미.영.불.스위스는 8.2. 이라크 및 쿠웨이트 자산 동결 조치
o 프 랑 스 : 대이라크 무기 금수 조치
o 네덜란드 : 이라크 유조선의 입항 금지
o G C C : 대 이라크 비난 자제, 아랍 정상들과의 외교를 통한 사태
             해결 노력
o E   C : 외무 고위 회담(로마, 8.4)에서 이라크 자산 동결을 포함한
             일련의 대응조치 검토
o UN 안보리 : 대 이라크 경제 제재 가능성 논의
o 아랍연맹, OAU : 이라크의 쿠웨이트 침공 비난 및 조속 철군 촉구 성명

3. 조치사항

  o 주한 이라크 대사대리 초치 (Mr. Burhan Ghazal)
  - 8.4. (토) 11:00 중동아 국장 면담
  - 쿠웨이트 및 이라크내 아국인 신변 안전, 보호조치 요청
  - 억류 또는 소재 미상인 아국 근로자(3명) 조기 귀환 협조 요청

0050

長 官 報 告 事 項

1990 . 8 . 6 .
國際機構條約局
國際法規課(22)

題目 : UN 안보리 대 이라크 경제제재 조치에 대한 법적 검토

1. UN 안보리 채택 결의안 요지

　가 . 이라크가 결의안 660호를 이행하지 않았음 .

　나 . 이라크 또는 쿠웨이트 상품의 수입 전면금지

　다 . 이라크 또는 쿠웨이트 상품의 수출 촉진활동 또는 환적 금지, 동
　　　목적의 대이라크, 쿠웨이트자금 이동 금지

　라 . 무기등 군사장비를 포함한 모든 상품의 대이라크, 쿠웨이트 판매
　　　또는 공급 및 동 촉진활동 금지

　마 . 모든 국가에 의한 이라크 또는 쿠웨이트내 상업적, 산업적 또는
　　　공공 사업기관에 대한 어떠한 자금이나 재정적, 경제적 자원 제공
　　　금지

　바 . 유엔 비회원국을 포함한 모든 국가가 동 결의안 이전의 계약이나
　　　허가에도 불문하고 동 결의안의 제규정을 엄격히 준수할 것을 요청

　사 . 동 결의안 규정에도 불구하고 쿠웨이트의 정당한 정부에 대한 지원
　　　을 금지하는 것은 아님 .

　아 . 모든 국가들이 점령국에 의하여 수립된 어떠한 정권도 승인치 않을
　　　것과 쿠웨이트의 정당한 정부의 자산을 보호하기 위해 적절한 조치
　　　를 취할 것을 요청함 .

　※ 안보리 표결에서 13:0:2(기권 :쿠바, 예멘)로 채택

0051

2. 법적근거

o UN 안보리는 헌장 41조의 규정에 따라 평화를 파괴하거나 위협하는
   사태를 해결하기 위하여 비군사적 강제조치를 취할 수 있음.

o 헌장 41조는 비군사적 강제조치의 법위로 "경제관계 및 수송, 통신의
   중단 또는 외교관계의 단절"을 규정하고 있음.

3. 사례

가. 대 로데지아(현 짐바부웨) 제재 결의
   - 1965.11.11 백인 소수 정권 수립
   - 1966.12.16 안보리 결의 232호 채택
     · 로데지아와 모든 통상관계 단절을 회원국에 요청(call upon)
     · 비회원국의 결의에 따른 조치 촉구(urge)

나. 대 남아공 제재 결의
   - 1963. 남아공에 대한 무기급수 결의
   - 1979. 군사적 핵협력 금지 결의 (누기급?)
     * 남아공에 대한 제재는 로데지아와 달리 포괄적 제재조처는 아님.

다. 기타
   1980.1.10. 이란 주재 미국 대사관 점거사건시 미국이 제출한 대 이란
   제재 결의안은 소련의 거부권 행사로 부결됨.

0052

4. 아국과의 관련

　가. 아국이 UN 회원국이 아니더라도 안보리의 대 이라크 경제제재 결의를
　　　준수하여야 할 규범적 의무가 발생한다고 볼 수 있음.

　　　(근거)

　　　- 금번 결의안은 UN 비회원국의 동 결의안 준수도 요청(call upon)
　　　　하고 있음.

　　　- 아국은 UN 헌장을 준수하고 제결의를 존중한다는 입장을 일관되게
　　　　취하여 옴.

　　　- UN 헌장 제2조 제6항은 유엔이 비회원국의 협조를 확보하도록
　　　　규정하고 있음.

　나. 경제제재 조치를 취할 수 있는 국내법적 근거는 대외무역법 제4조
　　　"무역에 관한 제한등 특별조치"가 있음.

　　　※ 대외무역법 제4조

　　　　"상공부장관은 우리나라 또는 우리나라 무역상대국에 전쟁·사변
　　　　또는 천재·지변이 있을 때 대통령령이 정하는 바에 의하여
　　　　물품의 수출·수입의 제한 또는 금지에 관한 특별조치를 할 수
　　　　있다".

　다. 1966.3.10 아국정부는 상공부고시를 통하여 대로데지아 통상관계
　　　단절조치를 취한 바 있음.

　라. 결론

　　　o 아국은 유엔 안보리의 경제 제재조치의 준수를 강력히 요구받게
　　　　될 것이며, 상기한 유엔헌장 및 유엔각기관의 결의에 대한 아국
　　　　입장에 비추어 유엔 비회원국임을 이유로 규범적 의무를 부인
　　　　하기는 곤란할 것임.

0053

ㅇ 특히 결의안 내용이 유엔비회원국의 제재 참여를 명시적으로
요청하고 있음에 비추어 정치적으로도 이를 거부하기 어려울
것으로 판단됨.

5. 관찰 및 평가

가. 유엔 안보리가 포괄적 경제제재 조치를 채택한 것은 상기 1966년
로데지아에 대한 조치 이래 두번째임.

나. 유엔 안보리 5개 상임이사국이 모두 찬성한 것은 국제평화와 안전의
유지를 위한 안보리의 역할을 재확인한 것이며, 이는 금후 지역
분쟁처리의 본보기로 작용할 것으로 판단됨.

다. 동 결의는 유엔 비회원국에 의한 이행을 요청하고 있음에 비추어
아국이 취할 조치 내용 및 동 조치의 안보리 통보 필요성에 대한
검토가 요망됨.

첨부: 안보리결의 전문 사본. 끝.

0054

~규정, UNW(F)-ㅡ (중앙, 중동, 등이, 경험2-기정)
UNW-1465 00806 17군)

UNITED NATIONS

SECURITY

COUNCIL

PROVISIONAL

S/21441
6 August 1990

ORIGINAL: ENGLISH

Canada, Colombia, Côte d'Ivoire, Ethiopia, Finland,
France, Malaysia, United Kingdom of Great Britain
and Northern Ireland, United States of America
and Zaire: draft resolution

The Security Council,

Reaffirming its resolution 660 (1990),

Deeply concerned that this resolution has not been implemented and that the
invasion by Iraq of Kuwait continues with further loss of human life and material
destruction,

Determined to bring the invasion and occupation of Kuwait by Iraq to an end
and to restore the sovereignty, independence and territorial integrity of Kuwait,

Noting that the legitimate Government of Kuwait has expressed its readiness to
comply with resolution 660 (1990),

Mindful of its responsibilities under the Charter for the maintenance of
international peace and security,

Affirming the inherent right of individual or collective self-defence, in
response to the armed attack by Iraq against Kuwait, in accordance with Article 51
of the Charter,

Acting under Chapter VII of the Charter of the United Nations,

1.   Determines that Iraq so far has failed to comply with operative paragraph
2 of resolution 660 (1990) and has usurped the authority of the legitimate
Government of Kuwait;

2.   Decides, as a consequence, to take the following measures to secure
compliance of Iraq with operative paragraph 2 and to restore the authority of the
legitimate Government of Kuwait;

1484E

3-1

0055

3. Decides that all States shall prevent:

- (a) The import into their territories of all commodities and products
originating in Iraq or Kuwait exported therefrom after the date of this resolution;

- (b) Any activities by their nationals or in their territories which would
promote or are calculated to promote the export or transshipment of any commodities
or products from Iraq or Kuwait; and any dealings by their nationals or their flag
vessels or in their territories in any commodities or products originating in Iraq
or Kuwait and exported therefrom after the date of this resolution, including in
particular any transfer of funds to Iraq or Kuwait for the purposes of such
activities or dealings;

- (c) The sale or supply by their nationals or from their territories or using
their flag vessels of any commodities or products, including weapons or any other
military equipment, whether or not originating in their territories but not
including supplies intended strictly for medical purposes, and, in humanitarian
circumstances, foodstuffs, to any person or body in Iraq or Kuwait or to any person
or body for the purposes of any business carried on in or operated from Iraq or
Kuwait, and any activities by their nationals or in their territories which promote
or are calculated to promote such sale or supply of such commodities or products;

4. Decides that all States shall not make available to the Government of
Iraq or to any commercial, industrial or public utility undertaking in Iraq or
Kuwait, any funds or any other financial or economic resources and shall prevent
their nationals and any persons within their territories from removing from their
territories or otherwise making available to that Government or to any such
undertaking any such funds or resources and from remitting any other funds to
persons or bodies within Iraq or Kuwait, except payments exclusively for strictly
medical or humanitarian purposes and, in special humanitarian circumstances,
foodstuffs;

5. Calls upon all States, including States non-members of the United
Nations, to act strictly in accordance with the provisions of this resolution
notwithstanding any contract entered into or licence granted before the date of
this resolution;

6. Decides to establish, in accordance with rule 28 of the provisional rules
of procedure of the Security Council, a Committee of the Security Council
consisting of all the members of the Council, to undertake the following tasks and
to report on its work to the Council with its observations and recommendations:

- (a) To examine the reports on the progress of the implementation of this
resolution which will be submitted by the Secretary-General;

2

0056

- (b) To seek from all States further information regarding the action taken by them concerning the effective implementation of the provisions laid down in this resolution;

7. Calls upon all States to co-operate fully with the Committee in the fulfilment of its task, including supplying such information as may be sought by the Committee in pursuance of this resolution;

8. Requests the Secretary-General to provide all necessary assistance to the Committee and to make the necessary arrangements in the Secretariat for the purpose;

9. Decides that, notwithstanding paragraphs 4 through 8, nothing in this resolution shall prohibit assistance to the legitimate Government of Kuwait, and calls upon all States:

- (a) To take appropriate measures to protect assets of the legitimate Government of Kuwait and its agencies; and

- (b) Not to recognize any régime set up by the occupying power;

10. Requests the Secretary-General to report to the Council on the progress of the implementation of this resolution, the first report to be submitted within thirty days;

11. Decides to keep this item on its agenda and to continue its efforts to put an early end to the invasion by Iraq.

3

0057

원 본

외 무 부

종 별 : 지 급

번 호 : UNW-1465 일 시 : 90 0806 1730

수 신 : 장 관(국연,중동,통이,경협이,기정)

발 신 : 주 유엔대사

제 목 : 안보리(이락-쿠웨트 분쟁)

1. 금 8.6 14:00-16:00 표제건 토의를 위한 안보리가 속개됨.이라크에 대한 포괄적인 경제제제 조치를 주내용으로 한 결의안이 찬 13-반0-기권2(큐바,예멘)로 채택됨2.카나다,콜롬비아,코트디브와르,이디오피아,핀랜드,미,영,불   말레이지아, 자이레등10개국이 공동제안한 동 결의안의 주요내용은 아래와 같음 가. 이라크가 결의안 660호를 이행하지 않았음.

나. 이라크 또는 쿠웨이트 상품의 수입전면금지

다. 이라크 또는 쿠웨이트 상품의 수출 촉진활동 또는 환적 금지. 동 목적의 대이라크, 쿠웨이트자금 이동 금지

라. 무기등 군사장비를 포함한 모든 상품의 대이라크,쿠웨이트 판대 또는 공급및 동 촉진활동 금지

마. 모든 국가에 의한 이라크 또는 쿠웨이트 내상업적,산업적 또는 공공 사업기관에 대한 어떠한 자금이나 재정적,경제적 자원 제공금지.

바. 유엔 비회원국을 포함한 모든 국가가 동 결의안 이전의 계약이나 허가에도불문하고 동결의안의 제규정을 엄격히 준수할것을 촉구

사. 동 결의안 규정에도 불구하고 쿠웨트의 정당한정부에 대한 지원을 금지하는것은 아님.

아. 모든국가들이 점령국에 의하여 수립된 어떠한 정권도 승인치 않을것과 쿠웨트의 정당한정부의 자산을 보호 하기 위해 적절한 조치를 취할것을 촉구함.

3. 안보리 회원국 발언 요지

0 쿠이이트

이라크에 대한 제제조치 촉구

0 이라크

국기국	장관	차관	1차보	2차보	중아국	경제국	통상국	안기부

PAGE 1

90.08.07   08:50 WH

외신 1과 통제관

0053

이라크군의 철수가 개시되었음. 동 결의안은 분쟁해결에 도움이 되지 않음.

0 미국   이라크는   결의안 660호를   계속 이행치 않고 있으며 점령군을
철수하기보다는 장기체류 준비를하고있음. 헌장 7장 에의한 강제조치가 필요함.

0 핀란드

유엔헌장상의 기본원칙 준수 필요

0 말레이지아

동결의안 채택이 역외국가에 의한 무력 사용의전조가 되어서는 안됨.

0 자이레

비동맹운동의 원칙에 따라 이라크에 의한 결의안 660호 이행을 촉구함. 자이레의
금번결의안 지지는 미래 무력사용국에 대한 하나의경고임.

0 큐바

이라크가 결의안 660호에 따른 철수의사를 밝혔음. 금번 결의안은 분쟁해결에
기여하기보다는 미국에 의한 중동지역 지배 목적에 기여하는것임.

0 예멘

예멘이 동 분쟁 해결을 위해 적극 중재에 나서고있음. 중동지역 내부문제에 외세가
개입해서는 안됨.

0 영,불,중,소등 여타국:

유엔헌장상 원칙 준수촉구

4. 관찰 및 평가

0 유엔 안보리가 결의안 661호 같은 포괄적인 경제제제 조치를 채택한것은
1965로데지아에 대한 제제조치 이래 두번째임.

0 유엔 안보리 5개 상임이사국이 동 조치에 모두찬성 표결함으로써 이들 강대국이
지역분쟁의 평화적 해결 원칙 준수 촉구 및 국가간 분쟁해결 목적의 무력 불사용원칙
위반국에 대한 강력한 제제조치 결의를 공동 표명한바, 이는 국제평화와 안전의유지를
위한 최근 점증하는 안보리의 역할을 재확인하고 금후 지역분쟁 처리의 본보기로 작용
할 것으로 판단됨.

0 일부 안보리 국가는 금번 제제조치 결의안 채택이 금후 미국등에 의한
군사적제제조치의 전단계조치 또는 군사조치의 발판으로 이용될 가능성에 대해 우려를
표명하였음.

0 금번 결의안은 모든 유엔 비회원국에 의한 동일한 제제조치의 이행을

PAGE 2

촉구하고있는바, 아국이 취해야할 사항에 대한 검토가 필요한 것으로 사료됨. 금번 결의안에따라 안보리내에 설치될 위원회에 아국이 취한 조치를 통보해야할 필요성에도 대비하여야 할 것으로 사료됨.

    첨부:동결의안 전문 UNW(F)-120

    끝

    (대사 현홍주-국장)

유첨 UNW(F)- ⇒ (중연, 중동, 동이, 경협2-기정)
UNW-1465 00806 17전

UNITED NATIONS

SECURITY

COUNCIL

PROVISIONAL

S/21441
6 August 1990

ORIGINAL: ENGLISH

<u>Canada, Colombia, Côte d'Ivoire, Ethiopia, Finland,
France, Malaysia, United Kingdom of Great Britain
and Northern Ireland, United States of America
and Zaire: draft resolution</u>

The Security Council,

<u>Reaffirming</u> its resolution 660 (1990),

<u>Deeply concerned</u> that this resolution has not been implemented and that the invasion by Iraq of Kuwait continues with further loss of human life and material destruction,

<u>Determined</u> to bring the invasion and occupation of Kuwait by Iraq to an end and to restore the sovereignty, independence and territorial integrity of Kuwait,

<u>Noting</u> that the legitimate Government of Kuwait has expressed its readiness to comply with resolution 660 (1990),

<u>Mindful</u> of its responsibilities under the Charter for the maintenance of international peace and security,

<u>Affirming</u> the inherent right of individual or collective self-defence, in response to the armed attack by Iraq against Kuwait, in accordance with Article 51 of the Charter,

<u>Acting</u> under Chapter VII of the Charter of the United Nations,

1.   <u>Determines</u> that Iraq so far has failed to comply with operative paragraph 2 of resolution 660 (1990) and has usurped the authority of the legitimate Government of Kuwait;

2.   <u>Decides</u>, as a consequence, to take the following measures to secure compliance of Iraq with operative paragraph 2 and to restore the authority of the legitimate Government of Kuwait;

1484E

3-1

S/21441
English
Page 2

3.   Decides that all States shall prevent:

-   (a) The import into their territories of all commodities and products
originating in Iraq or Kuwait exported therefrom after the date of this resolution;

-   (b) Any activities by their nationals or in their territories which would
promote or are calculated to promote the export or transshipment of any commodities
or products from Iraq or Kuwait; and any dealings by their nationals or their flag
vessels or in their territories in any commodities or products originating in Iraq
or Kuwait and exported therefrom after the date of this resolution, including in
particular any transfer of funds to Iraq or Kuwait for the purposes of such
activities or dealings;

-   (c) The sale or supply by their nationals or from their territories or using
their flag vessels of any commodities or products, including weapons or any other
military equipment, whether or not originating in their territories but not
including supplies intended strictly for medical purposes, and, in humanitarian
circumstances, foodstuffs, to any person or body in Iraq or Kuwait or to any person
or body for the purposes of any business carried on in or operated from Iraq or
Kuwait, and any activities by their nationals or in their territories which promote
or are calculated to promote such sale or supply of such commodities or products;

4.   Decides that all States shall not make available to the Government of
Iraq or to any commercial, industrial or public utility undertaking in Iraq or
Kuwait, any funds or any other financial or economic resources and shall prevent
their nationals and any persons within their territories from removing from their
territories or otherwise making available to that Government or to any such
undertaking any such funds or resources and from remitting any other funds to
persons or bodies within Iraq or Kuwait, except payments exclusively for strictly
medical or humanitarian purposes and, in special humanitarian circumstances,
foodstuffs;

5.   Calls upon all States, including States non-members of the United
Nations, to act strictly in accordance with the provisions of this resolution
notwithstanding any contract entered into or licence granted before the date of
this resolution;

6.   Decides to establish, in accordance with rule 28 of the provisional rules
of procedure of the Security Council, a Committee of the Security Council
consisting of all the members of the Council, to undertake the following tasks and
to report on its work to the Council with its observations and recommendations:

-   (a) To examine the reports on the progress of the implementation of this
resolution which will be submitted by the Secretary-General;

2

0062

-    (b) To seek from all States further information regarding the action taken by them concerning the effective implementation of the provisions laid down in this resolution;

7. Calls upon all States to co-operate fully with the Committee in the fulfilment of its task, including supplying such information as may be sought by the Committee in pursuance of this resolution;

8. Requests the Secretary-General to provide all necessary assistance to the Committee and to make the necessary arrangements in the Secretariat for the purpose;

9. Decides that, notwithstanding paragraphs 4 through 8, nothing in this resolution shall prohibit assistance to the legitimate Government of Kuwait, and calls upon all States:

-    (a) To take appropriate measures to protect assets of the legitimate Government of Kuwait and its agencies; and

-    (b) Not to recognize any regime set up by the occupying power;

10. Requests the Secretary-General to report to the Council on the progress of the implementation of this resolution, the first report to be submitted within thirty days;

11. Decides to keep this item on its agenda and to continue its efforts to put an early end to the invasion by Iraq.

3

0063

유엔안보리의 대이라크 경제제재조치 결의

90. 8. 7.
국제연합과

1. 결의안 채택

   o 유엔 안전보장이사회는 90.8.6.(월) 오후 10개국(미, 영, 불,
   카, 콜롬비아, 코트디브와르, 이디오피아, 핀랜드, 말레이지아,
   자이르)이 공동 제안한 대이라크 경제제재조치 결의안(안보리
   결의 661조)을 13:0으로 채택 (쿠바, 예멘은 기권)

2. 결의안 주요내용 (전문 별첨)

   o 이라크, 쿠웨이트 상품수입의 전면금지

   o 무기등 군사장비를 포함한 모든 상품(all commodities and
   products)의 대이라크, 쿠웨이트 판매 또는 공급금지

   o 인도적, 의학적 목적이외에 이라크, 쿠웨이트에 대한 재정적,
   경제적 자원제공 금지

   o 유엔 비회원국을 포함한 모든 국가가 본 결의안 이전의 계약이나
   허가에 불문하고, 본 결의안의 제규정을 엄격히 준수할 것을 촉구

   o 모든 국가들이 점령국에 의하여 수립된 어떤 정권도 승인치 않을
   것과 쿠웨이트의 정당한 정부의 자산을 보호하기 위해 적절한
   조치를 취할 것을 촉구

3. 아국의 조치검토

   o 금번 안보리의 경제제재 조치는 헌장 41조에 의한 비군사적
   제재조치로서, 유엔회원국은 헌장 48조 및 49조에 의하여

0064

안보리가 결정한 조치의 이행에 상호 원조를 제공(affording mutual assistance in carrying out the measures)"할 의무가 있음.

* 1966년 대로데지아 제재조치시, 동의무 불이행국인 남아공과 폴투갈에 대한 제재문제가 논의된바 있음.

o 유엔 비회원국은 유엔헌장에 의한 제재조치 이행의무는 없으나, 금번결의가 비회원국의 결의내용 준수도 촉구하고 있는 점에 비추어, 제재조치에 참여치 않을 경우, 유엔의 집단조치에 대한 비협조적인 태도로 간주될 것이므로 정치적 부담을 지게 될것임.

* 아국은 1966년 유엔의 대로데지아 경제제재 조치시, 상공부 고시(66.3.10.)로 대로데지아 통상관계 단절을 발표한 바 있음.

안보리 결의 661호

90. 8. 6.

The Security Council,

Reaffirming its resolution 660 (1990),

Deeply concerned that this resolution has not been implemented and that the invasion by Iraq of Kuwait continues with further loss of human life and material destruction,

Determined to bring the invasion and occupation of Kuwait by Iraq to an end and to restore the sovereignty, independence and territorial integrity of Kuwait,

Noting that the legitimate Government of Kuwait has expressed its readiness to comply with resolution 660 (1990),

Mindful of its responsibilities under the Charter for the maintenance of international peace and security,

0066

Affirming the inherent right of individual or collective self-defence, in response to the armed attack by Iraq against Kuwait, in accordance with Article 51 of the Charter,

Acting under Chapter VII of the Charter of the United Nations,

1. Determines that Iraq so far has failed to comply with operative paragraph 2 of resolution 660(1990) and has usurped the authority of the legitimate Government of Kuwait ;

2. Decides, as a consequence, to take the following measures to secure compliance of Iraq with operative paragraph 2 and to restore the authority of the legitimate Government of Kuwait ;

3. Decides that all States shall prevent :
   (a) The import into their territories of all commodities and products originating in Iraq or Kuwait exported therefrom after the date of this resolution ;

0067

(b) any activities by their nationals or in their territories which would promote or are calculated to promote the export or transshipment of any commodities or products from Iraq or Kuwait ;/ and any dealings by their nationals or their flag vessels or in their territories in any commodities or products originating in Iraq or Kuwait/and exported therefrom after the date of this resolution, including in particular any transfer of funds to Iraq or Kuwait for the purposes of such activities or dealings ;

(c) The sale or supply by their nationals or from their territories or using their flag vessels of any commodities or products, including weapons or any other military equipment, whether or not originating in their territories but not including supplies intended strictly for medical purposes, and, in humanitarian circumstances, foodstuffs, to any person or body in Iraq or Kuwait or to any person or body for the purposes of any business carried on in or operated from Iraq or Kuwait, and any activities by

0068

their nationals or in their territories <u>which</u>
<u>promote or are calculated to promote such sale or</u>
<u>supply of such commodities or products</u> ;

4. <u>Decides</u> that <u>all States shall not make available</u> to
the Government of Iraq or to any commercial, industrial
or public utility undertaking in Iraq or Kuwait, <u>any</u>
<u>funds or any other financial or economic resources</u>
and <u>shall prevent their nationals and any persons</u>
within their territories from removing from their
territories or otherwise making available to that
Government or to any such undertaking <u>any such funds</u>
<u>or resources and from remitting any other funds to</u>
persons or bodies within Iraq or Kuwait, <u>except</u>
<u>payments exclusively for strictly medical or humani-</u>
<u>tarian purposes and, in special humanitarian</u>
<u>circumstances, foodstuffs</u> ;

5. <u>Calls upon</u> <u>all States, including States non-members</u>
<u>of the United Nations, to act strictly</u> in accordance
with the provisions of this resolution <u>notwithstanding</u>
<u>any contract entered into or licence granted before</u>
<u>the date of this resolution</u> ;

0069

6. _Decides_ to establish, in accordance with rule 28 of the provisional rules of procedure of the Security Council, a Committee of the Security Council consisting of all the members of the Council, to undertake the following tasks and to report on its work to the Council with its observations and recommendations :

(a) To examine the reports on the progress of the implementation of this resolution which will be submitted by the Secretary-General ;

(b) To seek from all States further information regarding the action taken by them concerning the effective implementation of the provisions laid down in this resolution ;

7. _Calls upon_ all States to co-operate fully with the Committee in the fulfilment of its task, including supplying such information as may be sought by the Committee in pursuance of this resolution ;

8. _Requests_ the Secretary-General to provide all necessary assistance to the Committee and to make the necessary arrangements in the Secretariat for the purpose ;

0070

9. Decides that, notwithstanding paragraphs 4 through 8,
    nothing in this resolution shall prohibit assistance
    to the legitimate Government of Kuwait, and calls upon
    all States :

    (a) To take appropriate measures to protect assets
        of the legitimate Government of Kuwait and its
        agencies ; and

    (b) Not to recognize any regime set up by the
        occupying power ;

10. Requests the Secretary-General to report to the
    Council on the progress of the implementation of
    this resolution, the first report to be submitted
    within thirty days ;

11. Decides to keep this item on its agenda and to
    continue its efforts to put an early end to the
    invasion by Iraq.

0071

안보리 결의 660호

90. 8. 2.

The Security Council,

Alarmed by the invasion of Kuwait on 2 August 1990 by the military forces of Iraq, determining that there exists a breach of international peace and security as regards the Iraqi invasion of Kuwait,

Acting under articles 39 and 40 of the Charter of the United Nations.

1. Condemns the Iraqi invasion of Kuwait

2. Demands that Iraq withdraw immediately and unconditionally all its forces to the positions in which they were located on August 1, 1990

3. Calls upon Iraq and Kuwait to begin immediately intensive negotiations for the resolution of their differences and supports all efforts in this regard, and especially those of the Arab League

4. Decides to meet again as necessary to consider further steps to ensure compliance with this resolution

0072

이라크,쿠웨이트 사태 속보
(8.7. 06:00) <5>

1. 상 황

- ㅇ 이라크, 미국 군사 행동 대비 전군에 비상 경계령 및 대규모 소개 훈련 실시 (바그다드 외신 종합)
  - 18개 사단, 사우디 국경선 배치
  - 이라크, 터어키 경유 송유관 1개 폐쇄
- ㅇ 사우디 쿠웨이트 접경지역 군사력 강화
- ㅇ 유엔 안보리 회의 개회 (8.6)
  - 대 이라크 모든상품 수출입 금지
  - 신규 투자 금지
  - 금융자산 유입 금지등 검토
- ㅇ 쿠웨이트 임시정부, 제재 국가의 자국민 신변 안전 문제 경고(8.6)
- ㅇ 이라크군 쿠웨이트내 2개 호텔 체류 외국인 (미.영) 366명 체포, 이라크 이송 준비 (영국 외무부 대변인 6일 발표)
  - BA 항공사 747기 탑승객
- ㅇ 이집트 및 사우디 외세 개입 막기위한 사담후세인과 타협안 제시 준비

2. 각국 추가 반응

- ㅇ 미 국 : 채니 국방장관 사우디 파견 화드 국왕과 회담(8.6)
    (이라크군 철수 아랍 세계 설득)
  - 미군함 추가 배치 발표
- ㅇ 프 랑 스 : 프랑스 선박에 의한 이라크산 원유 수송 금지
    "뒤플렉스"호 페르샤 항진
  - 엑소세 함대함 미사일, 크로탈 대공 미사일등 최신예 무기 적재

0073

o 일   본 : 원유 수입 금지 조치 실시 (8.6)

　　　　　　　　교역 금지

　　　　　　　　부 융자, 자본거래 정지

　　　　　　　　경제 협력 동결

o 이   란 : 이란과 시리아는 이라크 침공에 더이상 무관심하지 않을

　　　　　　　　것이며 양국은 이라크 군대의 전면 철수 촉구(외무장관 표명)

o 터 어 키 : 터어키내 이라크 송유관 폐쇄 가능성 시사 (NATO 대사 긴급

　　　　　　　　회의시)

3. 추가 조치 사항

o 관계부처 대책회의 (8.6. 16:00 외무부)

　- 서방의 대 이라크 제재 조치 관련, 관계부처 문제점 검토

o 주 이라크 대사관에 아국인 근로자 3명 소재 확인(압송 여부) 및

　　확인시 석방 교섭 지시 (8.6)

o 외국인 이라크 압송 보도 관련, 주 영 대사관에 사실 확인 지시

　- 8.5. BBC 보도 관련, 주 영 대사관이 BBC측에 확인 결과, 8.5. 오전

　　방송에서 아국인 압송 관계 부분을 발견하지 못하였다 함

　- 본건 외무성에 문의 결과 아국인을 포함한 외국인 이라크 압송 사실

　　아는바 없다 함

o 사우디, UAE 등 걸프 지역 주재 공관장에 비상 대비 계획 수립 지시

　- 교민 신변 안전 보호

　- 비상 대피 및 철수

　- 비상 식량, 식수, 연료 준비

4. 전   망

o 이라크, 쿠웨이트 사태는 계속 확대 내지 장기화 전망

　- 이라크는 점령군의 즉각 철수 및 쿠웨이트 왕정 원상 복구 의도 전무

　　(쿠웨이트 예속화)

　- 미국 및 서방 각국의 대이라크 무력 사용 경고 및 군사 개입 태세와

　　대 이라크 경제 제재 조치를 취하므로써 사태 악화 우려

　- 이집트 및 사우디가 아랍권 내부 문제에 외세 개입 배제 전제로

　　협상을 통해 수습 노력을 펴고 있으나 아랍 제국간 깊은 이해 관계 및

　　심한 분열로 힘을 배경으로 한 결집력이 없기 때문

0074

외 무 부

종 별 :

번 호 : UNW-1471   일 시 : 90 0806 1820

수 신 : 장관(중근동,국연,경협,기정)

발 신 : 주유엔대사

제 목 : 이라크-쿠웨이트 침공 관련 기사

　　이라크의 쿠웨트 침공과 관련, 당지 주요 신문의 관계 해설기사등을 별첨 FAX 송부
하니 참고바람.

　　첨부

　　1. NY TIMES (90.8.6) 'EXPERTS SAY EMBARGO MAY WORK IFNATIONS MAINTAIN
COMMITMENT'

　　2. THE CHRISTIAN SCIENCE MONITOR (90.8.6)'GULF CRISIS PUTSARABS IN
DIPLOMATIC BIND'

　　3. WALL STREET JOURNAL (90.8.6) 'AS IRAQ EMBARGO GAINSSUPPORT, RISK GROW
FOR US AND ITS ALLIES'

　　4. WSJ(90.8.6) 'ARAB WORLD SORELY DIVIDED OVER IRAQ'S SHOW OFFORCE' 끝

　　(대사 현홍주-국장)

　　첨부: UNW(F)-121

중아국　　국기국　　경제국　　안기부　　1차보　　2차보

90.08.07　　08:19 CG

외신 1과 통제관

0075

1

Experts Say Embargo May Work If Nations Maintain Commitment

NY Times
90.8.6

By STEVE LOHR

(A.1)

With Japan joining the United States and Europe yesterday by agreeing to halt oil imports from Iraq and Kuwait, the industrialized world has begun an economic campaign against Baghdad that for the moment relies on an embargo but holds out the possible use of a naval blockade.

While economic embargoes have rarely succeeded, oil analysts and Middle East experts say the sanctions against Iraq could hobble its economy as long as Western unity and commitment to enforcing the embargo holds.

The modern history of economic embargoes is checkered at best. The effectiveness of an embargo is sometimes blunted by a lack of international cooperation and enforcement, so that the target nation can still buy and sell in the global marketplace. And breaking sanctions against oil trade is often made easier by the fact that oil is a commodity, not branded or labeled for easy identification.

But the embargo against Iraq is different in certain crucial respects, Middle East experts and oil analysts say. It has enlisted a larger measure of international support than previous sanction efforts and is aimed at a war-weakened economy whose income is almost solely derived from one product — oil — that is shipped abroad from a few easily monitored locations.

Still, the embargo plan appears to have broad international appeal. The United Nations Security Council is expected to approve a worldwide ban on oil purchases from Iraq and occupied Kuwait on Monday and to prohibit all other trade and financial dealings with those countries. [Page A6.]

"Tracking and enforcing an embargo against Iraqi-controlled oil exports should not be a big problem," said Henry Schuler, director of the energy program at the Center for Strategic and International Studies in Washington. "The problem will be sus-

Continued on Page A6, Column 3

101

0076

82   걸프 사태 유엔안전보장이사회 동향 1

Experts Say Embargo Could Work if Unity Against Iraq Is Uph

Continued From Page A1

taining the commitment."

The real test of the West's commitment may well come if the embargo is successful. Iraq has been exporting about 2.6 million barrels of oil a day, while Kuwait ships about 1.2 million barrels. Together, they account for more than 20 percent of OPEC exports.

If the oil from Kuwait and Iraq is taken off the world market, energy prices will jump unless other producers increase their output. The nation most capable of filling the oil shortfall is Iraq's oil-rich neighbor, Saudi Arabia, which now produces 5.5 million barrels of oil a day. But, experts estimate, it could quickly increase its output by another 2 million barrels a day.

The Saudis, the experts agree, will be unlikely to pump more oil and risk antagonizing President Hussein without a guarantee that the West will come to Saudi Arabia's defense if it is attacked.

"For this embargo to work without driving up oil prices and slowing economic growth, the Saudis will have to produce more oil," said Joseph Stanislaw, managing director of Cambridge Energy Research Associates, an oil consultant. "The Saudis will only cooperate if the international consensus that has emerged in the past few days is backed up with Western — and specifically, American — military power."

Different Restrictions

The boycott of oil imports from Iraq and Kuwait is also different in that previous economic embargoes tried mainly to restrict the flow of goods from many different countries to one nation, such as Rhodesia or South Africa. By contrast, the sanctions against Iraq are an attempt to put pressure on a nation by refusing to buy its main export.

Iraq's oil is shipped to the West by just three routes: a pipeline through Turkey to the Mediterranean; a pipeline across Saudi Arabia that runs to the Red Sea port of Yanbu, and loaded directly into tankers in the Persian Gulf. Kuwait's oil is exported via tankers in the gulf.

So if Turkey and Saudi Arabia, assured of Western military protection, shut down the pipelines across their territory, most of Iraq's economic lifeline would be gone. Even if they do not, the ship movements to and from the ports handling Iraqi and Kuwaiti oil in the Mediterranean, the Red Sea and the Persian Gulf can be monitored without too much trouble, according to oil experts, both by observation and tracking ship movements by Western military satellites.

A naval blockade would insure that Iraqi and Kuwaiti oil never reach foreign buyers. Should Washington and its allies try a naval blockade, the task would not be too daunting because the "choke points" are few and in comparatively narrow waterways, according to one shipping analyst.

Without a blockade, there are several techniques oil traders can use to disguise the identity of an oil shipment, including falsifying documents that show a tanker's identity, switching oil from one tanker to another and bribing port officials to allow oil from an embargoed nation to be unloaded. Concealing the origin of an oil shipment is made easier by the freewheeling nature of the international oil business. The ownership of a tankerload of oil can frequently change hands several times from the time it leaves its home port to the time it unloads weeks later, halfway round the world.

All these gambits have been employed since 1979 to sidestep the voluntary embargo, backed by the United Nations General Assembly, on oil shipments to South Africa to protest its apartheid policies. The oil embargo against South Africa has increased its oil bill, because it has paid millions in fees to middlemen to help Pretoria elude the sanctions. But the voluntary embargo did not stop oil from reaching South Africa.

Veterans of the South African oil trading curbs say the embargo against Iraq should be much more difficult to circumvent. "This is a much more concerted international action than the restrictions on trade with Pretoria," said a Rotterdam oil trader, who asked not to be identified. "It should be much

Japan joined the United S and Europe in halting all o ports from Iraq and Kuwait oji Sakamoto, chief cabinet s tary of Japan, made the nouncement yesterday in To!

easier to track shipments out o especially if American military nology is being used, than it has l monitor oil tankers from all o world heading for South Africa."

Syrian Likens Invasion to Law of the Jur

NICOSIA, Cyprus, Aug. 5 (Reuters) — President Hafez al-Assad of Syria, denouncing Iraq's invasion of Kuwait, was quoted today as saying Baghdad was following the law of the jungle.

"If every country were to impose its illegitimate viewpoints through aggression and the use of force, the world would resemble a jungle," Iranian television quoted Mr. Assad as saying.

The Iranian Foreign Minister, Ali Akbar Velayati, meeting Mr. As Damascus, also criticized the inv

"Ten years ago, when Iraq att Iran, we said that if no serious were taken against the aggressi dangerous consequences would other countries in the future," th vision station, monitored by quoted Mr. Velayati as having sa

Iraq and Iran began an eig war in 1980.

THE CHRISTIAN SCIENCE MONITOR Monday, August 6, 1990

4

THE WORLD ★★★ IRAQI ★★★ POWERPLAY

Gulf Crisis Puts Arabs in Diplomatic Bind

Jordan's bid to arrange Arab minisummit involving Iraq cut short by Arab League condemnation

By Gerald Butt
Special to The Christian Science Monitor

NICOSIA, CYPRUS

THE Iraqi invasion of Kuwait has presented Arab diplomacy with its biggest challenge.

Arab reaction to the invasion, in sharp contrast to that from outside the region, has been both slow and divided.

"The rest of the world was quick to condemn the attack," commented Al-Ahram, the authoritative Egyptian newspaper, "while the Arabs wasted two days in consultations."

The shock of what had happened in Kuwait was felt most keenly in the Arab Gulf states, whose reticence to condemn Iraq, according to Western diplomats, was based on fear. To provoke Iraqi anger, it was felt, might be to court a visit from the Iraqi Army.

However, in the end the Gulf states had no choice but to condemn Iraq. The Gulf Cooperation Council had been humiliated by its inability to come to the assistance of one of its members at a time when its territorial integrity had been challenged. "For them to have remained silent," a diplomat in Bahrain said, "would have been impossible."

The Gulf states made their protest once

How the Military Stacks Up in the Middle East

Country	Troops*	Tanks**	Combat Aircraft***
Iraq	1mil.	5,500	670
Kuwait	20,300	275	54
Bahrain	3,350	54	29
Egypt	445,000	2,250	494
Iran	600,000	500	300
Israel	140,000	3,900	676
Oman	25,500	39	62
Qatar	7,000	24	~9
Saudi Arabia	65,700	550	180
United Arab Emirates	43,000	131	79

*Men under arms
**Main battle tanks
***Aircraft plus armed helicopters
Source: International Institute for Strategic Studies

SHIRLEY HORN, GUT STUART - STAFF

Middle Eastern OPEC Nations

Oil production, millions of barrels per day
■ OPEC quota
▫ July actual
Source: Platt's Week

6 5 4 3 2 1 0
Iraq Kuwait Iran Qatar Libya UAE Saudi Arabia

they were assured that a similar stand was being taken by Egypt and other powerful states in the region.

Arab League foreign ministers in Cairo, meanwhile, could not agree on a resolution on the Kuwait crisis that would win the support of all 21 members.

"They frankly did not know what to do about Iraq," an Arab diplomat in Cairo said. "Getting 14 Arab countries to condemn Iraq and call for the invasion force to be withdrawn was the best they could come up with."

Significantly, Jordan voted against the resolution. King Hussein did not agree with other Arab leaders on how Saddam Hussein should be handled.

King Hussein is a frequent visitor to Baghdad. Throughout the Gulf war with Iran he was a loyal supporter of Saddam Hussein. He allowed vital supplies for the Iraqi war effort to be imported through Aqaba on the Red Sea when Iraq lost its access to the Gulf.

The King considered it essential to keep open at least one avenue to Baghdad in the hope that Saddam Hussein could be persuaded to join diplomatic efforts to defuse the Gulf crisis.

Jordan's role of go-between was confirmed yesterday when Jordanian Prime Minister Mudar Badran said that both President Bush and Saudi King Fahd had asked King Hussein to mediate.

King Hussein flew to Baghdad the day after the invasion began and convinced the Iraqi leader that he should take part in the talks with other Arab leaders – and possibly even the deposed Emir of Kuwait – in the Saudi city of Jeddah at the weekend.

However, the Jeddah summit was scut-

tled, Mr. Badran said yesterday because of the premature Arab League censure of Iraq, Arab League states – including Egypt and Saudi Arabia – came out with a strong condemnation of Iraq Saturday, leaving Hussein with little enthusiasm for the talks in Jeddah, Western diplomats said.

THAT same day the Iraqis made it clear that the ruling Sabah family would never be allowed to hold power in Kuwait again, referring to them contemptuously as "the extinct regime."

In this atmosphere, reconciliation talks were out of the question. And the Kuwaitis were left increasingly frustrated that their appeals for help from their Arab brothers had not been answered.

"Those states which voted against the Arab League resolution," a minister in the former Kuwaiti government, Abdel Rahman al-Awadi said in Cairo, "have good relations with Saddam Hussein and think they might benefit from what has happened. But I am sure that those countries are going to be next in line for his deception and aggression."

The new Iraqi-supported "free government" in Kuwait, meanwhile, expressed its "deep gratitude and thanks" for what it called Iraq's "pan-Arab decision and lofty Arab initiative" in sending in its troops.

"Therefore," a senior Arab official admitted privately, "the regimes have to be careful what they say about Saddam Hussein." Furthermore, the confiscation of the riches of the ruling family of Kuwait will not be universally condemned by the Arab public.

But the hard truth was that the Arabs had run out of options.

Kuwait wanted a military response.

However, no single Arab state, Western diplomats noted, offered to take on the might of the Iraqis.

Saddam Hussein has shown that he is willing to sweep aside conventional restraints and use whatever force may be necessary to achieve his goals. To incur Iraqi wrath, therefore, would be a dangerous gamble.

"You should know by now how Saddam Hussein behaves," Mr. Awadi said. "He promised us a week ago through all the Arab leaders that he was not intending any military action. One day we were discussing our problems with his delegation in Jeddah. The next day he was invading us."

Another reason for Arab reluctance in confronting Iraq stems from a different fear. While Saddam Hussein is viewed negatively in the West and is disliked and feared by most Arab leaders, among sections of the ordinary Arab population he enjoys considerable support. He is admired for his militant attitude toward Israel and its Western supporters, particularly the United States.

The threat made by the Iraqi leader earlier this year to use chemical weapons to wipe out "half of Israel" if the Israelis launched an attack on Iraq won loud applause in the Arab world.

This statement was clearly based on fanciful thinking. Such pan-Arab reaction as there was had been critical of the Iraqi move.

garded with both envy and contempt by many Arabs. In the Israeli-occupied Gaza Strip, Palestinian sources say, there was "a certain degree of satisfaction" at the Iraqi invasion. "Here was an Arab leader backing up his words with actions. He seems to be the only political leader in the Arab world who could stand up to Israel."

In general, though, the Palestinians will get little satisfaction from the events in Kuwait. The crisis deflects international attention from the search for a solution to the Arab-Israeli conflict.

DIPLOMATS in the Middle East expect another side effect of the Kuwait crisis to be the emergence from political isolation of Syria and Iran – both enemies of Iraq. Each expects to benefit from the need felt by Arab states for counter-balances to Iraq. Both hope too that the West will court their friendship for the same reasons.

[According to Reuters, a Kuwaiti diplomat said yesterday that Iraq had moved from Kuwait to Baghdad 15 Shiite Muslim prisoners whose freedom has long been demanded by Lebanese groups holding Western hostages in Beirut.

"They are going to use them as bargaining counters," said Faisal Mukhlaizen, Kuwait's chargé d'affaires in Amman.

A Western witness told Reuters from Kuwait City yesterday that the 15 Shiites were among 1,300 inmates who had broken out of Salidia Central Prison after the Iraqi invasion.]

Lamis Andoni in Amman, Jordan, contributed to this article.

Wall Street Journal

90. 8.6

VOL. CCXVI NO. 25 ★

(A·1)

Crisis Decisions

As Iraq Embargo Gains Support, Risks Grow For U.S. and Its Allies

Americans Will Feel Pain Of Boycott; Military Role Poses Even More Dangers

Massing on the Saudi Border

By GERALD F. SEIB and JOHN J. FIALKA
Staff Reporters of THE WALL STREET JOURNAL.

WASHINGTON—Iraqi strongman Saddam Hussein has left President Bush with a very unattractive set of options. The economic sanctions the president is attempting to impose may inflict as much pain on the U.S. as they do on Iraq, yet there was growing concern last night that the president may have to resort to even more drastic military measures to keep Iraq's hands off Saudi Arabia.

Mr. Bush is having surprising early success on the economic front, getting both Western Europe and Japan to sign on to the U.S.-led global embargo of oil exports from Iraq and the Kuwaiti oil fields Iraq seized last week.

The administration is now considering a move to gain United Nations support for a plan to blockade Iraqi oil shipments

---

Moving Against Iraq

Japan and the European Community decided to support a U.S. call for an economic embargo against Iraq for its invasion of Kuwait. Story on page A8.

In other developments:

■ Baghdad's incursion into Kuwait has sundered the Arab world, page A8.
□ U.S. and Soviet cooperation against Iraq has its limits, page A9.

---

through the Persian Gulf or either of two major pipelines carrying oil out through Saudi Arabia and Turkey. The blockade, which would be carried out in international waters, would be accomplished by an international fleet, including U.S. warships.

But the more the embargo succeeds, the more painful it will be for American consumers. In all likelihood, there isn't enough extra oil capacity in other countries to make up for the more than 4 million barrels a day of oil that a boycott and such a blockade would bottle up in Iraq and Kuwait.

Under such a scenario, world oil prices could skyrocket, at least temporarily, perhaps to as high as $35 a barrel, 40% higher

than they are today, an increase of about 25 cents a gallon American gas pumps.

The resulting disruptions could, in the short run, wreak havoc on industrial economies world-wide.

The president yesterday used his toughest language yet condemning the Iraqi move against Kuwait. Mr. Bush declared that "these are outlaws—international outlaws and renegades," and he flatly pledged to roll back the Iraqi invasion: "This will not stand. This will not stand, this aggression against Kuwait."

And though Iraq claimed yesterday that it had begun pulling troops out of Kuwait, Mr. Bush charged that Baghdad "lied" and that its forces remained. He declared that Arab leaders had "failed" to find their own solution within 48 hours of the invasion, as promised.

Defending the Saudis

The president again refused to rule out the use of military force against Iraq, and it seems clear that the U.S. would move militarily if Saudi Arabia were attacked. U.S. intelligence officials yesterday told the White House of signs Iraq is actually preparing to seize the so-called neutral zone on the Saudi-Kuwaiti border or to invade Saudi Arabia itself, according to officials familiar with the intelligence reports.

In one sign that the U.S. is preparing to react to such an event, Defense Secretary Richard Cheney was dispatched for talks to Saudi Arabia, which still doesn't want to allow American forces on its soil as a precaution.

In the event of Iraqi aggression against Saudi Arabia, the U.S. would have to hope that the quick dispatch of jet fighters and big B-52 bombers from distant domestic and foreign bases and the rapid deployment of a small contingent of light ground forces would be enough to offset Iraqi troops, who would be far closer to Saudi oil fields and more heavily armed.

Tracking Iraqi Troops

One option under study in the Pentagon, according to defense officials who asked not to be identified, is the possibility of bombing secret Iraqi facilities where Mr. Hussein has scientists and foreign mercenaries working on nuclear and biological weapons research. Iraq also has underground storage sites for chemical weapons that are vulnerable to U.S. bombs, some of which have the capacity to penetrate deeply into the earth. Mr. Hussein "has a great deal to lose here," says one expert.

Yet the complications facing any American military move are sobering. In addition to the U.S.'s inability to position forces ahead of time in the region, the puppet government Iraq has installed appeared to raise a new obstacle yesterday by hinting that it is prepared to take reprisals against foreigners trapped in Kuwait, including an estimated 3,800 Americans.

There is disagreement among U.S. officials and Arab diplomats about the chances of Mr. Hussein actually ordering his troops to drive on into Saudi Arabia. Some diplomats reported that Iraq has moved into at least part of the neutral zone.

The intelligence assessment was based

Please Turn to Page A8, Column 1

0080

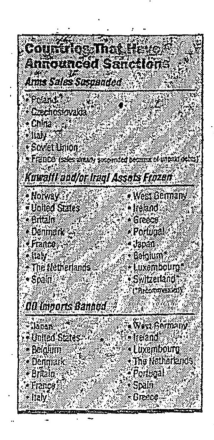

Countries That Have Announced Sanctions

Arms Sales Suspended

- Poland
- Czechoslovakia
- China
- Italy
- Soviet Union
- France (sales already suspended because of unpaid debts)

Kuwaiti and/or Iraqi Assets Frozen

- Norway
- United States
- Britain
- Denmark
- France
- Italy
- The Netherlands
- Spain
- West Germany
- Ireland
- Greece
- Portugal
- Japan
- Belgium*
- Luxembourg*
- Switzerland

(*Recommended)

Oil Imports Banned

- Japan
- United States
- Belgium
- Denmark
- Britain
- France
- Italy
- West Germany
- Ireland
- Luxembourg
- The Netherlands
- Portugal
- Spain
- Greece

6

Crisis Decisions: Iraq Poses Risks for U.S.

Continued From First Page

on satellite photos and human intelligence reports showing the configuration of Iraqi troops, movements between Iraq and Kuwait and the types of arms and logistical supplies soldiers near the Kuwaiti-Saudi border are receiving. Publicly, the White House said Iraqi forces are five to 10 miles from the border.

But some American officials discount the new warnings of a possible Iraqi move against the desert kingdom and its enormous oil reserves. Middle Eastern diplomatic sources say the Saudis themselves doubt that Iraq is preparing to move and don't see the evidence in either satellite photos—which the U.S. has begun providing to them in the last few days—or movements on the ground.

Although the movement toward meaningful sanctions picked up momentum over the weekend, there remains doubt that the international community has the will to make such measures severe or long-lasting enough to be truly painful to Iraq.

The European Community agreed to impose broad sanctions, including embargos on oil purchases from Iraq and Kuwait and on arms sales to Iraq. And, crucial to hopes for a meaningful trade embargo, Japan announced yesterday that it also will embargo oil imports from Iraq and Kuwait.

But Japan seemed to want further international political cover, suggesting its move depends on the United Nations Security Council passing a resolution calling for broad sanctions. American diplomats were busy trying to draft such a resolution for quick passage. And there were hints that China, though it has joined the international move to cut off arms shipments to Iraq, may balk at endorsing broad trade sanctions. As a Security Council member, China could block a resolution it didn't approve of.

Even if a boycott is successfully assembled, bottling up all crude exports from Iraq and Kuwait would drain more than 4 million barrels from the world's daily flow of oil. Other oil exporters have 4.5 million to 5.5 million barrels a day in currently spare surge capacity, estimates

Daniel Yergin, president of Cambridge Energy Associates, a Massachusetts-based research and consulting firm. But perhaps 2 million barrels of that is in Saudi Arabia and another 800,000 barrels in the United Arab Emirates, both sources that might be reluctant to pump full out while looking down the barrels of Saddam Hussein's guns, Mr. Yergin notes.

As a result, the world could quickly find itself short more than a million barrels a day in total crude supplies, a situation almost certain to set off a price-boosting scramble. In time, the higher prices would call forth increased supplies and would help induce conservation. And in the interim the U.S. and other countries could let some oil out of their strategic stockpiles to ease the shortage. For a time, however, the turmoil would likely be intense.

Meanwhile, there's no way of telling precisely how quickly a full-scale embargo would pinch Iraq. But over time, the sting would become painful, particularly because the country already is in sad economic shape.

On the military front, two U.S. naval task forces are converging on the Persian Gulf area. One, including the U.S. carrier Eisenhower, is expected to take a position in the eastern Mediterranean. A second, led by the carrier Independence, is moving from the Indian Ocean toward a position near the Strait of Hormuz, at the mouth of the Persian Gulf.

Crucial Airfields

A third U.S. naval task force, which will include the cruise-missile-carrying Wisconsin and the carrier Saratoga, is scheduled to leave Norfolk tomorrow for the Mediterranean. A Defense Department spokesman asserted, though, that the move was planned as part of the normal rotation to replace the Eisenhower task force.

While attack aircraft from the carriers could reach targets in Kuwait and Iraq with in-flight refueling, military experts believe that the Saudis would let them operate from Saudi airfields if the desert

7

0082

kingdom were attacked. Airfields at King Khalid Military City, near the Saudi border with Kuwait, have been equipped with spare parts and fuel for such a contingency.

Such landing privileges would be seen by Iraq as a serious provocation, and so far the Saudis have been reluctant to give them, raising concerns in Washington. Sen. David L. Boren (D., Okla.), chairman of the Senate Intelligence Committee, said yesterday on ABC-TV's "This Week with David Brinkley" that the Persian Gulf countries at risk "have to give us forward basing rights, to put the air power and other kinds of military forces physically into the region."

The U.S. could fly in heavier aircraft, such as tankers, transports and bombers, to a staging point in Oman. The Pentagon has spent over $300 million preparing an airfield there, however the Omani government must approve U.S. use during a crisis.

Mr. Hussein's tank columns, which have operated with little air cover up to now, according to U.S. analysts, would be extremely vulnerable to U.S. precision-guided weapons. If the Iraqi dictator was tempted to use his missiles against Saudi oil installations, the U.S. could retaliate with heavier strikes against Iraqi targets, using FB-111's based in the United Kingdom or B-52's from the U.S.

Squadrons of U.S. fighters based in Europe also could be ferried quickly into the Persian Gulf region, once permission is given to use the Saudi bases. Some planners think the combined U.S. and Saudi air forces could defeat Iraq's Soviet-equipped air forces within a day or two, barring political constraints that would force the U.S. to operate from distant bases.

Radar Support

The U.S. would probably move quickly into Saudi Arabia some additional tactical radar equipment and operators, to coordinate with American-made Airborne Warning and Control System planes to monitor skies over Saudi Arabia and direct Saudi and American fighter planes.

Far more difficult than air or sea support, military planners say, would be to quickly get any significant American ground force into Saudi Arabia to defend against Iraq's heavily armored ground troops. Former Defense Secretary Harold Brown says that a contingent of Marines or troops from the 82nd or 101st Airborne Divisions could be flown in, perhaps in as little as one day, because they travel lightly.

"The trouble is that because they're light they wouldn't do well against heavy forces," says Mr. Brown. And, he notes, Iraq's Mr. Hussein "isn't Gen. Noriega," and his troops wouldn't be as easy to repel as the Panamanian leader's forces were. Though American and Saudi air forces have worked closely together to plan and practice moves that would have to be taken in a crisis, the U.S. doesn't have any experience in moving significant ground forces to the kingdom.

Military planners say the Saudis are confident, though, that they have the ability—using fighter aircraft, helicopter gunships and ground forces of their own—to cut the two main roads that lead from Kuwait down the Saudi coast to the kingdom's giant Persian Gulf oil fields. If those roads were cut, the tanks would be forced onto the desert to travel, slowing them down and making them far easier targets for air attack by the Saudi's American-made F5 and British-made Tornado aircraft.

One of the Iraqis' most inviting early targets would be an industrial city the Saudis have built up through investment of billions of dollars at Jubail, on the Persian Gulf coast. But invading forces would have to move much further down the gulf coast to reach the biggest Saudi oil fields and refining facilities near Dhahran.

—Walter S. Mossberg and James Tanner contributed to this article.

Wall Street Journal '90. 8. 6

THE MIDEAST CONFLICT (A8)

Total Armed Forces

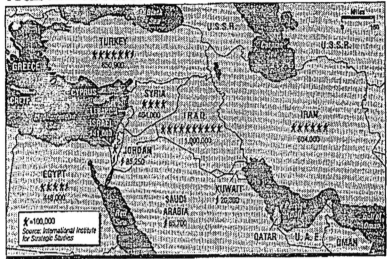

Arab World Sorely Divided Over Iraq's Show of Force

At a restaurant in Amman, the Jordanian capital, Dawood Ibrahim is so agitated he spills Turkish coffee in his lap.

"Every true Arab is for Saddam Hussein, except prostitutes and emirs," says the businessman. To prove his point, he

This article was prepared by Geraldine Brooks in Cairo, Egypt, and Tony Horwitz in Amman, Jordan.

polls passing waiters, and diners at adjoining tables. The vote is unanimous. "You see," he says, "we are all soldiers for Saddam now."

The view from a sidewalk cafe in Cairo is precisely the opposite. "We all know Saddam is the son of a dog," says Atif Khalid, who like many Egyptians worked in Iraq during its war with Iran. A dozen men bang tables to show their assent. "If he comes here," shouts one, "we will cut his throat."

Saddam Hussein's invasion of Kuwait has sundered the Arab world, separating two of America's closest allies in the region and pushing the Middle East toward further conflict. While Egyptian President Hosni Mubarak leads a campaign—backed by Saudi Arabia and Syria—to condemn and contain the Iraqi leader, Jordan has thrown itself into the Iraqi camp, joined by the Palestine Liberation Organization and Libya.

Saddam Hussein

The rift bodes poorly for American influence in the region and confirms what leaders across the Arab world have been warning: that U.S. neglect of moderates such as Mr. Mubarak has paved the way for Iraqi extremism.

"Demagoguery plays to the gallery. Moderation doesn't play unless it brings results," says Tahseen Bashir, a veteran Egyptian diplomat. "We were bringing home empty baskets."

In Jordan, where the population is half Palestinian, the failure of both diplomacy and the Palestinian uprising to gain any ground has bred despair, and fervent anti-Americanism. The almost unanimous view of both officials and ordinary people is that strong leadership and a strong show of force is now the only way to break the stalemate.

Saddam Hussein has become the symbol of that defiance. Jordanians appear remarkably unconcerned by both the plight of Kuwait, and Mr. Hussein's brutality at home and abroad. "We do not have the luxury to concern ourselves with democratic niceties," says Hazem Nuseibeh, a veteran Jordanian diplomat. "The need for Arab unity and pride overrides all that."

Jordanian officials repeatedly liken Mr. Hussein to Otto von Bismarck, who unified Germany with iron and blood. If Mr. Hussein needs oil and territory to advance Arab nationalism,

King Hussein

0084

so be it. Many Jordanians go so far as to suggest that Iraqi tanks would be welcome in Amman.

"The colonial powers vivisected the Arab world to make us weak," says Mr. Nuseibeh, voicing a common view. Adds Deeb Marji, a member of Parliament: "If Saddam can put the Arab map together again, who will regret what he did in Kuwait?"

In Egypt, the overwhelming view is that Mr. Hussein's action has destroyed hopes for Arab unity. And they fear it will provoke foreign intervention that will cause a lasting rift in the region.

On Saturday night in Cairo, a group of senior military officers drew up a list of winners and losers in the wake of Iraq's action. Israel topped everyone's list of winners. All reasoned that the invasion will likely increase U.S. military aid to Israel and harden Israeli attitudes toward ceding land to Palestinians.

Mr. Mubarak tended to turn up on the list of losers. Last week, he frantically tried to defuse the conflict and even assured both the Kuwaitis and the West that Iraq wouldn't invade. Iraq's action humiliated Mr. Mubarak, and the Arab world's divided response suggests that his leverage as a regional power broker is waning.

Egypt also appears to have lost its role as the PLO's go-between with America and Israel. "Iraq is the PLO's godfather now," says a senior Jordanian official.

Both the PLO and Jordan were among those who refused to join an Arab League vote condemning Iraq. And PLO Chairman Yasser Arafat helped scuttle plans for an Arab summit yesterday.

But not everyone is comfortable with the PLO's tilt toward Baghdad. At a seaside lunch in Tunis just before the invasion, a PLO official tried to justify the shift, saying, "The West talks about Saddam's lack of human rights, but what about human rights in Saudi Arabia? They're abysmal too."

His wife shook her head in disbelief. "You know very well Saddam is a butcher," she said. The couple lived in Iraq for several months until she insisted they leave. "I couldn't stand the repression," she says.

Arab acquiescence to Iraq's action also reflects resentment of Kuwait's vast oil wealth. A Jordanian official who often went begging to the deposed emir calls Kuwait and other gulf states, "oil wells with flags." A legislator says "what they spend in one year on houses, women and cars could pay off our entire national debt."

In fact, the Kuwaitis have given quite a bit to Jordan, including most of $125 million promised this year in aid. But Jordanian officials say Saudi Arabia has paid much more, and they feel confident Saddam Hussein will do the same if he controls Kuwait's oil wealth.

Palestinian officials, who say Kuwait pays a meager $2 million dollars a month to the PLO, also expect largesse from Mr. Hussein. There is some concern, though, that support of Iraq by Jordan and the PLO could spark a backlash against hundreds of thousands of Jordanians and Palestinians working in the gulf states.

Kuwait's gulf neighbors responded to the invasion with predictable alarm. State-controlled media in some states failed to even mention the invasion for more than 24 hours after it occurred. Saudi television showed the deposed Kuwaiti emir in Saudi Arabia, but noted only that he was "visiting" the kingdom.

While some impoverished Egyptians resent the Kuwaiti tourists who flock to expensive Cairo hotel suites, many have been enriched by work in the emirate.

"It's a luxury life there," says Jamaa Abdul-Fadil, who arrived home in Cairo on his annual vacation just four days before the invasion. Eight years of work as a legal clerk in Kuwait has comfortably furnished his apartment and allowed him to buy a small shop in Cairo.

By contrast, Egyptian workers' experiences in Iraq often have been bitter. More than a million Egyptians flocked to bolster Iraqi manpower during the eight-year gulf war. "Saddam used us up, and when the war was over he tossed us aside," says Atif Khalid, who worked in Baghdad as a waiter. Some Egyptians were beaten and shot at by Iraqis, and others haven't been able to

Hosni Mubarak

transfer home their earnings as part of a campaign to clear the way for Iraqi jobseekers returning from the front. Many Egyptians also served and died in the war with Iran and more than 10,000 are believed to still be prisoners of war.

Egyptians, deeply religious, also identify with Kuwait's Islamic character. They are outraged that Iraq has once again breached the Koranic prohibition against Moslems killing Moslems, as it did when it attacked Iran in 1980.

If Iraq's action has forced Arab enmities into the open and forced countries to choose sides, the fate of its invasion also is likely to determine the Arab world's winners and losers. Some analysts think King Hussein may be repeating the error he made in 1967, when he entered the war against Israel on the side of the Egyptian president, Gamal Abdel Nasser. Then, the king mistook bluster for strength and lost half his kingdom—the West Bank—to Israeli occupation.

A senior Jordanian official, though, says Iraq's ascent marks a return to a much more potent Arab nationalism after two decades during which Islamic fundamentalism had become the dominant ideology. Unlike Mr. Nasser, "who bragged of missiles and had only tin," the official says, "Saddam has real force and is willing to use it."

He also has oil, and by not sharing a border with Israel, he is safer than Mr. Nasser was from Israeli reprisals. And Western military action against Iraq is widely viewed in the Arab world as potentially disastrous, because it would make a martyr of Mr. Hussein and confirm suspicions that many gulf states are little more than American protectorates. But the situation is in such flux that many Arabs fear violence could erupt from unexpected directions.

"People are thinking with their hearts, not their brains," says Asad Abdul Rahman, a member of the Palestinian National Council, the Palestinian parliament in exile.

원 본

외 무 부

종 별 :

번 호 : UNW-1476   일 시 : 90 0807 1700

수 신 : 장관(중근동,국연,경협,기정)

발 신 : 주유엔대사

제 목 : 이라크-쿠웨이트 침공 관련기사

　　이라크의 쿠웨이트 침공과 관련, 당지 주요 신문의 관계해설 기사등을 별첨 팩스 송부하니 참고바람.

　　첨부:

　　1. NY TIMES (90.8.7)'COPING WITH THE ECONOMIC CONSEQUENCES'

　　2. THE CHRISTIAN SCIENCE MONITOR (90.8.7) 'BEHIND IRAG'SGRAB FOR KUWAIT'

　　3. THE CHRISTIAN ACIENCE MONITOR (90.8.7) 'JORDAN'S HUSSEIN PLAYS IRAQ'S MIDDLE MAN' 끝

　　유첨: UNW(F)-122

　　(대사 현홍주-국장)

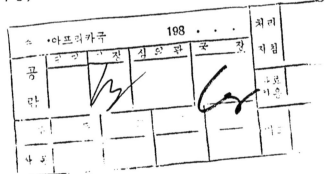

중아국　　국기국　　경제국　　안기부　　차보　　김문국　　차관　　장관

PAGE 1   90.08.08   09:07 CG

외신 1과 통제관

0086

UNW(F)-122

UNW-1476   0807 170 (중근동, 국면, 정책 기획)

Coping with the Economic Consequences NYT (A 18) 90. 8. 7

President Bush has rallied the U.N. Security Council to vote a trade embargo against Iraq and Kuwait. This is the right response to Baghdad's heinous invasion, but it raises two troubling questions for the U.S.: Will the embargo block Iraqi oil exports? And will it throw the U.S. into a devastating recession?

There is cause for muted optimism on both scores. Iraq relies upon a single export, oil, whose shipment is easily monitored. The oil importing nations, if they cooperate, can make sure they buy only from non-Iraqi sources.

The more successful the embargo, the worse the danger for the U.S. economy. The loss of oil from Iraq and Kuwait would drive up oil prices and throw a limp U.S. economy into recession. But Mr. Bush can mitigate this danger by marshaling Saudi support and releasing oil from large U.S. stockpiles. That way the embargo can cripple Iraq without crippling the U.S. too.

●

Iraqi oil is shipped through pipelines across Turkey and Saudi Arabia and in tankers through the Persian Gulf. The limited number of outlets makes the oil easy to track, and check. The proof may already be in hand. Even before the U.N. vote, the industrialized countries had announced an embargo. Iraq then suspended most of its oil shipments through Turkey apparently because it would be unable to find buyers.

Iraq and Kuwait sold between four and five billion barrels a day before the invasion. If that entire output is lost, the price of oil could, at worst, double. But even that scenario would be far less damaging to the U.S. economy than the quadrupling of oil prices in 1973-74 or their tripling in 1979. Inflation would rise by several percentage points; the unem-

ployment rate might approach 8 percent from its present 5.5 percent. These are very serious but manageable consequences — especially when compared with the possible costs of inaction.

Mr. Bush has ways to lessen the economic harm. By providing military guarantees against Iraqi reprisal, he might be able to persuade Saudi Arabia and the United Arab Emirates to step up production. If Venezuela also raises output, most of the shortfall could be offset.

And there is a powerful antidote within Mr. Bush's control: the Strategic Petroleum Reserve, a 600-million-barrel stockpile created in the aftermath of the 1970's oil crises. Japan and Western Europe created similar stockpiles.

These reserves were established to smooth over a temporary crisis just like the one triggered by Iraq's invasion. The Western stockpiles are large enough to offset a sizable portion of the shortfall even if the crisis lasts as long as a year.

The loss of U.S. oil imports during the 1970's never exceeded 5 percent. The reason that such a modest supply shock caused havoc was that consumers panicked, and hoarded available oil. By immediately releasing oil from stockpiles, the West can calm jittery markets.

Western economies are less vulnerable to OPEC now than in the 70's. Energy use — compared with the size of Western economies — is lower and there are more supplies of natural gas and other non-oil energy sources. For these reasons, and because the price shock will be much smaller, the U.S. and its allies can withstand the embargo.

Only panic can turn this very difficult situation into a catastrophe. By addressing the nation now, explaining the price of inaction and the costs of his proposed actions, Mr. Bush has it in his power to prevent that and reassure the American people.

5-1

THE CHRISTIAN SCIENCE MONITOR

AN INTERNATIONAL DAILY NEWSPAPER

TUESDAY, AUGUST 7, 1990   50¢ [$1.00 CANADIAN]

Cuba Activists Seek 'Dignified Way' to End Castro's Rule

By Michael White
Special to The Christian Science Monitor

— HAVANA —

AS young men, Gustavo Arcos and Jesús Yanez Pelletier stood on opposite sides in the battle that launched the Cuban revolution and placed Fidel Castro on the road to power.

Now, 37 years later, they fight together in a dangerous and seemingly quixotic campaign to expose human rights abuses and muster opposition to Mr. Castro's communist government.

Mr. Arcos and Mr. Yanez both concede Castro is firmly in control of Cuba and that

VOL 37, NO 176

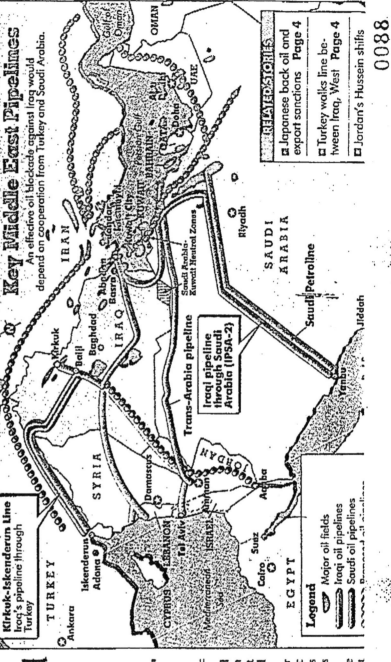

JOHN VAN PELT – STAFF

Key Middle East Pipelines

An effective oil blockade against Iraq would depend on cooperation from Turkey and Saudi Arabia.

Kirkuk-Iskenderun Line
Iraq's pipeline through Turkey

Iraqi pipeline through Saudi Arabia (IPSA-2)

Trans-Arabia pipeline

Saudi Petroline

Saudi Arabia–Kuwait Neutral Zones

Legend
- Major oil fields
- Iraqi oil pipelines
- Saudi oil pipelines

TURKEY — Ankara, Adana, Iskenderun
SYRIA — Damascus
LEBANON
ISRAEL — Tel Aviv, Amman
JORDAN
CYPRUS
Mediterranean Sea
EGYPT — Cairo, Suez
IRAQ — Kirkuk, Bajī, Baghdad, Basra
IRAN
SAUDI ARABIA — Riyadh, Jiddah, Yanbu
KUWAIT
BAHRAIN — Manama
QATAR — Doha
UAE — Abu Dhabi, Dubai
OMAN
Persian Gulf
Gulf of Oman
Aqaba
Abadan

RELATED STORIES
- Japanese back oil and export sanctions Page 4
- Turkey walks line between Iraq, West Page 4
- Jordan's Hussein shifts

0088

0089

Behind Iraq's Grab for Kuwait

Sagging economy, stalemate on POWs, and heavy debt prompted move, analysts say

By Amy Kaslow
Staff writer of The Christian Science Monitor

WASHINGTON

IRAQI President Saddam Hussein's invasion of Kuwait is the latest measure of his quest for power at home and abroad.

At home, he faces a population increasingly frustrated over soaring inflation, the country's heavy international debt, and the government's inability to negotiate the return of prisoners-of-war held in Iran.

Abroad, he faces oil-exporting neighbors to whom he owed billions and whose high-gear production in effect cut his own oil revenues. He also faces a vacuum in the leadership of the Arab world and sees it as an opportunity, analysts say.

"The vistors [of supremacy] he articulated before the Gulf war were never abandoned," says Richard Murphy, former assistant secretary of state for Near East and South Asian affairs.

Two years after Iraq's cease-fire with Iran, Baghdad's policies remain war-related. Estimates of Iraqi military spending range from $7 billion to Gulf-war levels of $10 billion a year. The other key area of investment is the oil sector, which helps pay the bills.

Iraq's sluggish economy is straining to absorb even a portion of the 1 million soldiers returning from the war, analysts say.

Workers have found that dramatic wage increases – as much as 25 percent by one measure – register no impact against escalating prices.

"The country's snowballing foreign debts – over $80 billion – and rampant inflation have created an economic crisis," says Tom Kono, a former Japanese foreign service officer in Baghdad who is now a fellow at Columbia University and is writing a book on Iraqi domestic affairs. "The Iraqi people have become increasingly disgruntled by their regime's inability to deliver a 'peace dividend' and repatriate some 70,000 prisoners of war."

By invading Kuwait, Hussein both engaged the Iraqi military and renewed his

See IRAQ next page

Unseen Diversity

tension of the trial of Marion Barry highlights erroneous perceptions of black America **8**

Einstein's Theory Put To the Test

Gravity Probe-B and laser-beam observatories will measure unproved relativity predictions **12**

A Designer in the Age of Mass Production

Marianne Straub's fabrics are sat upon in London's underground trains, Trident aircraft, public buildings, and ordinary homes **14**

Film Ticket Prices Soar

They're rising faster than Warren Beatty's bank account – up to $5 this summer in Des Moines and $7.50 in Los Angeles **15**

Beatrix Potter, the Writer

Artist, yes, but even more, a delightful writer lurked behind Peter Rabbit and friends **16**

---

they can do little in the near term to change that. Nevertheless, they say they are determined to resist a repressive dictatorship, if only by speaking out.

"This regime has cost much blood, much suffering," says Arcos. "We think that information about the situation in the country is critical."

Arcos, a former ambassador, and Yanez, who once served as Castro's military attaché, are founding members of the Cuban Committee for Human Rights. In the past 18 months, such activities have been sharply curtailed, apparently in response to communism's fall in Eastern Europe.

Only, 11 human rights activists were sentenced to prison terms of up to 15 years for alleged terrorist conspiracies. In 1989, 60 Cuban dissidents were imprisoned, according to Amnesty International. Despite such measures, Arcos and Yañez believe forces of change will catch up to Castro.

"The Marxist system has failed," Arcos says. "Cuba, China, North Korea, and North Vietnam are the last representatives. . . . Now, every time something happens, it's a stimulus for us."

Although Arcos and Yanez are free at

See CUBA next page

Closed or nonoperational

Support to Iraq   Page 5

Source: Petroleum Economist;
Times Atlas of World History;
Reuters.

INSIDE

3 THE WORLD
6 THE ECONOMY
8 THE US
12 SCIENCE
14 PEOPLE
15 THE ARTS
16 THE HOME
    FORUM
18 OPINION
20 EDITORIAL

Tuesday, August 7, 1990

5

0090

Jordan's Hussein Plays Iraq's Middle Man

By Lamis Andoni
Special to The Christian Science Monitor

— AMMAN, JORDAN —

THE eruption of the Gulf crisis has once again boosted the role of Jordan's King Hussein as the only acceptable mediator in negotiations for a withdrawal of Iraqi troops from Kuwait.

However, his alliance with Iraqi President Saddam Hussein – who has come to be viewed as "the No. 1 enemy of the West" placing Hussein and his tiny kingdom at a dangerous crossroads.

Saudi King Fahd and President Bush reportedly called King Hussein immediately after the invasion to ask him to mediate an Iraqi pullout from Kuwait.

But Jordan's refusal to condemn Baghdad is provoking the resentment of both Washington and Riyadh – his two main financial backers.

Mr. Bush has already criticized King Hussein's "apologetic" associations. The public attitude has also been hostile to the ruling royal family in Kuwait.

In public meetings and discussions organized by professional unions, the Iraqi challenge to US regional interests and the Gulf states are described as the start of a revolution against the US.

The euphoria which has swept Jordan since the Iraqi invasion – reflected in the press and public plans to boycott US imports – show the accumulation of anger and humiliation of the Arab "poor" against the "rich" Gulf states and their ruling sheiks' pursuit of pleasure and luxury in the West.

"The entire population of Qatar, Kuwait, and the United Arab Emirates is no more than one and a half million people living in abundant luxury, conspicuously consuming and mostly in the West, while the other 200 million Arabs are caught in the grip of poverty and anger," writes leading Jordanian political scientist Kamel Abu Jaber.

Viewed in this context, Saddam Hussein's dictatorship and position of King Hussein, who as a young man in the mid-1950s defied tremendous pressures from powerful Egyptian President Gamal Abdel Nasser and anger at home, to consolidate his association and alliance with the West and Washington.

Now he is standing against greater odds to side with the perhaps uncontrollable Saddam Hussein.

For Jordanian politicians – both loyalists and opposition – what seems to be a riddle for the stunned West is understandable.

"It is simply his only option," says a former Jordanian minister echoing a widely held conclusion.

According to Jordanian politicians, including former senior officials, Washington's inability or unwillingness to pressure Israel to withdraw from the occupied Arab territories, the mass influx of Soviet Jewish immigrants to Israel, the formation of the right-wing government in Israel, and the loss of valuable Soviet support to the Arab cause have completely undermined peace prospects in the region.

The euphoria which has swept Jordan since the Iraqi invasion of Kuwait show the accumulation of anger and humiliation of the Arab 'poor' against the 'rich' Gulf states.

endorsing its transformation into a substitute homeland for the Palestinians – if that was necessary to ensure Israel's security.

His strongly worded warning to the Arab and, particularly, oil-rich Gulf states, that the very entity of Jordan – which hitherto has acted as a buffer state between Israel and the Gulf – was in danger of demise went unheard despite verbal support and enthusiastic rhetoric.

The Arab reaction further con-

of an Arab block to face a changing international political map.

Consequently, the King fears that an outright Jordanian condemnation of Iraq, despite his declared opposition to the use of force by one Arab country against another, would torpedo an Arab solution to the crisis, invite foreign intervention, and undermine the prospect of forming an Arab bloc, the former official said.

This scenario clearly contravened that of his Egyptian ally and of Saudi Arabia and most Arab countries, who according to Arab officials, have reached the conclusion that, since they cannot beat the only superpower left, the alternative was to join it.

The King's option, however, has boosted his negotiating status as the only acceptable mediator with the formidable Saddam Hussein.

But this very same position – that of a guarantor of the Iraqi president's behavior and of dependency on Baghdad's support – has plunged King Hussein into a very risky gamble.

...rich Gulf states indicate that they might deport 300,000 Jordanian expatriates working there. Such a step coupled with a possible cutoff of Gulf states' financial aid – which has drastically dropped in the last few years – would aggravate Jordan's acute economic crisis and rising unemployment, already over 20 percent.

Jordanians are concerned that Israel, which has repeatedly criticized Amman's closeness with [Baghdad], would seize the opportunity to strike against their country. But despite these fears and the possibility that Jordan would be caught in a fatal war between its two strong neighbors, Israel and Iraq, Hussein seems undeterred.

The King launched a new round of Arab diplomacy yesterday, according to Jordan radio. Meanwhile, Prime Minister Mudar Badran left for Damascus for talks likely to be dominated by the Iraqi invasion.

In interviews with international television networks the King has described the Iraqi president as "patriotic" and "trustful," challenging Arab and international censure of Baghdad.

At home the King is enjoying unprecedented and overwhelmingly popular support for what is widely seen as a refusal to bow to US pressure and for his firm opposition to foreign intervention. Jordanians in general have expressed strong support for Iraq through leaflets, and statements by the press and professional as-

...for the moment, beside the point. "He is portrayed here more or less as some kind of a modern Robin Hood, while King Hussein is the brave poor man who dares to stand against the rich and the mighty," a Western expert here comments.

But such explanations fall short of clarifying the complex ...

... warned that the new accord between Washington and Moscow has left Israel a free hand to pursue its ambitions in the area.

Some well-informed politicians even say that King Hussein has washed his hands of US support and does not rule out the possibility that Washington would be ready to sacrifice Jordan – by

strong, united Arab block to preempt Israel from filling the political gap and the US from improving its total hegemony in the region, senior government officials say.

Iraq, being the only potential military deterrent to counter Israel, has been central to King Hussein's idea of the foundation

he will boost his country's strategic status; if not, he might be risking his country and his throne," a Western specialist says.

"It seems that we shall either sink with Iraq or ensure the continuity of the country," a Jordanian politician says.

US Readies Broad Response to Iraqi Invasion

NICOSIA, CYPRUS

UNITED States Defense Secretary Richard Cheney arrived in Jeddah, Saudi Arabia, Monday for talks on the Gulf crisis, a US Embassy spokesman in Riyadh said.

Mr. Cheney was seeking King Fahd's permission to base US troops and air power inside Saudi Arabia to help repel any invasion and facilitate sorties against Iraq if Washington opts for a military response, ABC News reported Monday.

Cheney was also said to be aiming to persuade Saudi leaders that US President Bush was sincere in his commitment to defend Saudi Arabia.

In the past, the Saudis have feared that Washington might fail to come to their rescue if they adopted an aggressive posture toward Iraq and were attacked by Baghdad.

Cheney is leading a delegation including Gen. Norman Schwarzkopf, commander-in-chief of the US Central Command, and Deputy National Security Advisor Robert Gate.

"He will discuss with Saudi leaders the situation in the Gulf," said the embassy spokesman, contacted by phone from Nicosia.

Saudi Arabia, the world's biggest oil exporter, is Washington's most important ally in the region and provides the US with nearly 18 percent of its oil needs.

Washington has warned Iraq's invasion Army in Kuwait against any attack on Saudi Arabia. Gulf oil sources said Monday they had seen Saudi troops moving close to the border with Iraqi-occupied Kuwait. Earlier reports by Kuwaiti officials abroad said Iraqi forces were poised on the other side of the border.

Saudi Arabia's King Fahd has given refuge to Kuwait's emir, Sheikh Jaber al-Ahmed al-Sabah, ousted by Baghdad's predawn invasion last Thursday.

Mr. Bush, pushing for an international embargo on Iraqi and Kuwaiti oil, sent Cheney to the kingdom. Gulf officials and Western analysts say Washington is pressing Saudi Arabia and Turkey to shut pipelines that carry nearly 90 percent of Iraqi oil exports.

The oil sources said Saudi troop movements had been observed in the past 48 hours near the oil port of Khafji in the so-called Partitioned Neutral Zone. Oil in the zone was shared before the invasion by Saudi Arabia and Kuwait.

On Monday, Iraq's senior diplomat in Europe said that international sanctions against Iraq could delay Baghdad's troop pullout from Kuwait. "Their withdrawal may well be disrupted by any threats that may arise to both Kuwait and Iraq," Abdul Razzak Al-Hashimi, the Iraqi ambassador in France, told reporters.

Meanwhile, Iraq prepared for possible outside attack by drilling millions for mass evacuation of Baghdad and other cities. Hussein has warned Iraq's 17 million people to be on alert for possible US or Israeli attacks.

Bush has ordered US government agencies to draw up plans for possible covert action to topple President Hussein, the Washington Post reported Monday.

Bush, who vowed Sunday to roll back Iraq's conquest of Kuwait, initiated the effort after receiving a Central Intelligence Agency evaluation that Hussein already was in a position to manipulate world oil prices, the Post said, quoting informed sources.

— Reuters

발 신 전 보

WUN-0977   900808 1803 AO

번   호 :   종별 :

수   신 : 주 유엔   대사. *청영씨*

발   신 : 장 관   (국연)

제   목 : 안보리 결의(661호) 통보

8.8. 유엔사무총장은 대이락 경제제재에 관한 안보리 결의(661호)

내용을 *장관앞* Telex 로 통보하여 온바, 참고바람. 끝.
   본직

(국제기구조약국장 문동석)

0092

↓ ○
↑ WOIMUBU K24651

↓ IIX2508101-0688(UNNY:WUCB0688)
  TXC266 78724651
  WUCB0688 NYKT655 UNNY:WUCB0688
  TLXCAB
  78724651 24651

  WUCB0688 MIR7397
  SS CABKS
  .NEWYORK (UNNY) 06 2017Z
  ETATPRIORITE
  HIS EXCELLENCY
  MINISTER FOR FOREIGN AFFAIRS OF THE REPUBLIC OF KOREA
  MINISTRY OF FOREIGN AFFAIRS
  SEOUL (REPUBLIC OF KOREA)
BT
37230-08
    I HAVE THE HONOUR TO TRANSMIT HEREWITH THE TEXT OF RESOLUTION
661 (1990) ADOPTED BY THE SECURITY COUNCIL AT ITS 2933RD MEETING
ON 6 AUGUST 1990. -QUOTE-

    ''THE SECURITY COUNCIL,
    REAFFIRMING ITS RESOLUTION 660 (1990),
    DEEPLY CONCERNED THAT THIS RESOLUTION HAS NOT BEEN IMPLEMENTED
AND THAT THE INVASION BY IRAQ OF KUWAIT CONTINUES WITH FURTHER
LOSS OF HUMAN LIFE AND MATERIAL DESTRUCTION,
    DETERMINED TO BRING THE INVASION AND OCCUPATION OF KUWAIT BY
IRAQ TO AN END AND TO RESTORE THE SOVEREIGNTY, INDEPENDENCE AND
TERRITORIAL INTEGRITY OF KUWAIT,
    NOTING THAT THE LEGITIMATE GOVERNMENT OF KUWAIT HAS EXPRESSED
ITS READINESS TO COMPLY WITH RESOLUTION 660 (1990),
    MINDFUL OF ITS RESPONSIBILITIES UNDER THE CHARTER FOR THE
MAINTENANCE OF INTERNATIONAL PEACE AND SECURITY,
    AFFIRMING THE INHERENT RIGHT OF INDIVIDUAL OR COLLECTIVE SELF-
DEFENCE, IN RESPONSE TO THE ARMED ATTACK BY IRAQ AGAINST KUWAIT,
IN ACCORDANCE WITH ARTICLE 51 OF THE CHARTER,
    ACTING UNDER CHAPTER VII OF THE CHARTER OF THE UNITED NATIONS,

0093

1. DETERMINES THAT IRAQ SO FAR HAS FAILED TO COMPLY WITH OPERATIVE PARAGRAPH 2 OF RESOLUTION 660 (1990) AND HAS USURPED THE AUTHORITY OF THE LEGITIMATE GOVERNMENT OF KUWAIT=

N0 2

2. DECIDES, AS A CONSEQUENCE, TO TAKE THE FOLLOWING MEASURES TO SECURE COMPLIANCE OF IRAQ WITH OPERATIVE PARAGRAPH 2 OF RESOLUTION 660 (1990) AND TO RESTORE THE AUTHORITY OF THE LEGITIMATE GOVERNMENT OF KUWAIT=

3. DECIDES THAT ALL STATES SHALL PREVENT:

(A) THE IMPORT INTO THEIR TERRITORIES OF ALL COMMODITIES AND PRODUCTS ORIGINATING IN IRAQ OR KUWAIT EXPORTED THEREFROM AFTER THE DATE OF THIS RESOLUTION=

(B) ANY ACTIVITIES BY THEIR NATIONALS OR IN THEIR TERRITORIES WHICH WOULD PROMOTE OR ARE CALCULATED TO PROMOTE THE EXPORT OR TRANSSHIPMENT OF ANY COMMODITIES OR PRODUCTS FROM IRAQ OR KUWAIT= AND ANY DEALINGS BY THEIR NATIONALS OR THEIR FLAG VESSELS OR IN THEIR TERRITORIES IN ANY COMMODITIES OR PRODUCTS ORIGINATING IN IRAQ OR KUWAIT AND EXPORTED THEREFROM AFTER THE DATE OF THIS RESOLUTION, INCLUDING IN PARTICULAR ANY TRANSFER OF FUNDS TO IRAQ OR KUWAIT FOR THE PURPOSES OF SUCH ACTIVITIES OR DEALINGS=

(C) THE SALE OR SUPPLY BY THEIR NATIONALS OR FROM THEIR TERRITORIES OR USING THEIR FLAG VESSELS OF ANY COMMODITIES OR PRODUCTS, INCLUDING WEAPONS OR ANY OTHER MILITARY EQUIPMENT, WHETHER OR NOT ORIGINATING IN THEIR TERRITORIES BUT NOT INCLUDING SUPPLIES INTENDED STRICTLY FOR MEDICAL PURPOSES, AND, IN HUMANITARIAN CIRCUMSTANCES, FOODSTUFFS, TO ANY PERSON OR BODY IN IRAQ OR KUWAIT OR TO ANY PERSON OR BODY FOR THE PURPOSES OF ANY BUSINESS CARRIED ON IN OR OPERATED FROM IRAQ OR KUWAIT, AND NY ACTIVITIES BY THEIR NATIONALS OR IN THEIR TERRITORIES WHICH PROMOTE OR ARE CALCULATED TO PROMOTE SUCH SALE OR SUPPLY OF SUCH COMMODITIES OR PRODUCTS=

4. DECIDES THAT ALL STATES SHALL NOT MAKE AVAILABLE TO THE GOVERNMENT OF IRAQ OR TO ANY COMMERCIAL, INDUSTRIAL OR PUBLIC UTILITY UNDERTAKING IN IRAQ OR KUWAIT, ANY FUNDS OR ANY OTHER FINANCIAL OR ECONOMIC RESOURCES AND SHALL PREVENT THEIR NATIONALS AND ANY PERSONS WITHIN THEIR TERRITORIES FROM REMOVING FROM THEIR TERRITORIES OR OTHERWISE MAKING AVAILABLE TO THAT GOVERNMENT OR TO ANY SUCH UNDERTAKING ANY SUCH FUNDS OR RESOURCES AND FROM REMITTING ANY OTHER FUNDS TO PERSONS OR BODIES WITHIN IRAQ OR KUWAIT, EXCEPT PAYMENTS EXCLUSIVELY FOR STRICTLY MEDICAL OR HUMANITARIAN PURPOSES AND, IN SPECIAL HUMANITARIAN CIRCUMSTANCES, FOODSTUFFS=

0094

5. CALLS UPON ALL STATES, INCLUDING STATES NON-MEMBERS OF THE UNITED NATIONS, TO ACT STRICTLY IN ACCORDANCE WITH THE PROVISIONS OF THIS RESOLUTION NOTWITHSTANDING ANY CONTRACT ENTERED INTO OR LICENCE GRANTED BEFORE THE DATE OF THIS RESOLUTION=

No.

6. DECIDES TO ESTABLISH, IN ACCORDANCE WITH RULE 28 OF THE PROVISIONAL RULES OF PROCEDURE OF THE SECURITY COUNCIL, A COMMITTEE OF THE SECURITY COUNCIL CONSISTING OF ALL THE MEMBERS OF THE COUNCIL, TO UNDERTAKE THE FOLLOWING TASKS AND TO REPORT ON ITS WORK TO THE COUNCIL WITH ITS OBSERVATIONS AND RECOMMENDATIONS:

(A) TO EXAMINE THE REPORTS ON THE PROGRESS OF THE IMPLEMENTATION OF THIS RESOLUTION WHICH WILL BE SUBMITTED BY THE SECRETARY-GENERAL=

(B) TO SEEK FROM ALL STATES FURTHER INFORMATION REGARDING THE ACTION TAKEN BY THEM CONCERNING THE EFFECTIVE IMPLEMENTATION OF THE PROVISIONS LAID DOWN IN THIS RESOLUTION=

7. CALLS UPON ALL STATES TO CO-OPERATE FULLY WITH THE COMMITTEE IN THE FULFILMENT OF ITS TASK, INCLUDING SUPPLYING SUCH INFORMATION AS MAY BE SOUGHT BY THE COMMITTEE IN PURSUANCE OF THIS RESOLUTION=

8. REQUESTS THE SECRETARY-GENERAL TO PROVIDE ALL NECESSARY ASSISTANCE TO THE COMMITTEE AND TO MAKE THE NECESSARY ARRANGEMENTS IN THE SECRETARIAT FOR THE PURPOSE=

9. DECIDES THAT, NOTWITHSTANDING PARAGRAPHS 4 THROUGH 8, NOTHING IN THIS RESOLUTION SHALL PROHIBIT ASSISTANCE TO THE LEGITIMATE GOVERNMENT OF KUWAIT, AND CALLS UPON ALL STATES:

(A) TO TAKE APPROPRIATE MEASURES TO PROTECT ASSETS OF THE LEGITIMATE GOVERNMENT OF KUWAIT AND ITS AGENCIES= AND

(B) NOT TO RECOGNIZE ANY REGIME SET UP BY THE OCCUPYING POWER=

10. REQUESTS THE SECRETARY-GENERAL TO REPORT TO THE COUNCIL ON THE PROGRESS OF THE IMPLEMENTATION OF THIS RESOLUTION, THE FIRST REPORT TO BE SUBMITTED WITHIN THIRTY DAYS=

11. DECIDES TO KEEP THIS ITEM ON ITS AGENDA AND TO CONTINUE ITS EFFORTS TO PUT AN EARLY END TO THE INVASION BY IRAQ."

-UNQUOTE-

HIGHEST CONSIDERATION.

JAVIER PEREZ DE CUELLAR

SECRETARY-GENERAL

COL 37230-08

GBS 3520 NAV M8313

CC95

=0807900426GMT

UN 제재 결의에 대한 각국 반응

서 독 : 교역금지 및 이라크, 쿠웨이트 자산 포함한 추가 제재 조치 예정

호 주 : UN 제재 결의에 부분적 제재 동참 발표

유 고 : - 이라크의 침공은 현 국제정세 발전에 역행
          - Al-Sabah 쿠웨이트 정부의 주권 및 적법성을 보존하기 위한
            지원 필요성 인식

터어키 : - 2개의 송유관중 1개를 폐쇄하고 잔여 1개도 75% 감량 조치
          - 쿠웨이트·이라크 자산 동결 결정
          - UN 제재 결의에 동참 예정 발표

스위스 : - 이라크, 쿠웨이트 자산 동결
          - 대 이라크 교역 금지
          - 무역, 재정자금 거래 금지

스페인 : - 자금거래 금지

스웨덴 : 이라크, 쿠웨이트 자산 동결

홍 콩 : 이라크, 쿠웨이트 자산 동결

노르웨이 : 제재 조치 강구중

※ 말   련 : 이라크, 쿠웨이트 자산 동결 불고려

0096

2. 각국 반응 및 제재 조치 현황

국명	반응	제재 (제재정책)	내용 (군사)	비고
미국	o 이라크 군대의 무조건 철수 요구 o UN 안보리 긴급 소집 요구 o 걸프지역내 미국의 중요이익 보호 위해 모든 필요 조치 강구 예정	o 미국내 모든 이라크 및 쿠웨이트 동결 및 교역 금지 o 사우디.터이키에 자국 등과 이라크 송유관 폐쇄 요구	o 미군함 걸프만 파견 o 걸프 분쟁이 행시 UN에 의한 군사 조치 추구 o 역타국 첨공시 군사력 사용	o 이라크 및 쿠웨이트 체류 4,000 명
소련	o 이라크군 무조건 철수 요청 o 사태 해결 위한 미국과의 긴밀 협력 의사 표명	o 대이라크 무기 금수 조치	o 군함 걸프만 파견	o 철수 요구 특별 서한 이라크에 송부
EC (영국)	o 이라크군 즉각적 철수 요구 o UN 안보리 대이라크 제재 조치 지원 응의 표명 o 이라크군 즉각 철수 요구	o 이라크 및 쿠웨이트 자산 동결 조치 o 이라크 원유 수입 금지	o 군함 걸프만 파견	o 쿠웨이트 체류 3,000 명
(프랑스)		o 이라크 및 쿠웨이트 자산 동결 지원 o 대이라크 무기 금수 조치	o 대 이라크 무기 금수 조치	o 이라크 대구불단서 50억불 채무
(이태리)	o 이라크 철수에 의문 제기 o EC의 대이라크 제재 촉구	o 쿠웨이트 이라크 자산 동결 등 조치		o 이라크 대이태리 10억불 채무

국가	찬성	경제제재	군사	비고
일	○ 이라크의 쿠웨이트 침공에 유감 표명, 평화적 해결 희망 ○ UN 안보리 제재 결의 동참	○ 이라크 및 쿠웨이트 자산 동결 ○ 이라크 및 쿠웨이트 원유 도입 수출 금지 ○ 이라크에의 경제 협력 정지 (엔차관 동결) ○ 이라크와의 자본 거래 금지		○ 이라크 석유 도입 전체 8% ○ 쿠웨이트 석유 도입 전체의 5.9%
중	○ UN 결의안 지지 ○ 미·다국적군은 주둔 및 이라크 자산 동결 조치로 중동지역 긴장 고조 비난		○ 대 이라크 무기 판매 중지	
이스라엘	○ 이라크의 침공은 걸프지역내 위협 상황 표명 ○ 이라크의 요르단 침공시 자국의 모든 필요행동 개시 시사 ○ UN 결의안 지지	○ UN 안보리 결의 준수		
기타	○ UN 결의안 지지	○ 자산 동결	○ 순유관 1개 폐쇄	

0098

관리	
번호	fo-1686

외 무 부

종 별 : 지 급

번 호 : UNW-1480

일 시 : 90 0808 1800

수 신 : 장관(국연,동구일,기정)

발 신 : 주 유엔 대사

제 목 : 안보리담당 사무차장 면담

1. 금 8.8 본직은 SAFRONCHUK 안보리 담당 유엔 사무차장 (소련인)과 오찬,상호 관심사에 대해 논의한바 동면담 요지를 아래 보고함.

2. 동인은 이라크 침공사태와 관련한 유엔 안보리 결의 661 호는 유엔이 23 년만에 채택한 포괄적 경제제제 조치로서 유엔내 주요 회원국 및 세계 여론의 적극적인 호응으로 성공할 가능성이 높은 것으로 전망한다고 하였음. 동인은 금일아침 데꾸에야르 유엔 사무총장이 사무국 작성 세계 뉴스 요약자료에 한국이 안보리 결의 661 호상 제제조치 이행에 미온적인 반응을 보였다는 내용이 포함되어 있다고 자신에게 지적하면서 의아해 하였다고 밝혔음.

3. 동 사무차장은 외신보도 내용이 사실이라면 유엔가입을 추진하고있는 한국에 대해 좋지않는 인상을 줄 우려가 있다고 언급하고, 상금 어느나라도 안보리결의에 대해 부정적이거나 미온적인 반응을 보였다는 보도가 없었는데 유독 한국에서 이러한 보도가 나오는데 대해 이외로 느낀다고 말하였음. 본직은 이에대해 언론이 앞질러 기사를 게재하는 경향이 있어 문제라고 말하고 이라크내의 이천명 이상의 한국 근로자의 안전에 대한 대책 강구등으로 본국 정부가 신중히 검토하고 있다는 사실이 "미온적 반응" 으로 확대 해석되어 보도된 것으로 보인다고 해명 하였음.

4. 동인은 금번 안보리 결의는 중.소 서방국가들의 의견에 찬동하여 안보리회원국간 별다른 이견이나 대립없이 신속히 채택 되었는바, 동.서 화해에 따라지역분쟁 처리에 있어 안보리가 신속히, 단호한 조치를 취하였다는 점에서 주목되는 현상으로 평가 하였음.

5. 북한의 단일의석 가입안과 관련 동인은 아래와 같이 언급하였음.

0 박길연 대사로부터 직접 동방안에 대해 설명을 들었음. 본인이 선례가 있는지, 법적으로 문제점이 없는지, 현실적으로 가능성이 있는지등 질문하였으나, 북한대사는

국기국	장관	차관	1차보	2차보	구주국	정문국	정와대	안기부
미주국								

PAGE 1

90.08.09   08:11

외신 2과 통제관 BN
0099

충분히 답변치 못하였음.

　O 그러나 북한의 방안이 통일전 가입 가능성을 논의하고 있고 단일 의석이라고 하드라도 2 개 한국 모두를 대표하는 결과를 낳게 되므로 한국측에서 <u>단순히선전적 술책이나 지연전술로 무시하지 말고 대화로 이끌어 나가는것이 바람직하다고 봄</u>. 단일 의석안을 유엔에 재기하면 유엔으로서는 난처한 입장이 될것이므로 어떤 다른 형태의 합의에 도달하기 바람.

　O 북한의 방안과 직접 유사한 선례는 없으나, 북한측이 현재 캄보디아 사태해결책의 일환으로 논의되고 있는 SUPREME NATIONAL COUNCIL (총선거 실시까지의 과도기간중 캄보디아의 주권을 명목상 행사하고 유엔 대표권을 가질 캄보디아각정파 대표로 구성될 기구)을 유사 사례로 활용하여 단일의석 가입 방안이 현실적, 실제적 방안이라고 주장하는 논거로 내세울 가능성이 있는바, 한국측의 대비가 필요할 것임. (본직은 캄보디아 SNC 케이스는 캄보디아 정파간 합의에 따라 성사될 경우이나, 북한의 단일의석 가입안의 경우에는 남. 북한간에 통합에 관한기본적인 합의가 전혀 상정되지 않은 상태이므로 비교할수 없는 것이라고 설명한바, 동인은 이에 찬동하였음.)

　O 북한대사는 북한이 유엔과 함께 한국 휴전협정의 당사국 이므로 남. 북한이 통일 이전인 현단계에서 휴전협정을 평화협정으로 대치함이 없이 북한이 유엔에 가입하는 경우에는 북한은 유엔과 전쟁상태에서 유엔에 가입하게 되는것이라고 본인에게 주장한바 있음. 기묘한 논리이기는 하나 북측의 이러한 주장에 대해서도 대비할 필요가 있을것임.

　6. 아국의 유엔가입 문제와 관련하여 동인은 아래사항을 언급하였음.

　O 한. 소 수교가 금차 총회기간중 성사될 경우, 한국이 바로 이어서 유엔가입을 신청한다고 하드라도 소련은 반대치 않을것으로 봄. 이경우 중국도 난처해질것임. 중국이 현실적인 입장을 취하도록 여러나라가 설득 노력을 전개하는것이필요하나 쉬운일은 아닐것으로 봄.

　O 어느 일방을 몰아부치고 당황케 하는것은 긴 안목으로 볼때 바람직하지 않으며, 일방적으로 추진할 경우 반대하는 축에서는 절차문제에 있어서의 요건을세밀히 적용코자 할것임.

　O 예멘 리셉션에서 귀하가 북한 대사와 직접 대화를 나누는것을 목격하였는바, 북측을 대화로 유도토록 노력하는것은 바람직한 것으로 봄.

PAGE 2

0100

0 유엔 사무총장은 남. 북한이 동시에 요청한다면 가입문제에 대해서도 중재에 나설 용의가 있다는것을 사적으로 표명하였음. 동인은 개인적으로 큰 관심을 가지고 있으며 총회나 안보리의 위임이 없이도 그러한 중재는 사무총장의 고유권능으로 할수 있다고 믿고있음.

7. 동인은 사무차장직 임기말료로 10월중 귀국예정이라 하며 모스코 국제관계 연구소에 강사로 나가게될 것이라함. 기회가 나는대로 한국을 방문, 유엔에서의 경험을 아측과 나누는 기회가 있기 바란다고 한바, 동인은 그러한 기회가 있기를 희망한다고 말하였음.

8. 관찰 및 평가

0 상기 동인의 언급으로 보아·유엔 사무국내에서는 아국의 안보리 결의안 661호에 미온적이라는 국내 언론 및 외신보도에 대해 이외라는 반응을 보이고 있고, 여사한 보도가 아국의 입장을 두드러지게 하고 있는바 이에대한 대책을 시급히 강구할 필요가 있을것으로 판단됨.

0 동 대책의 일환으로 결의안 661호와 관련 아국의 금후 조치 내용이 확정될 경우 이에관한 당관 PRESS RELEASE 를 즉시 유엔에 배포코자 하니 동 조치내용이 확정될시 당관에도 회시바람. 끝

(대사 현홍주-차관)

예고:90.12.31 일반

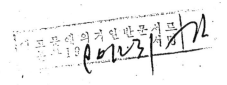

PAGE 3

0101

원 본

외 무 부

종 별 : 긴 급

번 호 : UNW-1482   일 시 : 90 0808 1900

수 신 : 장관(국연,동구일,기정)

발 신 : 주 유엔 대사

제 목 : 아국의 안보리 결의 661호 이행문제

연:UNW-1480

1. 금 8.8 17:20 SAFRONCHUK 유엔 안보리 담당 사무차장은 본직에게 전화, 연호 언급 표제건 관련 유엔사무국 내부 회람문서 내용은 "THE REPUBLIC OF KOREAREFUSES TO COMMIT ITSELF TO THE U.N. RESOLUTION. VICE FOREIGN MINISTER YOO CHONG-HA SAID HIS GOVERNMENT OPPOSES ANY USE OF FORCE."로 되어 있다고함.

2. 동인은 명 8.9 오후 결의안 661 호에 따라 안보리내에 설치된 특별 위원회 1 차 회의가 소집될 예정이며, 동 위원회에서 각국의 결의안 이행상태가 점검될 것이라고 말하였음.

3. 본직은 상기 보도가 근거없는 부정확한 내용이라고 말하고 아국은 유엔 안보리 결의안을 준수할 것임을 밝혔음. 명일 개최될 특별 위원회에서도 본직의 해명을 적절히 보고하여 줄것과 아울러 데꾸에야르 사무총장에게도 보고하여 줄것을 요청한바, 동인은 알겠다고 대답하였음.

4. 동 보도관련 유엔에서 상당한 관심이 표명되고 있음에 비추어 특별위원회 1 차 회의가 있기전 (당지시간 8.9 아침 09:00 까지) 이에관한 우리정부의 입장을 분명히 하는 발표가 있는것이 필요할것으로 사료됨. 끝

(대사 현홍주-차관)

예고:90.12.31 일반

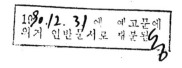
1990.12.31에 예고문에
의거 일반문서로 재분류

국기국   장관   차관   1차보   2차보   구주국   청와대   안기부

공보관실
90. 8. 9.
19:30시

유종하 외무부차관 발표문

(총리주재 관계 부처 장관 대책회의 내용)

유엔 안보이사회 결의 661호와 관련한 "데 꾸에야르" 유엔사무총장의 요청을 받고, 정부는 8.9. 오후 총리 주재하에 관계 부처 장관 회의를 개최하였음. 이 회의에는 부총리,안기부(차장), 외무(차관), 재무, 국방, 상공, 동자, 건설, 노동, 교통부와 공보처 장관이 참석하였음.

이 회의에서 정부는 유엔 안보이사회 결의에 충분히 부응하는 조치가 필요 하다는 결정을 내리고 구체적으로 다음 분야에 있어서 즉시 조치를 취하기로 하였음.

1. 이라크와 쿠웨이트 지역으로 부터 오는 원유 수입은 금지한다.

2. 이 지역과의 상품교역도 의약품등 인도적인 소요에 해당하는
    물품을 제외하고는 수입과 수출을 공히 금지한다.
    유엔 결의에는 특히 무기 수출 금지를 요청하고 있는 바, 한국은
    무기를 수출한 적도 없고 앞으로도 수출하지 않는다.

3. 이 양 지역에 있어서 건설 공사는 수주하지 않는다.

4. 이라크와 쿠웨이트 정부 자산의 동결 요청에 대하여는 이러한
    자산이 한국내에는 없음을 확인한다.

이와 별도로 오늘 회의에서는 현지 근로자를 포함한 우리 진출 인원의 안전 대책을 세밀히 검토하였는 바, 현지와 긴밀히 연락하여 모든 가능한 안전 조치를 강구해 나가기로 하였음.

이러한 제재 조치의 이행과 현지 교민의 안전 대책을 위하여 외무부 權丙鉉 본부대사를 장으로 하고 관계 부처 국장으로 구성되는 대책반을 설치 금 8.9. 부터 운영키로 하였음. 끝.

0103

유종하 외무차관 언급내용

(90.8.9. 기자 브리핑시)

○ 한국은 8.6자 이라크에 대한 유엔 안보리의 제재조치 결의 661호를
   지지하며, 이의 이행 방안에 관하여 금 8.9. 오후 관계부처 회의를
   가질 예정임.

○ 유엔 안보리의 8.2.자 660호 결의에 대하여는 8.2.자 외무부 대변인
   성명을 통하여 이라크군이 쿠웨이트 영토로 부터 즉각 철수해야
   한다는 입장을 천명하였으며, 이러한 입장을 재강조하는 바임.

○ (질문에 대하여) 한국 정부는 이라크에 의한 쿠웨이트 합병을
   인정할 수 없음을 분명히 밝힘.

0104

COMMENTS BY VICE FOREIGN MINISTER YOO CHONG-HA
(AT A PRESS BRIEFING AT 10:00 A.M., AUG. 9, 1990)

1. The Republic of Korea supports United Nations Security Council
   Resolution 661 adopted on August 6, 1990, regarding collective
   economic measures against Iraq.

   An inter-ministerial meeting for implementation of this
   resolution will take place in the afternoon of August 9.

2. We have already called for, in a statement on August 2 by the
   Foreign Ministry Spokesman, the immediate withdrawal of Iraqi
   troops from the Kuwaiti territory in accordance with UN Security
   Council Resolution 660 of August 2, 1990, and we reemphasiz
   this position.

3. (To a question)   The Government of the Republic of Korea makes it
   clear that the annexation of Kuwait by Iraq is unacceptable.

0105

관리	
번호	

분류번호	보존기간

발 신 전 보

WUN-0979　900809 1140 FC

번　호 : _____　　종별 : 긴급(암호)

수　신 : 주　유엔　　　대사. 총영사/////

발　신 : 장　관　　　　　(국연)

제　목 : 이락.쿠웨이트 사태관련 ~~~~~~~ 논평

대 : UNW-1480, 1482

1. 유종하 외무차관은 8.9. 오전 10:00시 이락.쿠웨이트 사태관련 하기
내용의 논평을 발표하였으니 귀지 활동에 활용바람.

COMMENTS BY VICE FOREIGN MINISTER YOO CHONG-llA
AT THE PRESS BRIEFING ON AUG. 9, 1990

The Republic of Koreas supports United Nations Security Council
Resolution 661 adopted on August 6, 1990, regarding collective economic
measures against Iraq.

An inter-ministerial meeting ~~to discuss the~~ for implementation of this
resolution by the Republic of Korea will take place in the ~~this~~ afternoon of August 9.

보 안 통 제	앙고재 90년 8월 9일	4 과	기안자 성명 홍영각	과 장	국 장	차 관	장 관	외신과통제

0106

We have already called for, in a statement on August 2 by the
Foreign Ministry Spokesman, the immediate withdrawal of Iraqi troops
from the Kuwaiti territory, in accordance with UN Security Council
Resolution 660 of August 2, 1990, and we ~~reiterate~~ *reemphasize* this position.

2. 기자의 질문에 대하여 이락의 쿠레이트 合倂에 대하여 아주기 ~~논~~) 답변하였다.
~~(To a question.)~~ The Government of the Republic of Korea believes that 並에바던
the annexation of Kuwait by Iraq is unacceptable to peace-loving States of
the world.

~~예 고 : 00.12.31 일반~~

(국제기구조약국장 문동석)

0107

외 무 부

종 별 :

번 호 : UNW-1488   일 시 : 90 0809 1700

수 신 : 장 관(국연,해신,기정)

발 신 : 주 유엔대사

제 목 : 이락.쿠웨이트 사태관련 논평

   대: WUN-0979

   당대표부는 8.9 대호 외무차관 논평을 프레스릴리스로 제작,유엔사무국 및 출입기자등에 배포했음.끝

   (대사 현홍주-관장)

국기국   안기부   공보처

외 무 부

종 별 : 지 급

번 호 : UNW-1491

일 시 : 90 0809 1900

수 신 : 장 관(국연,중동,미북,기정)

발 신 : 주 유엔 대사

제 목 : 안보리(이라카-쿠웨이트 사태)

1. 금 8.9 오전 안보리가 속개되어 이라크의 쿠웨트합병을 무효로 간주하는 요지의결의안을 찬 15-반0 로 만장일치 채택함(결의안 662호)

2. 안보리 회원국간 사전 협의에서의 양해에따라 공식회의에서는 토의없이 동 결의안의 표결을 바로 실시하였으며, 동 결의안 초안은 제안국을 명시함이 없이 안보리 문서로 사전배포되었음.

3. 결의안 요지(전문은 별전 훽스 송부함)

   0 어떤 형태 또는 어떤 구실하에서든 이라크에의한 쿠웨이트의 합병은 법적 근거가 없으며 무효로 간주함.

   0 모든국가,국제기구가 동 합병을 승인치 않을것과 간접적인 승인으로 간주되는조치를 취하지않을것을 촉구함.

   0 이라크가 동 합병과 관련한 모든 조치를 취소할것을 요구함.

4. 금일 주요국 발언 (표결후 발언)요지

   0 미국-헌장 51조에 따른 미군의 사우디 파병조치를안보리에 정식 봉고하는 절차를 취하고있음.이라크의 조치를 묵인하는것은 1930년대의 역사적교훈을 망각하는것임.

   0 소련-현 대결상황을 해결하기 위한 가장현명한 방법은 유엔기구나 유엔의 역량을 동원한 집단적 조치임. 소련은 일방에의한 무력조치를 반대함. 안보리내 군사위원회가 동위기 극복을 위한 조치를 강구하기 적합한 기구임.

   0 영국- 카이로,아랍 정상회의가 성과가 있기기원함. 안보리 결의 661 호 이행을위한 영국내 국내법적 조치가 지난 자정을 기해 발효되었음. 최근 안보리의 신속하고 효율적인 대응조치는 미래안보리의 역할의 본보기가 될것임.

   0 말레이지아-특정국가에 의한 일방적 조치는 사태해결에 도움이 되지 않음.

   0 중국- 모든 당사자가 사태를 더이상 악화시키지않도록 자제하여 줄것을 요망함.

국기국	차관	1차보	2차보	아주국	중아국	정문국	안기부	장관

아랍국가들의중재노력을 지지함.

0 큐바- 특정국가에 의한 일방적 또는 이기적조치를 반대함.

0 이라크-이라크는 철수를 발표하였고 철수를개시하였으나 이라크에 대한 군사적압력이 가중되었으므로 철수가 불가능하게 되었음. 과거 식민주의 국가들이 아랍지역을 자의적으로 분할하였음. 쿠웨이트는 원래 이라크에 속하는 영토였으나 식민주의자들이 자의적으로 분할해갔음. 이번 합병으로 원상회복 되었음.

4. 관찰 및 평가

0 큐바,예멘도 금번 결의안에는 찬성표결한바,이라크의 쿠웨이트 합병을 무효화하는 조치는반대할 명분이 없기 때문으로 보임.

0 금일 중.소 및 비동맹국 대다수가 미국을 직접 지칭하지 않았으나 미국이 일방적인 군사조치를 취하지 않을것을 촉구하였음. 특히 소련은 안보리내 군사위를 통하여 집단적으로 조치를 취하여야 한다고 강조하였음.

0 다수의 발언국이 금일 카이로에서 개최될 예정인 아랍정상회의가 동 사태해결에 긍정적인 기여를 하도록 기대한다는 뜻을표명하였음.

끝

첨부: UNW(F)-123

(대사 현홍주-국장)

UNITED NATIONS
SECURITY
COUNCIL

PROVISIONAL

S/21471
9 August 1990

ORIGINAL: ENGLISH

Draft resolution

The Security Council,

Recalling its resolutions 660 (1990) and 661 (1990),

Gravely alarmed by the declaration by Iraq of a "comprehensive and eternal merger" with Kuwait,

Demanding, once again, that Iraq withdraw immediately and unconditionally all its forces to the positions in which they were located on 1 August 1990,

Determined to bring the occupation of Kuwait by Iraq to an end and to restore the sovereignty, independence and territorial integrity of Kuwait,

Determined also to restore the authority of the legitimate Government of Kuwait,

1. Decides that annexation of Kuwait by Iraq under any form and whatever pretext has no legal validity, and is considered null and void;

2. Calls upon all States, international organizations, and specialized agencies not to recognize that annexation, and to refrain from any action or dealing that might be interpreted as an indirect recognition of the annexation;

3. Further demands that Iraq rescind its actions purporting to annex Kuwait;

4. Decides to keep this item on its agenda and to continue its efforts to put an early end to the occupation.

1504E

17

0111

```
관리
번호  PO-16PP
```

외 무 부

종 별 :

번 호 : UNW-1492   일 시 : 90 0809 1920

수 신 : 장관(민북,국연,중동,국법,기정)

발 신 : 주 유엔 대사

제 목 : 대이락 경제 제재 조치

대:WUN-0984

1. 대호 제재조치의 유엔 사무총장에 대한 통보는 아래사항을 고려, 추후 적절한 시기에 조치함이 좋을 것으로 생각되는바 본부 방침 회시바람.

   가. 현재까지 결의안 이행에 관한 세부조치를 공식 발표한 국가가 적은점

   나. 많은 유엔 회원국이 아직 제재조치의 구체적 내용에 대해서는 유엔에 통보하지 않은 싯점에서 비회원국인 아국이 먼저 통보함으로서 너무 두드러지게 나타날 필요가 없음. 특히 아국은 661 호 를 지지한다는 일반적 내용의 8.9 자 외무차관의 언론 브리핑을 당관 프레스릴리스로 유엔 요로에 기 배포한바 있어 아국입장에 대한 요해는 없음.

   다. 안보리내 특별위가 금 8.9 제 1 차 회의를 비공개로 개최하였는바 동의장국 (핀란드 유력), 또는 직접 유엔 사무총장이 각국의 제재 조치 이행 실태를 통보하여 줄것을 요청하는 서한을 발송해올 것이 예상되는점.

2. 대호 제재조치 이행에 따라 계약불이행으로 인한 배상문제등 아국과 이라크간 야기될 수 있는 법률적 문제점에 대한 연구와 대비를 위하여 실제 문제가제기될 가능성이 있는 관련부처와의 협의를 통하여 대책을 강구할 필요도 있다고 사료됨. 끝

   (대사 현홍주-국장)

   예고:90.12.31 일반

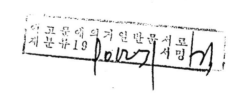

미주국	장관	차관	1차보	중아국	국기국	국기국	안기부

PAGE 1   90.08.10   08:45
                                            외신 2과 통제관 BN

                                            0112

발 신 전 보

번   호 : WUN-0987   900810 1817 AO   종별 :

                                            WUS -2653

수   신 : 주 유 엔 대사. 총영사 (사본 : 주미대사)

발   신 : 장 관 (미북)

제   목 : 대이락 경제 제재 조치

        대 : UNW-1492

        연 : WUN-0984

      대호, 유엔 사무총장에 대한 통보는 귀관 건의대로 현지사정을 감안 적절한 시기에 조치 바람. 단 연호 아측의 조치내용이 이미 국내언론에 공개 발표 되었고, 미측에 대한 공식 통보도 완료 되었음을 감안, 동건관련 미국등 우방국 및 안보리의 동향도 특히 참고 바람.   끝.

(미주국장 반 기 문)

예고 : 90.12.31. 일반

중동아국장:

국제기구조약국장:

	90 년 8 월 10 일	북 미 과	기안자 성명	과 장	국 장	차 관	장 관	
앙 고 재					전결			보안 통제
								외신과통제

0113

주 국 련 대 표 부

주국련(공) 35260- 661   1990. 8. 9.

수신 장관

참조 국제기구조약국장, 해외공보관장, 정보문화국장

제목 이락. 쿠웨이트 사태

1. UNW-1488 의 관련입니다.

2. 연호 관련 당 대표부의 프레스 릴리스를 별첨과 같이 송부합니다.

첨부 : 동 자료1부. 끝.

주   국   련   대

REPUBLIC OF KOREA

PERMANENT OBSERVER MISSION TO THE UNITED NATIONS
866 UNITED NATIONS PLAZA, SUITE 300, NEW YORK, N.Y. 10017. TEL: 371-1280

No. 31/90   9 August 1990

<u>PRESS RELEASE</u>

<u>THE REPUBLIC OF KOREA SUPPORTS</u>
<u>THE U.N. SECURITY COUNCIL RESOLUTIONS NOS. 660 & 661</u>

Following is the text of the press briefing by Vice Foreign Minister Yoo Chong-Ha on 9 August 1990 on the position of the Republic of Korea Government with regard to the United Nations Security Council Resolutions Nos. 660 and 661.

"The Republic of Korea supports the United Nations Security Council Resolution No. 661 of 6 August 1990. An inter-ministerial meeting for implementation of this resolution will take place in the afternoon of 9 August.

"We have already called for, in a statement on 2 August by the Foreign Ministry spokesman, the immediate withdrawal of Iraqi troops from the Kuwaiti territory, in accordance with United Nations Security Council Resolution No. 660 of 2 August 1990, and we reemphasize this position.

"The Government of the Republic of Korea believes that the annexation of Kuwait by Iraq is unacceptable to peace-loving states of the world."

0115

관리
번호 PO/851

원 본

외 무 부

종　별 :

번　호 : UNW-1493
일　시 : 90 0809 1920

수　신 : 장관(중동,국연,기정)

발　신 : 주 유엔 대사

제　목 : 아국 근로자 철수대책

1. 금 8.9 태국대표부 NOPPADON 서기관은 권참사관에게 이라크 및 쿠웨이트체류(특히 쿠웨이트 체류 근로자 철수대책)아국 근로자 철수 대책을 문의해왔는바, 참고로 보고함. 동인은 본국 훈령에 따라 아국, 일본, 영국, 미국 정부의 철수대책을 확인중에 있다고 함.

2. 동인이 밝힌바에 의하면 태국은 이라크에 <u>외무차관을</u> 파견 이라크내 근로자 철수는 이라크 정부와 직접 대책을 협의하고 있으며 쿠웨이트가 이라크에 합병되었으므로 쿠웨이트내 근로자 철수 대책 강구에 어려움이 있다고 말하였음. 끝

(대사 현홍주-국장)

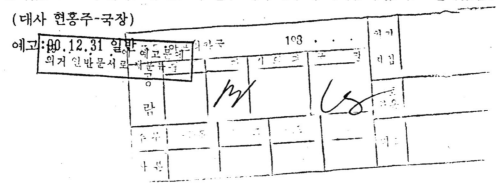

예고:90.12.31 일반

의거 일반문서로 재분류

국가국　중아국　안기부　국기국

PAGE 1

90.08.10　08:45

외신 2과　통제관 BN

0116

이라크, 쿠웨이트 사태 속보
(8.10. 07:00) ⟨10⟩

중동아프리카국
중근동과

1. 상 황

o UN 안보리, 15개 회원국 만장일치로,
  - 이라크의 쿠웨이트 병합이 무효
  - 쿠웨이트로 부터의 이라크군 무조건 철수 및 쿠웨이트 주권.독립.영토
    보존 회복을 결의
  - 모든 국가 및 국제기구의 쿠웨이트 병합에 대한 불인정과 간접적
    승인을 위한 어떠한 조치도 취하지 말것을 요청 (8.9)
o 긴급 아랍 정상회담 개최 연기 (8.10. 카이로 개최 예정)
  - 이라크군의 쿠웨이트 철수후 사태 해결 위한 아랍 연합군 파견 문제
    토의 예정
  - 이라크 참석 예정
o 소련 외무성, 소련은 UN 안보리에 의해 승인될 경우, 다국적군 및
   대 이라크 해상 봉쇄 참여를 고려할 것임을 발표 (8.9)
o 이라크, 화학무기를 보유, 외국 공격을 받을 경우, 무기 사용 시사
   (주 그리이스 이라크 대사 언급)
o 이라크 외무성, 쿠웨이트 소재 모든 외국 공관은 8.24 까지 폐쇄,
   바그다드로 옮겨 업무 개시할것을 요청 (8.9)
o 이라크군, 터어키 접경 지역으로 이동
o 영국 여객기(B.A) 탑승객중 36명의 승객 이라크군대에 의해 바그다드로
   이송
  - 잔여 승객 295명, 쿠웨이트 호텔에 억류)
o 이라크, 미 외교관 차량들의 요르단 국경지대 월경을 봉쇄
o 외국인 200명 이상, 이라크로 부터 요르단 국경 통과 출국
  - 휴가중인 주 이라크 영국 대사도 동 국경 통과 이라크로 귀임

0117

2. 각국 반응 및 조치

〈반 응〉

o 미 국 :
- NATO 회원국의 군사행동 동참 요청
- 바그다드 호텔내 억류된 38명의 미국인 안전에 낙관 표명 (부시 대통령)
- 자국인에게 쿠웨이트 인접 국경 이류 권고 및 걸프제국 진입 금지 권고

o 소 련 :
- 사우디에 군사 파병 의사 없음을 시사

o N A T O :
- 이라크의 터어키 위협시, 터어키 구원 예정 표명

o 중 국 :
- 강대국에 의한 간섭이 걸프만 위기 상황을 심화시킴을 경고

o 방글라데쉬 :
- 이라크 억류 쿠웨이트 체류 자국인 61명에 대해 석방 요구

o 아랍국가
- 이 집 트 : 이라크, 쿠웨이트 분쟁의 평화적 확신아래 자국의
              다국적군 참여 가능성 배제 표명
- 요 르 단 : 이라크의 쿠웨이트 병합 거부 천명
- 사 우 디 : 자국 방어에 아랍군 및 우방의 참여 희망을 표명(국왕)

o 이 란 :
- 이라크의 쿠웨이트 합병 비난

〈군사조치〉

o 미 국 : 폭격기 미사일 근접 배치
          지상군 5만명까지 증파 계획
o 영 국 : 사우디 및 걸프만 방어 위해 2개 편대 전투기, 지대공
          미사일 파견
o 호 주 : 미국 요청 의거 군함 1척 걸프만 파견
o 터 어 키 : 공군에 비상 경계령
o 이스라엘 : 이라크 위협 대응, 단거리 유도 미사일 첫시험 발사

0118

〈대 이라크 경제. 제재 조치〉

ㅇ 카 나 다 : UN의 대 이라크 경제 제재 결의에 동참 표명

ㅇ E C : UN의 대 이라크 제재 결의에 동참, 대 이라크 교역 중지

ㅇ 호 주 : 자국내 모든 이라크, 쿠웨이트 자산 동결 조치

ㅇ 뉴질랜드 : 대 이라크 교역 금지

ㅇ 태 국 : UN의 대 이라크 제재 결의 관련, 자국의 대 이라크 제재
조치 신중 검토

3. 교민 피해 현황 (8.10. 07:00 현재)

〈쿠웨이트 : 교민 648명〉

ㅇ 피해상황

- 미 귀환자 : 3명 (현대건설 소속 근로자)

※ 1명 - 이라크군 영내 억류 확인

2명 - 실종, 상금 생사 여부 미확인, 계속 추적중
(주 쿠웨이트 대사 보고)

ㅇ 북기사항

- 쿠웨이트 체류 아국인 2명 (김옥구 및 처), 이라크 국경 월경, 이라크로 피난
※ 쿠웨이트 체류 아국인으로서는 처음 (주 이라크 대사 보고)

4. 조 치 사 항

ㅇ UN 요청에 따른 아국의 UN 안보리 661호 지지 입장 불가피 조치에 대해
주재국에 설명코, 아국 교민 안전 조치를 요청토록 지시 (주 이라크 대사)

ㅇ 유종하 외무차관 기자 회견(8.9. 10:00)시의 기자 질문 답변사항을
주재국에 설명, 이해 요청을 지시
답변사항 : 이라크의 쿠웨이트 병합에 대한 아국 정부의 불수락 입장

ㅇ UN 안보리 결의 661호 관련한 아국 정부의 대 이라크 경제 제재 조치
결정사항, 관계부처에 통보

0119

외 무 부

종 별 :

번 호 : UNW-1496   일 시 : 90 0810 1730

수 신 : 장관(통상,중근동,국연,경협,기정)

발 신 : 주유엔대사

제 목 : 이라크-쿠웨이트 침공관련 기사

　　이라크의 쿠웨이트 침공관련, 당지 주요 신문의 해설기사를 별첨 송부하니
참고바람.

　　첨부

　　1. CHRISTIAN SCIENCE MONITOR(90.8.10.), MEXICO FINDS OILCRISIS A MIXED
ECONOMIC BLESSING´

　　2. CHRISTIAN SCIENCE MONITOR (90.8.10), AS COLD WAR ENDS, THE OIL WAR
BEGINS´ 끝

　　첨부: UNW(F)-125

　　(대사 현홍주-국장)

통상국　　1차보　　2차보　　중아국　　국기국　　경제국　　정문국　　안기부

PAGE 1   90.08.11   08:02 DN

나NW(가)125 (중근동, 뉴욕, 경협, 기정)
나NW-1496 00810 1730

CIENCE MONITOR   15

90. 8. 10

As Cold War Ends, The Oil War Begins

By Christopher Flavin

ON Aug. 2, Iraqi tanks rumbled into Kuwait and initiated the most profound change in the world oil picture in decades. In the space of a few hours, Saddam Hussein raised his share of world oil reserves from 10 percent to almost 19 percent. The petroleum reserves captured amount to nearly three times US reserves and almost double the Soviet total. In a night's work, Hussein altered not only the balance of power in the Middle East, but the balance of supply and demand in the world oil market.

In the short run, the world has already lost over 4 million barrels per day, or 15 percent of the oil traded on the world market. Given the military buildup in the Persian Gulf, it is unlikely that Saudi Arabia or any other country can fully make up for this loss. Future price increases are likely as long as this conflict persists.

Iraqi and United States forces now face each other across oil fields that represent about half of world oil reserves. Most of the nations that own those reserves – including Abu Dhabi, Dubai, and Qatar – possess tiny populations and military forces even weaker than Kuwait's. Even the military forces of the largest of the nearby oil states, Saudi Arabia, are no match alone for the large and battle-tested divisions that Iraq can bring to bear. It remains to be seen if the forces that the US and perhaps other countries are sending to Saudi Arabia will deter Hussein.

An open-ended period of extreme military and political instability now pervades the nerve center of the world's energy system. Indeed, the world is already seriously overdependent on Middle Eastern oil, which accounts for 27 percent of world production and 44 percent of world exports.

The Middle East's share of world oil exports is destined to increase steadily during the '90s. Global oil demand has been rising by more than 2 percent a year since 1985, and production by the two leading producers – the United States and the Soviet Union – is falling steeply. US oil imports have increased by 3 million barrels per day in just the last five years. Already Middle Eastern dominance of the world oil market is nearing the dangerously high proportions of the 1970s.

How has such a disastrous situation crept up on political leaders as unexpectedly as Hussein's tanks? The Western world's energy policymakers slept through the 1980s, slashing many of the government programs that could have reduced oil consumption.

In the United States, for example, the federal government allowed auto fuel-economy standards to lapse at the off Detroit's assembly lines in 1989 were actually less efficient than those of the year before. Meanwhile, home weatherization efforts have been gutted, as have energy efficiency R&D programs. Federal spending on improved energy efficiency fell from $700 million in 1981 to a budgeted $150 million in 1990.

President Bush, who finally discovered the words "energy conservation" in the midst of this military crisis, was part of an administration that attempted to eliminate virtually every program designed to reduce US oil dependence.

The folly of such moves has been evident for some time. Oil production in the continental 48 states has been declining for two decades, a trend interrupted only briefly by the massive drilling efforts of the '70s. Oil analysts have long warned that the old, depleted US fields were beginning to run dry. Yet the country's energy-guzzling habits have continued as if it were still in the

In the short run, the world has already lost over 4 million barrels per day, or 15 percent of the oil traded on the world market.

oil gusher days of the 1920s. Americans' per capita oil consumption is well over twice that of Europeans.

The military confrontation under way in the Persian Gulf will result in a substantial shortfall in world oil supplies for as long as it lasts. Beyond the oil lost from Iraq and Kuwait, oil companies will be reluctant to send tankers into the region to carry oil from Saudi Arabia, Iran, or any other country. The US action, while intended to bring Iraq's economy to its knees, could soon cripple the world economy as well.

The resting period between the cold war and the "oil war" of the '90s has proved shockingly short. This new conflict may well turn out to be equally tense and more difficult to contain. At stake is a sizable share of the world's energy resources. While the local players may be smaller states, the United States and other major powers have gotten involved. Chemical and perhaps nuclear weapons are available to the combatants.

The Middle East is and will remain a dangerous place. It is reckless to rely on such a region for the bulk of the Western world's future energy supplies. Unless efforts begin immediately to reduce oil dependence, we may soon long for the economic and military stability of the former superpower standoff. Not only the industrial countries, but the entire third world is now vulnerable to a serious oil shock.

□ Christopher Flavin is an energy analyst and vice president for research at the World-

0121
ZH

IE CHRISTIAN SCIENCE MONITOR   90. P. 10   3

IRAQI ▶▶▶ POWER PLAY

Mexico Finds Oil Crisis a Mixed Economic Blessing

By David Clark Scott
Staff writer of The Christian Science Monitor

MEXICO CITY

FOR Latin America's major oil producers – Mexico and Venezuela – tension in the Persian Gulf means more petrodollars sloshing into government coffers.

That may be a bonanza or a mixed blessing. Much depends on the height of the latest oil price geyser, analysts say.

If current prices hold, the state-owned monopoly Petroleos Mexicanos S.A. (Pemex) will pocket some $12 million per day more – $4.3 billion more annually – than projected this year.

Both debtor nations can use the extra income. Venezuela's bill, just to cover interest payments on its external debt, comes to about $4 billion annually. Economists reckon that at today's prices, the additional revenue could cover those payments.

And, unlike Mexico, Venezuela has the ability to boost production significantly. Venezuela announced Wednesday it would increase production by 500,000 barrels a day, up from 1.6 million.

"Venezuela is the best placed in the world to benefit from this crisis," says Bill Orme, editor of Latin Finance, a Miami-based publication.

Along with brightening the debt-service picture for Mexico, a gush of unexpected oil revenue may provide the economic reform program of President Carlos Salinas de Gortari with a needed fillip.

Just two weeks ago Banco Nacional de Mexico was warning that low oil prices and a ballooning current account deficit might force the government into sizable, unplanned budget cuts.

Mexico's non-oil exports rose by only .4 percent in the first half of this year. Meanwhile a domestic economy ticking along at about a 3 percent growth rate sucked in 15 percent more imported goods than during the same period last year. Rising oil exports will help redress the imbalance in the short term.

"Higher oil prices benefit Carlos Salinas. How big a benefit depends on where oil prices go in the future," says an economist with a Mexican bank. "Remember, oil revenue is government revenue. The government will have less need to borrow, and that could mean lower interest rates."

Another potential benefit for Mexico (and Mr. Salinas who is desperately seeking foreign investment) could be a much-needed injection of capital into Pemex. Pemex investment in drilling equipment and oil exploration has dropped 75 percent,

ROBERT HARDISON – STAFF

FILL'ER UP: *This Pemex station in Mexico City is part of a state-owned chain, whose prices are rising at border locations as Americans cross into Mexico in search of cheaper gasoline.*

stunted by eight years of economic crisis here and ebbing petroleum prices.

Production continues to fall, down from 3 million barrels a day in 1982 to 2.5 million today.

In Washington on Wednesday, Mexico's Foreign Minister Fernando Solana Morales offered the US 100,000 more barrels of oil during the next two months. Although at full capacity now, Mr. Solana said an extra effort would be made to increase production. Already, Pemex is selling about 55 percent of its exports to the US, exceeding Mexico's National Energy Plan which states no more than 50 percent of sales should be to a single country.

So far, this year Mexico supplied 8.5 percent of the US oil-import needs. And, analysts say more than 80 percent of US strategic reserves are Mexican crude.

But the ongoing slide in production coupled with growing domestic demand, means "Mexico's exports would have vanished by the end of the century," Mr. Orme says.

"Now, the US and Japan will be looking for reliable oil suppliers outside of the Middle East. That means Mexico will be receiving new investment, joint ventures to increase production. That translates into more export income down the road," he predicts.

But analysts say there is a point where high oil prices may be of dubious benefit.

"If oil prices don't stay above $25 per barrel for an extended period, then Mexico is a big winner," says a Los Angeles money manager with large investments in Mexico. "But over $25 for an extended period, it's a mixed bag: a one-year boom and then a real crunch as the US economy slows down."

Economists predict industrialized nations may slip into a recession if petroleum prices remain high. For developing nations, such as Mexico, that means fewer exports of raw materials and finished goods. It means less foreign investment (possibly less aid) and fewer new jobs since companies will not need to invest in new plants to expand production.

High oil prices could push up inflation and interest rates in developed countries. That translates into bigger loan payments for debtor nations such as Venezuela and Mexico. "We still owe US banks a lot of money. And a portion of those debt payments is based on floating interest rates," notes one Mexican economist.

Orme says Mexico is less vulnerable now to floating interest rates. "Mexico gets hurt more by losing the US economy as a market, than by a rising interest rate bill," he says.

On Tuesday, Pemex says gas stations near the 2,000 mile US border would raise prices to match US gas hikes. This runs counter to Salinas' efforts to curb inflation, but was prompted by a sudden influx of Americans crossing the border this past weekend to top off tanks with cheaper Mexican gas.

0122
2-2

관리 번호	90 -1452

외 무 부

종 별 :

번 호 : UNW-1498   일 시 : 90 0810 1820

수 신 : 장관(국연,중근동,통일,기정)

발 신 : 주 유엔 대사

제 목 : 이라크내 근로자 철수 대책

연:UNW-1493

1. 금 8.10 태국대표부 NOPPADON 서기관은 권참사관에게 전화, 태국 대표부는 본국 훈령에 따라 이라크의 외국인 출입금지 조치에 대응하여 외국인 출국을 허용토록 촉구하는 안보리 결의안 채택을 추진하고 있다고 통보하고 동 추진에 아국이 동참할것을 요청하여 왔음.

2. 태국대표부는 안보리 회원국인 말레지아 대표부와 협의하여 동건을 추진하고 있으며, 이라크 및 쿠웨이트내 대사관을 유지하지 않고 있는 국가들의 경우에도 고려 (예:싱가폴) IRC, ILO 등 국제기구와도 협의 결의안 초안을 작성중에 있으며 아국도 동 결의안 작성에 참여할것과 아울러 아국도 안보리회원국들에게 동 결의안 채택을 위해 필요한 영향력을 발휘해 줄것을 요청하여 왔음. 태국대표부에서 일본, 중국등 대표부와도 접촉하였는바 호의적인 반응을 얻었다고함. 3. 안보리는 당초 금 8.10 17:00 비공식 협의회를 개최코자 하였으나 큐바의 요청으로 8.13 11:30 비공식 협의회를 개최키로 하였다함.

4. 권참사관은 일단 본국에 보고후 지침을 받아 협력하겠다고 말하였음.

5. 상기에 대한 본부 지침 및 이라크 및 쿠웨이트내 아국 근로자 철수 관련방침에 대해 참고로 회시하여 주시기 바람. 끝

(대사현홍주-국장)

예고:90.12.31.일반

1990. 12. 31. 예고문에
의기 일반문서로 재분류됨

국기국	차관	1차보	2차보	중아국	통상국	안기부

원 본

외 무 부

종 별 :

번 호 : UNW-1500   일 시 : 90 0810 1830

수 신 : 장관(미북,국연,통일,기정)

발 신 : 주 유엔 대사

제 목 : 대이락 경제 제재조치

대:WUN-0987

1. 안보리 결의 661 호를 이행하기 위한 아국의 조치에 대해 가능한한 조기에, 늦어도 8.24 까지 통보하여 줄것을 요청하는 유엔사무총장의 8.8 자 외무장관앞 서한 (동문 회람 NOTE)이 금 8.10 당관에 송부 되어 왔음.

2. 유엔 사무국에 확인한바 금일 현재 일본, 브라질, 뉴질랜드등이 661 호이행 조치에 관하여 유엔 사무국에 통보 하였다함.

3. 대호 및 상기 1,2 항에 비추어 아국의 조치 내용을 본직 명의의 8.10 자서한을 유엔 사무총장에게 통보하였음. 유엔 사무국은 동 서한을 내주초 안보리 문서로 배포하고자 한다함)

4. 유엔 사무총장은 8.8 안보리에서 채택된 결의안 662 의 텍스트 사본을 외무장관앞으로 당관에 송부 하여 왔으니 참고 바람.

첨부: 661 호 이행조치 통보 요청 유엔사무총장 서한 (UNW(F)-126)끝

(대사 현홍주-국장)

예고:90.12.31 일반

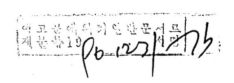

미주국	차관	1차보	2차보	중아국	국기국	통상국	안기부

UNITED NATIONS ⊛ NATIONS UNIES

POSTAL ADDRESS—ADRESSE POSTALE UNITED NATIONS, N.Y. 10017
CABLE ADDRESS—ADRESSE TELEGRAPHIQUE· UNATIONS NEWYORK

REFERENCE: SCPC/7/90(1)

The Secretary-General of the United Nations presents his compliments to the Minister for Foreign Affairs of the Republic of Korea and has the honour to refer to resolution 661 (1990), which was adopted by the Security Council at its 2933rd meeting, on 6 August 1990, in connection with the item entitled "The situation between Iraq and Kuwait", the text of which was transmitted to His/Her Excellency's Government by telegram on the same date.

The Secretary-General wishes, in particular, to draw attention to paragraphs 6, 7 and 10 of resolution 661 (1990), which read as follows:

"The Security Council,

...

"Acting under Chapter VII of the Charter of the United Nations,

...

"6. Decides to establish, in accordance with rule 28 of the provisional rules of procedure of the Security Council, a Committee of the Security Council consisting of all the members of the Council, to undertake the following tasks and to report on its work to the Council with its observations and recommendations:

"(a) To examine the reports on the progress of the implementation of the present resolution which will be submitted by the Secretary-General;

Annex enclosed

"(b) To seek from all States further information regarding the action taken by them concerning the effective implementation of the provisions laid down in the present resolution;

"7. Calls upon all States to co-operate fully with the Committee in the fulfilment of its task, including supplying such information as may be sought by the Committee in pursuance of the present resolution;

...

"10. Requests the Secretary-General to report to the Council on the progress of the implementation of the present resolution, the first report to be submitted within thirty days".

In light of his reporting responsibility under paragraph 10, the Secretary-General would appreciate receiving as early as possible, but no later than 24 August 1990, information on the measures taken by His/Her Excellency's Government in accordance with the provisions of the resolution.

8 August 1990

S. B.

0126

	분류번호	보존기간

발 신 전 보

WUN-0997   900811 1722 FA

번   호 :   종별 :

수   신 : 주 ^{유엔}   대사 . 총영사
               (국연)

발   신 : 장 관

제   목 : 아라크내 근로자 철수대책

대 : UNW-1498

1. 대호 관련, 교민안전대책 논의를 위한 8.11. 관계부처회의 토의 사항을
   하기 통보하니 두선 <u>참고하</u>바랍.

   가 . 8.10. 현재 교민현황 (총 1380명 체류중)

      ㅇ 이   락 : 근로자 660명등 732명 체류

      ㅇ 쿠웨이트 : 근로자 319명등 648명 체류

   나 . 교민 안전관련 조치현황

      ㅇ 교민안전에 만전을 기하도록 현지공관에 기지시(아직 아측 피해 없음)

      ㅇ 안전철수에 대비, 국제적십자사, 이락당국 및 우방국과 접촉중

      ㅇ 협조요청 우방국 : 영, 불, 독, 일, 이태리, 인도, 파키스탄,

                              요르단, 더키, 이집트등

   다 . 급후 조치 예정사항

      ㅇ 교민 비상철수에 대비, 교통부는 KAL 예비기 사전 확보예정

      ㅇ 건설부, 노동부에서 이락.쿠웨이트 진출업체와 협의, 내주중

      비상철수시기, 방법등 구체적 방안 강구 예정

///계속...

앙고재	90년8월11일 UN과	기안자	과 장	국 장	차 관	장 관	보안통제	외신과통제

2. 태국측의 동참요청과 관련, 동 결정에 참고코자 하니 대국측이 의미하는 동참의 구체적 내용에 대해서 파악 보고바람.

3. 한편, 안보리 의사규칙에는 옵서버의 결의안 제출 또는 공동 참여에 관한 규정이 없으므로 안보리 결의안 제출시 동참은 불가할 것으로 사료되는 바, 옵서버의 안보리 결의안 동참 가능여부 및 선례등에 관하여 조사보고 바람. 끝.

예고 : 90.12.31. 일반

(국제기구조약국장 문동석)

0128

외 무 부

관리
번호 90-
1459

종 별 :

번 호 : UNW-1502 일 시 : 90 0811 0930

수 신 : 장관(국련,중근동,기정)

발 신 : 주 유엔 대사

제 목 : 아국근로자 철수 대책

대:WUN-0997

연:UNW-1498

1. 태국측의 안보리 결의안 추진에 아국동참은 연호 보고와같이 아래사항을의미함.

가. 결의안 총안작성(결의안에 포함될 내용, 표현방식등)과정에서 이해관계국으로 참여함(동 결의안이 성안되면 태국이나 아국등이 제안국이 되는것이 아니라 말련등 안보리 회원국에 제시, 이들 국가들로 하여금 결의안 제안국이 되게거나 결의안 제안국을 명시함이 없이 안보리 전체 회원국의 콘센서스로 결의안을채택되게 한다는 구상임)

나. 안보리에서 동 결의안이 채택되도록 사전 안보리 회원국을 개별접촉, 동 취지.필요성등을 설명, 비공식 협의하는 과정에 아국이 참여함.

2. 대호와같이 안보리 비회원국이 안보리 결의안의 제안국에 포함될수 없으며, 포함된 사례도 없음.

3. 안보리 회원국들은 당초 8.10. 비공식협의회를 개최 동건을 협의코자 하였으나, 다수 국가들이 동건은 서두를 필요가 없고 사태를 관망해가며 결정할 문제라는 의견을 제시하여 8.13. 로 협의회를 연기했다함을 참고바람.

일본도 현단계에서는 사태진전을 관망하면서 추진하자는 신중한 입장을 보이고 있다함.

(대사 현홍주-국장)

예고:90.12.31. 일반

국기국 안기부	장관	차관	1차보	2차보	중아국	정문국	영교국	청와대

PAGE 1

90.08.12 01:37

외신 2과 통제관 CW

0129

WIRTSCHAFTSMASSNAHMEN GEGENUEBER DER REPUBLIK IRAK UND DEM
STAAT KUWAIT.

DER BUNDESRAT HAT MIT WIRKUNG VOM 7. AUGUST 1990, 11.00 UHR,
EINE VERORDNUNG UEBER DIE RANDERWAEHNTEN WIRTSCHAFTSMASSNAHMEN
IN KRAFT GESETZT. DARIN WIRD IN ANLEHNUNG AN DIE UNO-RESOLU-
TION VOM 6. AUGUST 1990 JEGLICHER HANDEL (EIN-, AUS- UND
DURCHFUHR) MIT DEM IRAK UND KUWAIT SOWIE DAMIT IN VERBINDUNG
STEHENDE ZAHLUNGEN UND DARLEHEN VERBOTEN. DER SCHUTZ KUWAITI-
SCHER GUTHABEN WIRD DURCH EINE GESONDERTE VERORDNUNG GEREGELT.

ZU IHRER INFORMATION UEBERMITTELN WIR IHNEN NACHFOLGEND DIE
NEUTRALITAETSRECHTLICHE UND -POLITISCHE BEGRUENDUNG FUER DIESE
WIRTSCHAFTSMASSNAHMEN, WIE SIE VON BUNDESRAT FELBER DER PRESSE
MITGETEILT WURDE:

1. NEUTRALITAETSRECHTLICHE BEURTEILUNG

DER NEUTRALE STAAT HAT SICH IM FALLE EINER BEWAFFNETEN AUSEIN-
ANDERSETZUNG ODER EINES KRIEGES AN DIE REGELN DES NEUTRALI-
TAETSRECHTS ZU HALTEN, WIE ES VOR ALLEM IM V. HAAGER ABKOMMEN
VOM 18. OKTOBER 1907 BETREFFEND DIE RECHTE UND PFLICHTEN DER
NEUTRALEN MAECHTE UND PERSONEN IM FALLE EINES LANDKRIEGES (SR
0.515.21) NIEDERGELEGT IST. SO DARF ER DEN KRIEGFUEHRENDEN
KEINE FINANZIELLE UNTERSTUETZUNG - IM SINNE VON ANLEIHEN UND
FINANZIELLEN LEISTUNGEN ZUR DIREKTEN VERWENDUNG FUER DIE
KRIEGSFUEHRUNG - GEWAEHREN UND KEINE WAFFEN UND MUNITION LIE-
FERN. IM UEBRIGEN BESTEHEN ABER KEIN WIRTSCHAFTLICHEN NEUTRA-
LITAETSPFLICHTEN, INSBESONDERE TRIFFT DEN NEUTRALEN KEINE
PFLICHT, DIE WIRTSCHAFTSBEZIEHUNGEN MIT EINER KONFLIKTPARTEI
AUFRECHTZUHALTEN. WAEHREND DAHER DIE TEILNAHME AN MILITAERI-
SCHEN SANKTIONEN MIT DER NEUTRALITAET ZUM VORNHEREIN NICHT
VEREINBART WERDEN KANN, IST ES GRUNDSAETZLICH DURCHAUS ZULAES-
SIG, DASS EIN NEUTRALER STAAT UNTER BESTIMMTEN VORAUSSETZUNGEN
WIRTSCHAFTSMASSNAHMEN ERGREIFT. DIES IST IN ERSTER LINIE SACHE
SEINER NEUTRALITAETSPOLITIK, DIE ER NACH FREIEM ERMESSEN GE-
STALTEN KANN.

대이락경제제재조치 이행관련
스위스 연방정부 발표성명
(UNW-1511) 90. 8. 13.

8

0130

NEUTRALITAETSPOLITISCHE BEURTEILUNG

DER VORLIEGENDE FALL UNTERSCHEIDET SICH IN GRUNDLEGENDER WEISE
VON ANDEREN SITUATIONEN, IN DENEN DIE SCHWEIZ ZUR VERHAENGUNG
VON WIRTSCHAFTSMASSNAHMEN AUFGEFORDERT WURDE. DURCH SEINE MI-
LITAERISCHE INVASION HAT DER IRAK DAS IM VOELKERGEWOHNHEITS-
RECHT UND IN ART.2 ABS.4 DER UNO-CHARTA VERANKERTE GEWALTVER-
BOT VERLETZT. DIESES SCHREIBT VOR, DASS ALLE STAATEN IN IHREN
INTERNATIONALEN BEZIEHUNGEN JEDE GEGEN DIE TERRITORIALE UNVER-
SEHRTHEIT ODER DIE POLITISCHE UNABHAENGIGKEIT EINES STAATES
GERICHTETE ANDROHUNG ODER ANWENDUNG VON GEWALT ZU UNTERLASSEN
HABE. DER IRAK HAT DAMIT GEGEN FUNDAMENTALES VOELKERRECHT VER-
STOSSEN. DIE STAATENGEMEINSCHAFT IST SICH - ANDERS ALS ETWA IM
FALLE SUEDAFRIKAS, AFGHANISTANS ODER DES FALKLAND-KONFLIKTS -
IN DER VERURTEILUNG DES RECHTSBRECHERS UND IN DER VERHAENGUNG
VON WIRTSCHAFTSSANKTIONEN BIS AUF WENIGE AUSNAHMEN EINIG. WEIL
DIE INTERNATIONALE STAATENGEMEINSCHAFT AUF EINER UNIVERSELLEN
DURCHFUEHRUNG DER WIRTSCHAFTSMASSNAHMEN BEHARRT, KANN DIE
SCHWEIZ DABEI NICHT ABSEITS STEHEN. ES IST NICHT MOEGLICH, DEN
UNSERER NEUTRALITAETSPOLITIK ZUGRUNDELIEGENDEN GLEICHBEHAND-
LUNGSGRUNDSATZ AUF ZWEI SO UNGLEICH KONFLIKTPARTEIEN WIE EINEN
EINZELNEN RECHTSBRECHER EINERSEITS UND DIE GANZE UEBRIGE
STAATENGEMEINSCHAFT ANDERERSEITS ANZUWENDEN.

DEN IN ANDEREN FAELLEN VON SANKTIONEN PRAKTIZIERTEN ''COURANT
NORMAL'' (STABILISIERUNG DES HANDELSVOLUMENS AUF DEN DURCH-
SCHNITT EINER DEN SANKTIONEN VORANGEGANGENEN REPRAESENTATIVEN
BASISPERIODE) VERMAG HIER NICHT ZU GENUEGEN. DIE EINFUEHRUNG
DIESER MASSNAHME GEGENUEBER DEM RECHTSBRECHER IRAK WAERE ZWAR
DURCHAUS MOEGLICH. HINGEGEN WAERE EINE ANWENDUNG DES ''COURANT
NORMAL'' GEGENUEBER DER ANDEREN ''PARTEI'', D.H. DER IN DER
UNO VEREINTEN UEBRIGEN WELT, NICHT DENKBAR.

NEUTRALITAETSPOLITIK IST WIE JEDE POLITIK INTERESSENPOLITIK.
SIE DIENT DER WAHRUNG DER SCHWEIZERISCHEN INTERESSEN IM AUS-
LAND. WENN DIE SCHWEIZ KEINE WIRTSCHAFTSSANKTIONEN GEGEN DEN
IRAK ERGREIFT, SO STELLT SIE SICH IN DEN AUGEN DER GANZEN
UEBRIGEN STAATENGEMEINSCHAFT AUF DIE SEITE DES RECHTSBRECHERS.
UNSERE HALTUNG WUERDE IM AUSLAND NICHT VERSTANDEN. UNSER AN-
SEHEN WUERDE WELTWEIT, INSBESONDERE ABER IN WESTEUROPA, GROS-
SEN SCHADEN ERLEIDEN. DIE SCHWEIZERISCHE NEUTRALITAETSPOLITIK
WUERDE IHRE GLAUBWUERDIGKEIT EINBUESSEN. DAS ERGREIFEN DIESER
WIRTSCHAFTSSANKTIONEN LIEGT DAHER IM AUSSENPOLITISCHEN INTE-
RESSE DER SCHWEIZ. ZUDEM WIRD AUF DIESE WEISE VERMIEDEN, DASS
DIE SCHWEIZ DURCH EIN ABSEITSSTEHEN ZUR DREHSCHEIBE FUER UM-

9

0131

3. RECHTSGRUNDLAGE

DIE WIRTSCHAFTSMASSNAHMEN GEGENUEBER DEM IRAK UND KUWAIT WERDEN GESTUETZT AUF ART.102 ZIFF.8 UND 9 BV ERLASSEN, WONACH DER BUNDESRAT DIE INTERESSEN DER EIDGENOSSENSCHAFT NACH AUSSEN ZU WAHREN HAT. AUF DER GRUNDLAGE DIESER BESTIMMUNGEN IST DER BUNDESRAT BEFUGT, NOTWENDIGE MASSNAHMEN ZU TREFFEN, UM DIE STOERUNG DER BEZIEHUNGEN DER SCHWEIZ ZU ANDEREN STAATEN ZU VERMEIDEN UND UM DIE ERHALTUNG DER INTERNATIONALEN STELLUNG UND DES ANSEHENS DER SCHWEIZ ZU GEWAEHRLEISTEN. DIE SCHWEIZ ERGREIFT DIESE WIRTSCHAFTLICHEN SANKTIONEN GEGENUEBER DEM IRAK UND KUWAIT ALS AUTONOME MASSNAHME. IM GEGENSATZ ZU DEN UNO-MITGLIEDERN TRIFFT DIE SCHWEIZ KEINE RECHTSPFLICHT ZU IHRER VERHAENGUNG.

0132

외 무 부

종 별 :

번 호 : UNW-1515   일 시 : 90 0813 1900

수 신 : 장관(국연,중근동,봉일,기정)

발 신 : 주 유엔 대사

제 목 : 근로자 철수 관련 안보리 결의추진

연:UNW-1498,1502

연호건에 관한 당관의 관찰 및 평가를 아래 보고함.

1. 이라크내 외국인 철수 문제는 8.13 현재 안보리 회원국간 비공식 협의의안건으로 제기되지 않았음.

2. 이라크 및 쿠웨이트 내 체제 국민의 국적, 동 체제 국민들의 규모, 체제성격등에 따라 안보리 회원국간 이해와 관심의 심도가 다르며, 미국의 경우에도 현재 억류되고 있는 자국민들을 "HOSTAGE"로 지칭하지 않으면서 양자가 외교적 협의와 교섭에 주력하고 있는 인상인바, 현 상황에서는 동건이 안보리의 주관심사항으로 제기되기 어려울것으로 보임.

3. 외국인 출국금지를 국적에 따라 선별적으로 집행할 것인지등 동건에 대한 이라크의 입장이 명확하지 않고, 동건 관련 사태 추이가 상금 분명치 않으므로 현 단계에서 안보리 결의 추진을 통하여 이라크에 압력을 행사하고자 할경우 역효과를 초래할 가능성도 예측할수 있을것임.

4. 상기 감안 당관에서는 동결의안 추진의 전면에 나서지 않고 실무차원에서 태국측에 상기 취지의 비공식 의견을 제시하며 관련 동향 파악에 임하는 것이바람직할것으로 판단됨. 끝

(대사 현홍주-국장)

예고:90.12.31 일반

1990.12.31 예고문에 의거 일반문서로 재분류됨

국기국 안기부	장관	차관	1차보	2차보	중아국	통상국	정문국	정와대

PAGE 1   90.08.14   08:41
                                            외신 2과 통제관 CW

0133

외 무 부

종 별 :

번 호 : UNW-1518   일 시 : 90 0813 1930

수 신 : 장 관(국연)

발 신 : 주 유엔 대사

제 목 : 안보리(이라크-쿠웨이트 분쟁)

1. 주유엔 PICKERING 대사는 8.9 자 서한으로 안보리 의장에게 미국의 자위권을 규정한 유엔헌장 51조에 근거하여 페스사만 지역에 군대를 배치하였음을 통보하였음.

2. 안보리 문서 (S/21492) 로 배포된 동 서한별첨 보고함.

별첨: UNW(F)-128

끝

(대사 현홍주-국장)

국기국   1차보   중아국   정문국   안기부   대책반   2과보   통상국   장가신

PAGE 1   90.08.14   09:08 WG

외신 1과 통제관

0134

UNITED NATIONS

유엔 UNW(가)-128 (총역)
     UNW-1518 008 13 1530

Security Council

Distr.
GENERAL

S/21492
10 August 1990

ORIGINAL: ENGLISH

LETTER DATED 9 AUGUST 1990 FROM THE PERMANENT REPRESENTATIVE OF THE UNITED STATES OF AMERICA TO THE UNITED NATIONS ADDRESSED TO THE PRESIDENT OF THE SECURITY COUNCIL

As I informed you yesterday, in accordance with Article 51 of the Charter of the United Nations, I wish on behalf of my Government, to report that the United States has deployed military forces to the Persian Gulf region. These forces have been dispatched in exercise of the inherent right of individual and collective self-defence, recognized in Article 51, in response to developments and requests from Governments in the region, including requests from Kuwait and Saudi Arabia, for assistance. The application of this inherent right in response to the Iraqi armed attack on Kuwait has been affirmed in resolution 661 (1990).

Since the invasion, Iraq has made statements and taken actions that threaten Saudi Arabia and other States neighbouring Kuwait. As the adoption of resolutions 660 (1990), 661 (1990) and 662 (1990) made clear, Iraq's invasion and the continued occupation of Kuwait do not simply concern Kuwait or the region, they concern the entire community of nations. The military forces dispatched by the United States to the Persian Gulf region will work together with those of Saudi Arabia and other nations.

I would be grateful if you could arrange for this letter to be circulated as a document of the Security Council.

(Signed) Thomas R. PICKERING

90-18800 2216a (E)

/-/

0135

외　무　부

종　별 :

번　호 : UNW-1520　　　　　　　　　　일　시 : 90 0813 1930

수　신 : 장　관(통일,국연,중근동,기정)

발　신 : 주 유엔 대사

제　목 : 대이락 경제제재 조치

　　연: UNW-1500

　　연호 본직의 유엔 사무초장앞 서한이 ' NOTE BYTHE SECRETARY-GENERAL' 제하 안보리 문서로 배포되었음 (S/21487) 동서한 텍스트 파편송부함.끝

　　(대사 현홍주-국장)

통상국　　1차보　　2차보　　중아국　　국기국　　안기부

PAGE 1

	분류번호	보존기간

발 신 전 보

번 호 : WUN-1028   900814 2001 DP   종별 :

수 신 : 주 유연   대사//총영사

발 신 : 장 관 (국연)

제 목 : 근로자 철수관련 안보리결의 추진

대 : UNW-1515, 1502

대호, 귀관 건의대로 실무차원에서 대처바라며, 관련동향 파악되는

대로 보고바람.   끝.

예 고 : 1990.12.31. 일반.

(국제기구조약국장 문동석)

1990. 12. 31 예고문에
의거 일반문서로 재분류됨

아중동국장 :					보 안 통 제	

앙 고 재	90 년 8 월 14 일 과	기안자 성명 유영완	과 장	국 장 전기원	차 관	장 관	외신과통제

0137

외 무 부

```
관리
번호   PO
     -14P2
```

종 별 :

번 호 : UNW-1522   일 시 : 90 0814 1600

수 신 : 장관(국연,봉일,중근동,기정)

발 신 : 주 유엔 대사

제 목 : 이라크의 쿠웨이트 침공

연:UNW-1516

1. 쿠웨이트 대사는 8.13 자 유엔 안보리 의장앞 서한에서 자국이 유엔헌장51 조 및 고유의 자위권 행사의 일환으로 일부국가들에게 안보리 결의 661 호의 효율적이고 신속한 이행에 필요한 군사적, 기타 조치를 취할것을 요청하였음을 봉보하였음.

2. 동 안보리 의장앞 서한은 연호와같은 서한의 발송을 안보리에 봉보한것으로 해상봉쇄 참여등 군사적 조치를 취하려는 국가들에게 그러한 조치를 취할수있는 정당한 법적 근거를 제공해주기 위한것으로 보임.

3. 영국도 안보리 의장앞 8.13 자 서한에서 유엔헌장 51 조에 따라 걸프지역에 군대를 배치하였음을 봉보하였음. 동 서한은 군대배치의 근거로서 쿠웨이트,사우디, 바레인의 지원 요청과 오만과의 합의를 또한 언급하였음. 끝

(대사 현홍주-국장)

예고:90.12.31 일반

19 90.12.31. 새 고문에 의거 일반문서로 재분류됨

국기국 안기부	장관	차관	1차보	2차보	중아국	통상국	정문국	청와대

PAGE 1   90.08.15   05:47
                                         외신 2과 통제관 CN

                                              0138

주 국 련 대 표 부

주국련 20313- 671   1990. 8. 14.

수신 장관

참조 국제기구조약국장

제목 대이라크 제재 조치

    아국의 표제 조치에 관한 본직의 유엔사무총장앞 서한이 8.10자 안보리
문서로 배포된바 동문서를 별첨 송부합니다.

    첨 부 : 상기 안보리 문서 1부.   끝.

발 송
No.
1990. 8. 16
주유.

주   국   련   대

OU 45809   0139

UNITED NATIONS

S

Security Council

Distr.
GENERAL

S/21487
10 August 1990

ORIGINAL: ENGLISH

NOTE BY THE SECRETARY-GENERAL

The attached letter dated 10 August 1990 from the Permanent Observer of the Republic of Korea to the United Nations has been addressed to the Secretary-General.

90-18794 1736e (E)

/...

0140

Annex

Letter dated 10 August 1990 from the Permanent Observer of the Republic of Korea to the United Nations addressed to the Secretary-General

I have the honour to bring to your attention the following economic measures against Iraq and Kuwait that my Government announced on 9 August 1990 in pursuance of the United Nations Security Council resolution 661 (1990). These measures are to take effect immediately.

1. An embargo on crude oil imports from Iraq and Kuwait;

2. The suspension of trade with the two countries in other commodities and products except items for medical and humanitarian purposes;

3. An embargo on sales of arms to Iraq (there has been no such sales);

4. The suspension of procurement of construction contracts in Iraq and Kuwait;

5. Establishment of a special inter-ministerial task force to monitor implementation of these measures.

As to the protection of assets of the legitimate Government of Kuwait and its agencies, it has been confirmed that there are no such assets in Korea.

I would highly appreciate it if you could have these measures brought to the attention of the special committee of the Security Council which has been set up under Security Council resolution 661 (1990).

(Signed) Hong-choo HYUN
Ambassador

0141

관리
번호 90
-1513

외 무 부

종 별 :

번 호 : UNW-1541   일 시 : 90 0816 1800

수 신 : 장관(국연,중근동,봉일,기정)

발 신 : 주 유엔 대사

제 목 : 이라크내 외국인 출국문제 유엔내 동향

　　대:WUN-1028

　　금 8.16 권종락 참사관이 태국, 일본, 유엔 사무국등과 접촉, 파악한 표제건 관련 동향을 아래 보고함.

　　1. 미, 영등이 표제건 관련 안보리 결의안 추진은 이라크를 자극할 것으로 보고있어 결의안 추진은 현 단계에서는 보류되고있음.

　　2. 태국은 말레이지아를 통하여 비동맹그룹이 표제건 관련 온건한 내용의 결의안을 채택하는 방안을 검토하고있음. 금후 사태진전을 보아가며 최종 결정할것이라함.

　　3. EC 의장국인 이태리의 주유엔대사가 EC, 호주, 오지리, 쳌코, 뉴질랜드,노르웨이, 스웨덴, 터키, 일본, 미국을 대표하여 유엔 사무총장이 이라크측에 대해 외국인의 출국을 허용토록 촉구하여줄것을 요청하였음.(유엔 사무초장의 부재로 금 8.16 13:00 유엔 사무총장실 PICCO 중동 담당관을 면담하였다함) 이태리 대사는 또한 유엔사무총장이 이라크에 특사를 파견하여 이를 촉구하여 줄것을요청하였음.

　　4. 아세안 그룹은 금일 오전 그룹회의에서 유엔 사무총장에게 개인사절을 이라크에 파견, 이라크 정부에 직접 외국인 출국허용을 촉구키로 결정하였다함. 끝

　　(대사 현홍주-국장)

　　예고:90.12.31 일반

90.12.31 고문에 의거 일반......서로 재분류됨

국기국	장관	차관	1차보	2차보	중아국	통상국	영교국	안기부

90.08.17　07:46

외신 2과 롱제관 FE

0142

발 신 전 보

번 호 : WUN-1057   900817 1944 DY   종별 :

수 신 : 주   유엔   대사 . 총영사

발 신 : 장 관   (국연)

제 목 : 이락.쿠웨이트 사태

대 : UNW-1488

대호. 안보리결의 661호 관련 경제 제재조치를 유엔에 통보한 국가
현황 및 북한과 이란의 조치내용을 파악. 보고바람.   끝.

(국기국장 문동석)

앙 고 재	90 년 8 월 17 일 외 과	기안자 송명옥	과 장	국 장 김재희	차 관	장 관	보안통제	외신과통제

0143

관리 번호	90 -1537

외 무 부

종 별 :

번 호 : UNW-1548

일 시 : 90 0817 1700

수 신 : 장관(국연,중근동,정일,기정)

발 신 : 주 유엔 대사

제 목 : 이라크-쿠웨이트 사태

연:UNW-1500

대:WUN-1057

1. 8.17 현재 경제제재 조치를 유엔 사무총장에 공식 통보한국가는 아래와 같음.(아국 포함 44 개국)

ARGENTINA, AUSTRALIA, AUSTRIA, BRAZIL, BULGARIA, CANADA, CHILE, COTE D'IVOIRE, CYPRUS, CZECH AND SLOVAK FEDERAL REPUBLIC, FINLAND, GERMAN DEMOCRATIC REPUBLIC, GERMANY, FEDERAL REPUBLIC, HUNGARY, ITALY (EC 대표), JAPAN, LUXEMBURG, MALAYSIA, NETHERLANDS, NEW ZEALAND, NORWAY, PANAMA, ROMANIA, SINGAPORE, SOLOMON ISLANDS, SPAIN, SWEDEN, TURKEY, UNITED KINGDOM OF GREATBRITAIN AND NORTHERN IRELAND, UNITED STATES OF AMERICA, URUGUAY

2. 금 8.17 현재 북한, 이란은 조치내용을 통보하지 않은것으로 파악됨.

3. 아국이 취하기로한 경제제재 조치의 이행에 필요한 국내법적 조치가 완료되는대로 (상공부 고시등) 외무장관 명의의 연호 8.8 자 유엔 사무총장 서한에대한 답신 (동 국내 법적조치내용을 주 내용으로함)을 가급적 8.24 이전 송부하는것이 좋을 것으로 사료됨. 끝

(대사 현홍주-국장)

예고:90.12.31 까지

1990. 12. 3 ...
의거 일반문서 ... 됨

국기국	장관	차관	1차보	2차보	중아국	정문국	청와대	안기부

90.08.18   07:11

외신 2과 통제관 FE

0144

외 무 부

종 별 :

번 호 : UNW-1550
일 시 : 90 0817 1730

수 신 : 장 관(국연,중근동,통일,기정)

발 신 : 주 유엔 대사

제 목 : 안보리(이라크-쿠웨이트 사태)

1. 금 8.17 안보리는 비공식 협의회를 개최 안보리 의장이 이라크 및 쿠웨트 체류 외국인의 안전문제에 관한 아래요지의 대언론 논평을 하기로 합의하였다함.

2. 안보리 의장의 대 언론논평

가. 이라크 및 쿠웨트내 외국인의 안전에 대한 안보리의 관심과 우려 표명

나. 외국인의 안전 보장을 위해 유엔 사무총장이 필요하다고 간주하는 조치를 취하도록 촉구.끝

(대사 현홍주-국장)

국기국   1차보   2차보   중아국   통상국   안기부   대책반   차관

90.08.18   09:44
외신 1과 통제관

0145

원 본

외 무 부 (사본:법정)

종 별 :

번 호 : UNW-1551   일 시 : 90 0817 1730

수 신 : 장 관(국연,중근동,통일,기정)

발 신 : 주 유엔 대사

제 목 : 이라크-쿠웨이트 사태

1. 미국 대표부는 차석대사 명의의 8.16 자 안보리 의장앞 서한에서 쿠웨이트 정부의 요청에 따라, 안보리 결의 661 호를 위반하여 이라크 또는 쿠웨이트와 무역에 종사코자 하는 선박을 차단하기 위한 쿠웨이트의 조치에 참여키로 하였음을 통보하였음. 미국은 동 조치가 헌장 51조상의자위권 행사로 취해지고 있음을 언급하였음.

2. 안보리 문서로 배포된 동 서한을 별첨 휄스송부함.

첨부: UNW(F)-134

끝

(대사 현홍주-국장)

| 국기국 | 1차보 | 2차보 | 중아국 | 통상국 | 안기부 | 대책반 | 차관 |

UNNW CF)-134   00817 1730
UNW-1551 (국예, 3UNB, 동일, 기경)

P.1

S

**UNITED
NATIONS**

Security Council

Distr.
GENERAL

S/21537
16 August 1990

ORIGINAL: ENGLISH

LETTER DATED 16 AUGUST 1990 FROM THE CHARGE D'AFFAIRES A.I. OF
THE UNITED STATES MISSION TO THE UNITED NATIONS ADDRESSED TO
THE PRESIDENT OF THE SECURITY COUNCIL

In accordance with Article 51 of the Charter of the United Nations, I wish, on behalf of my Government, to report that military forces of the United States, at the request of the Government of Kuwait, have joined the Government of Kuwait in taking actions to intercept vessels seeking to engage in trade with Iraq or Kuwait in violation of the mandatory sanctions imposed in Security Council resolution 661 (1990). These actions are being taken by the United States in the exercise of the inherent right of individual and collective self-defense, recognized in Article 51 of the Charter. The application of this inherent right in response to the Iraqi armed attack on Kuwait has been affirmed in resolution 661 (1990).

The United States has joined the Government of Kuwait and other Governments in taking these actions to ensure that the trade sanctions designed to secure the compliance of Iraq with resolution 660 (1990) and to restore the legitimate Government of Kuwait, are effective. The military forces of the United States will use force only if necessary and then only in a manner proportionate to prevent vessels from violating such trade sanctions contained in resolution 661 (1990).

I would be grateful if you could arrange for this letter to be circulated as a document of the Security Council.

(Signed) Alexander F. WATSON
Deputy Permanent Representative
of the United States of America
to the United Nations
Chargé d'affaires a.i.

90-19424   1826b (E)

0147

외 무 부

종 별 :

번 호 : UNW-1556   일 시 : 90 0817 2000

수 신 : 장관(국연)

발 신 : 주 유엔 대사

제 목 : 주유엔 자이르 대사 접촉

연 UNW-1311.

대:WUN-0851

본직은 금 8.17 유엔 본부에서 NZENGEYA 주유엔 자이르대사와 면담한바, 동대사 발언 요지를 아래 보고함.

1. 안보리 동향

가. 금일 안보리 결의안 661 호에 따라 설치된 대 이락. 쿠웨이트 재재조치이행 검토 위원회 회의가 개최된바, 동 회의시 영국 대사는 한국과 스위스가 유엔 회원국이 아님에도 불구하고, 유엔 결의안을 적극 이행키로 결정한 사실을 높이 평가하는 발언을 행함.

나. 금일 개최된 안보리 회원국간 비공식 협의회의 결론에 따라 동 회의 종료후 안보리의장 (MUNTEANU 루마니아대사)은 다른 발표문을 통해 이락 및 쿠웨이트가 동국에 체류하는 외국인 보호를 위해 필요한 조치를 취해 줄것을 촉구하였음. 또한 동 협의회시 안보리의장이 주유엔 이락대사를 접촉, 이락내 외국인의 안전에 대한 안보리의 관심과 우려를 전달하고 이락측의 적절한 조치를 촉구하도록함.

다. 현재 안보리내 분위기는 당초 안보리의 제재 결의안의 채택은 신속히 조치하였으나 시간이 경과함에 따라 미국의 해상봉쇄 조치에 대해서는 타이빙 및일반적 조치의 법적 근거등에 대해 일부 회의적인 의견도 대두되고 있는 상황임.

2. 자이르 대사 방한일정

가. 유엔총회 대책과 관련 본국 정부와 업무협의차 8.22 뉴욕출발예정이며, 항공일정상 9.9 서울도착, 9.14 출국 예정임(부인 동반)

나. 가급적 뉴욕 출발전 한국측에서 서울-뉴욕 왕복항공료에 해당 하는 T/C를 발급해 줄수 있으면 고맙겠음.

국기국 차관 1차보 중아국 대책반

PAGE 1   90.08.18   09:09

외신 2과 통제관 FE

0148

3. 상기 방한 항공편은 추보 예정안바, 상기 2 항 (나) 자이르 대사 요청을감안, 가급적 당지시간 8.20 (월) 동 대사에게 T/C 를 전달할수 있도록 조치바라며, 동 대사 체한일정(안)개요가 준비되는대로 당관에 봉보 바람. 끝

(대사 현홍주-국장)

예고 | 90.12.31 일반 예고 의
       | 의거 일반문서로 재분류됨

PAGE 2

0149

이라크, 쿠웨이트 사태 속보 <23>
(8.18. 07:00)

중근동과

1. 상 황

o 유엔 안보리 특별 회의(8.17)
  - 유엔의 대 이라크 제재 문제 토의
  - <u>유엔 사무총장에게 이라크 및 쿠웨이트 체류 외국인 철수를 위한</u>
    <u>적절한 모든 조치 취해줄것을 촉구</u>

o 부시, 후세인 요르단왕과 회담
  - 후세인 왕에게 이라크 선박의 아카바항 이용 기부 촉구
  - 후세인, 유엔의 대 이라크 제재 실행 의사 표명
  - 양측의 시각차로 회담 성과 별무

o 세바르드나제, 유엔이 걸프만 사태 해결을 위해 파병을 요청하는 경우
  수락 의사 표명

o 이라크, 사우디 및 서방인들에 대한 강경 조치 및 대 이란관계 개선 모색
  - 이라크 거주 일본인 278명에 대한 출국 금지 조치
  - 쿠웨이트내 미국인 35명 비밀장소로 강제 이동, 인질화 우려
  - 이라크, 쿠웨이트 거주 소련인 8,000 여명에 대한 출국 제한 조치
    (부녀자, 어린이는 제외)
  - 이라크, 사우디의 원유 증산 방침 및 이라크산 원유 선적 거부 비난
  - 이라크, 8.17 이란내 점령지로부터 철수, 1,000명의 이란 전쟁포로
    석방

o 중국, 이라크의 쿠웨이트로 부터의 조속 철수 및 미국의 걸프역내 군사
  개입 반대 입장 재강조

0150

o 이집트 - 이라크 관계 동향

  - 무바락, 이라크에 걸프만 사태의 평화적 해결 모색 촉구 및 카다피의
    사태 해결을 위한 중재 노력 언급

  - 이집트, 식량 적재 이라크 선박 1척에 대한 수에즈운하 통과 허용

o 일본, 사우디에 의료팀 파견 계획, 걸프 주변국에 대한 경협 원조 및
  다국적군의일부로서 비전투군사 요원 파견 검토

o 이스라엘, 이라크의 쿠웨이트 철군 거부로 이라크-미국간 전쟁 불가피 전망

2. 아국 교민 철수 관련 동향 (현지대사 보고)

o 8.17. 17:00 쿠웨이트 교민 95명 전원, 암만에 무사 도착
  (동 일행중 중환자인 임광웅씨는 병원에 긴급 입원 조치)

  - 이라크 주재 건설.상사직원 및 가족 27명도 암만 무사 도착

o 현대건설 제1진 한국인 170명, 태국인 692명, 8.17. 06:30 이라크로 출발

o 현대건설 제2진 한국인 105명, 태국인 455명은 8.18 아침 출발 예정

3. 조 치 사 항

o 쿠웨이트 주재 외교 공관 문제 철수 관련, 주 쿠웨이트 대사에 보고 지시

o 국방부에 방독면 공급에 관한 협조 의뢰

o 아국 교민 철수 문제 관련, 주 이라크 대사에 쿠웨이트 또는 바그다드 공항의
  사용 가능성 파악 보고 지시

0151

長 官 報 告 事 項

1990. 8. 18.

國際機構條約局
國際聯合課 (50)

題目 : 對이락 經濟 制裁措置에 관한 유엔 安保理 動向

安保理 決議案 661호 (經濟制裁措置)에 따라 設置된 對이락.쿠웨이트 制裁措置 履行 檢討委가 8.17. 開催된 바, 同 會議內容을 아대 報告합니다.

1. 經濟制裁措置 履行 檢討委 設置

가. 設置 및 構成

ㅇ 安保理決議 661호 第 6項에 따라 安保理 理事國 全體로 構成

나. 委員會 役割

ㅇ 各國의 安保理 決議 661호 履行 狀態 點檢, 安保理에 同內容 報告

2. 經濟 制裁措置 履行 檢討委 討議內容 (8.17. 개최)

가. 英國大使 發言內容

ㅇ 韓國과 스위스가 유엔 非會員國임에도 不拘하고 安保理決議 661호를 積極 履行키로 決定한 事實을 높이 評價함.

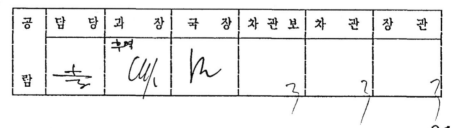

공	담 당	과 장	국 장	차 관 보	차 관	장 관
람						

0152

나. 이락.쿠웨이트 滯留 外國人 保護에 관한 發表文

　o 安保理議長은 會議終了後 發表文을 통해 이락.쿠웨이트가 同國에
　　滯留하는 外國人 保護를 위해 必要한 措置를 취할 것을 促求

　o 이와 관련, 安保理 會員國間 協議會에서는 安保理議長이 駐유연
　　이락大使를 接觸, 이락내 外國人의 安全에 대한 安保理의 關心과
　　憂慮를 傳達하고 이락側의 適切한 措置를 促求토록 合議함.

다. 安保理內 雰圍氣

　o 當初 安保理의 制裁 決議案의 採擇은 신속히 措置되었으나 시간이
　　經過함에 따라 英國의 海上封鎖 措置에 대해서는 타이밍 및 同 措置의
　　法的 根據等에 대해 일부 懷疑的인 意見도 擡頭되고 있음.

3. 對이락 經濟制裁措置 履行 現況

가. 對이락 經濟制裁措置 履行 促求 및 我國 措置事項

　o 安保理 決議 661호 履行을 위한 我國의 措置 內容에'대해 늦어도
　　8.24.까지 通報하여 줄 것을 要請하는 유연事務總長 書翰 (回覽
　　公翰) 8.10. 接受

　o 我國은 우선 유연大使 名義 8.10字 書翰을 통하여 我國 措置
　　內容을 유연事務總長에게 通報하였는 바, 同 書翰은 8.13字 安保理
　　文書로 配布됨.

나. 各國 措置現況

　o 8.17. 현재 經濟制裁措置를 유연事務總長에게 公式 通報한 國家는
　　我國 包含 44個國임.

　o 北韓, 이란은 措置內容 通報치 않음.

0153

4. 向後 措置 豫定事項

ㅇ 我國이 취하기로한 經濟制裁措置의 履行에 必要한 <u>國內法的 措置가</u>
<u>完了되는 대로 (상공부 고시등)</u> 外務長官 名義로 同 國內法的 措置
內容을 主 內容으로 하는 유엔事務總長 書翰에 대한 答信 送付 豫定

- 끝 -

0154

長 官 報 告 事 項

報 告 畢

1990. 8. 18.
國際機構條約局
國際聯合課 (50)

題目 : 對이락 經濟 制裁措置에 관한 유엔 安保理 動向

安保理 決議案 661호 (經濟制裁措置)에 따라 設置된 對이락.쿠웨이트 制裁措置 履行 檢討委가 8.17. 開催된 바, 同 會議內容을 아래 報告합니다.

---

1. 經濟制裁措置 履行 檢討委 設置

가. 設置 및 構成

　ㅇ 安保理決議 661호 第 6項에 따라 安保理 理事國 全體로 構成

나. 委員會 役割

　ㅇ 各國의 安保理 決議 661호 履行 狀態 點檢, 安保理에 同內容 報告

2. 經濟 制裁措置 履行 檢討委 討議內容 (8.17. 개최)

가. 英國大使 發言內容

　ㅇ 韓國과 스위스가 유엔 非會員國임에도 不拘하고 安保理決議 661호를 積極 履行키로 決定한 事實을 높이 評價함.

0155

나. 이락.쿠웨이트 滯留 外國人 保護에 관한 發表文

ㅇ 安保理議長은 會議終了後 發表文을 통해 이락.쿠웨이트가 同國에
滯留하는 外國人 保護를 위해 必要한 措置를 취할 것을 促求

ㅇ 이와 관련, 安保理 會員國間 協議會에서는 安保理議長이 駐유엔
이락大使를 接觸, 이락내 外國人의 安全에 대한 安保理의 關心과
憂慮를 傳達하고 이락側의 適切한 措置를 促求토록 合議함.

다. 安保理內 雰圍氣

ㅇ 當初 安保理의 制裁 決議案의 採擇은 신속히 措置되었으나 시간이
經過함에 따라 美國의 海上封鎖 措置에 대해서는 타이밍 및 同 措置의
法的 根據等에 대해 일부 懷疑的인 意見도 擡頭되고 있음.

3. 對이락 經濟制裁措置 履行 現況

가. 對이락 經濟制裁措置 履行 促求 및 我國 措置事項

ㅇ 安保理 決議 661호 履行을 위한 我國의 措置 內容에 대해 늦어도
8.24.까지 通報하여 줄 것을 要請하는 유엔事務總長 書翰 (回覽
公翰) 8.10. 接受

ㅇ 我國은 우선 유엔大使 名義 8.10字 書翰을 통하여 我國 措置
內容을 유엔事務總長에게 通報하였는 바, 同 書翰은 8.13字 安保理
文書로 配布됨.

나. 各國 措置現況

ㅇ 8.7. 현재 經濟制裁措置를 유엔事務總長에게 公式 通報한 國家는
我國 包含 44個國임.

ㅇ 北韓, 이란은 措置內容 通報치 않음.

0156

4. 向後 措置 豫定事項

ㅇ 我國이 취하기로한 <u>經濟制裁措置의 履行에 必要한 國內法的 措置</u>가
   完了되는 대로 (상공부 고시등) 外務長官 名義로 同 國內法的 措置
   內容을 主 內容으로 하는 유엔事務總長 書翰에 대한 答信 送付 豫定

- 끝 -

공   란

공   란

이라크.쿠웨이트사태 종합대책
(안보리 견의안 채택등)

1. 660호 채택(90.8.2)

    o 결의전문 : 별첨 1

    o 결의요지 및 채택시 각국 관련동향 : 별첨 2

2. 661호 채택 (8.6)

    o 결의전문 : 별첨 3

    o 유엔 안보리의 경제제재조치에 대한 검토 : 별첨 4

3. 662호 채택 (8.9)

    o 결의전문 : 별첨 5

4. 664호 채택 (8.18)

    o 결의전문 : 상금 미접

    o 내 용

        - 이라크, 쿠웨이트내 외국인의 즉시 출국허용 및 영사관

           직원과의 접촉 허용 촉구

        - 주쿠웨이트 각국대사관, 영사관 폐쇄 명령 철회 촉구

    o 이락.쿠웨이트내 외국인 안전 확보를 위한 안보리 동향

       : 별첨 6

    참고 안보리결의 663호(8.14)는 리히텐슈타인의 가입권고

          결의안임.

0160

걸프사태 관련 유엔안전보장이사회 동향, 1990-91. 전5권 (V.1 1990.8월)

이라크-쿠웨이트 事態 綜合 対策

1990. 8. 20

外 務 部

0161

1. 事態展望

   가. 現況

   나. 今後 展望

2. 當面 問題 處理 方案

   가. 基本 目標 ᴺ/ᴬ

       1) 我國人 安全,   迅速撤收
       2) 유엔 原則 遵守 및 美國等 友邦과의 關係 尊重
       3) 上記 基本 目標下,   我國의 쿠웨이트, 이라크所在
           利益 保全

   나. 現地 僑民 撤收 對策

   다. 쿠웨이트駐在 大使舘 撤收 問題

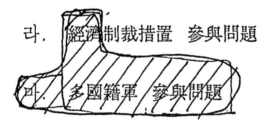
   라. 經濟制裁措置 參與問題

   마. 多國籍軍 參與問題

   마. 아국의 경제적이익보호문제

0162

3. 事後 對策

　가. 事態後 情勢展望

　　1) 國際情勢 全般 및 美.蘇關係

　　2) 아랍圈內 勢力판도 재편

　　3) 世界經濟 展望

　나. 韓半島 情勢에 대한 影響

　다. 우리의 對應策

　　1) 對아랍 對策

　　2) 對北韓 對策

　　3) 對유엔 對策

0163

이라크, 쿠웨이트 사태 속보 <25>
(8.20. 07:00)

중동아프리카국
중 근 동 과

1. 상 황

o 이라크 후세인 대통령, 이라크 TV 방송을 통해 억류 외국인 및
쿠웨이트 사태 관련 성명 발표

  - 적대국가와의 협상을 위해 수만명의 외국인이 억류

  - 걸프지역에서의 미군 철수 및 동 지역내 평화 안전에 대한
    UN 안보리 보장 조건하에 이들 외국인 석방 용의

  - 아랍 테두리 내에서의 쿠웨이트 사태 해결 표명

o 이라크, 걸프만 해상 봉쇄가 계속될 경우, 이라크 억류 유럽인을
  인질화 할 것임을 시사 (바그다드 통신)

  - 이라크 및 쿠웨이트 거주 유럽인, 군사시설에 억류 예정

o UN 안보리, 대 이라크 봉쇄 명령 및 이라크에 의한 점령된 쿠웨이트문제
  관련 결의 표결을 위해 긴급회의 소집 예정 (외교소식통 인용 보도 8.19)

o UN 사무총장, 이라크 억류 외국인 인질문제 해결 위해 특사 2명 8.21
  바그다드 파견 예정

o 이라크, 이라크 선박 가해 행위로 야기되는 어떠한 결과에 대해서도
  미국 및 그의 동맹국 책임을 경고

  - 이라크 외상, 대 이라크 해상 침략 및 음해 행위 중지를 국제사회에
    호소

o 이라크 의회, 스웨덴, 호주 및 스위스, 핀란드 및 폴투칼의 걸프지역내
  군사증강 불참여에 따라, 이라크 억류 이들 국가 국민의 이라크 출국
  허용을 결정

o 미국 부시 대통령,
  - 이라크내 억류 유럽인 인질화 결정은 국제법 위반이라고 강경 비난
  - 육.해.공군.예비군 동원령 발표 (육군 예비군 8만명 파병 예정)

0164

○ 미국, 이라크의 미국인 및 여타 외국인 억류는 있을수 없는 처사며,
  대 이라크 제재조치에 대응하여, 아무 죄없는 민간인들을 희생양으로
  삼는 이라크측 행위를 비난

○ 미.영.벨지움등 서방국가, 쿠웨이트 체류 자국민에게 외출 삼가 종용
  - 이라크 당국에 의해 외국인이 검거되는 호텔 출입 금지등

○ GCC(걸프 지역국가 협력기구) 동맹 국방장관들, 이라크 위협 대처 전략
  협의 위해, 회합 예정
  - 집단 방위문제 집중 거론

2. 교민 철수 동향

○ 이라크 및 쿠웨이트 교민 철수 총 609명(8.20 06:00 현재)
  - 이 라 크 : 100명 (잔류자 : 612명)
  - 쿠웨이트 : 509명 (잔류자 :   96명)

○ KAL 특별 전세기 1진 B 747 편 요르단 향발
  - 8.20 07:00 서울 출발
  - 8.20 15:00 (현지시간) 요르단 암만 착 예정
  - 378명 수송 예정

3. 조 치 사 항

○ 주 이라크 대사, 이라크 정부의 자국 주재 외교관 및 가족 출국 허용
  결정에 따라, 수일내 공관원 가족 철수 예정 (8.19)

○ 주 요르단 대사, KAL 특별 전세기 제2편(DC-10) 8.22 06:00 암만 도착
  예정으로의 연기 운항을 건의

○ 쿠웨이트 철수 교민 2진 120명 요르단 국경 무사 통과 (8.18 23:00)

○ KAL 특별기 요르단 공항 이.착륙 관련, 제반 필요 행정사항을 KAL에
  지원토록 지시 (주 요르단 대사, 8.19)

○ 주 쿠웨이트 공관의 최소 필수요원만 잔류, 나머지 전원 철수를 지시
  (주 쿠웨이트 대사관 8.19)

○ 교민 철수 취재 위해 당부 출입기자단 일행 23명, KAL특별기 1편(B 747)
  으로 요르단 향발

0165

ZCZC HKA036 INS028
OO LAE HAE

게야르유엔 사무총장,
페르시아만의 긴장 불구,
평화적해결의 희망적 견해 들며.
(8.20.)

R I
IRAQ-PEREZDECUELLAR 8-20
  U.N. CHIEF WANTS MIDDLE EAST CRISIS CONTROLLED
    SANTIAGO (UPI) -- UNITED NATIONS SECRETARY GENERAL JAVIER PEREZ DE
CUELLAR SAID SUNDAY SAID HE WAS STILL HOPEFUL FOR SOME KIND OF
PEACEFUL SETTLEMENT TO THE CURRENT CRISIS IN THE MIDDLE EAST DESPITE
RISING TENSIONS.
    HE SAID HE HAD NO PLANS TO TRAVEL NOW TO THE GULF AREA.
    PEREZ DE CUELLAR, 70, QUESTIONED BY REPORTERS UPON ARRIVING AT
SANTIAGO AIRPORT ON A FLIGHT FROM HIS NATIVE PERU, SAID THE MIDDLE
EAST +CONTINUES TO BE VERY TENSE AND EXPLOSIVE, BUT NOT EVERYTHING
THAT IS EXPLOSIVE ACTUALLY BLOWS UP.
    +ONE MUST HAVE HOPE THAT THIS SITUATION CAN BE CONTROLLED. I NEVER
LOST FAITH THAT HUMAN KINDNESS WILL PREVAIL AND THAT IT WILL BE
UNDERSTOOD THAT ONLY THROUGH DIALOGUE AND NEGOTIATION CAN PROBLEMS BE
RESOLVED.+
    HE NEVERTHRELESS CALLED THE CURRENT MIDDLE EAST CRISIS +ONE OF THE
MOST DIFFICULT THAT I HAVE HAD TO FACE IN THE NINE YEARS I HAVE BEEN
SECRETARY GENERAL.+
    ASKED IF THE UNITED NATIONS MIGHT SEND A MULTINATIONAL MILITARY
FORCE TO THE PERSIAN GULF REGION, THE SECRETARY GENERAL SAID HE DID
NOT EXPECT THE WORLD BODY TO TAKE A DECISION TO THIS EFFECT IN THE
NEAR FUTURE.
    PEREZ DE CUELLAR SAID TWO UNITED NATIONS EMMISARIES WILL ARRIVE IN
THE MIDDLE EAST TUESDAY AND WILL PAY SPECIAL ATTENTION TO THE +WHAT
PERTAINS TO THE FOREIGNERS,+ MEANING THOSE DETAINED BY IRAQ.
    HE SAID +THIS IS NOT THE APPROPRIATE MOMENT+ FOR HIS OWN VISIT TO
THE REGION.
    ASKED TO RESPOND TO SOME COMMENT THAT HE SHOULD BE VISITING THE
MIDDLE EAST NOW RATHER THAN CHILE, PEREZ DE CUELLAR SAID HE SAID HE
FELT PUBLIC OFFICIALS SHOULD BE +SERENE, IN THE PRESENT
CIRCUMSTANCES, AND BE WHERE YOU HAVE TO BE BE, MAYBE LIKE GOD, AND
COMPETE WITH GOD IN BEING IN A LITTLE BIT OF EVERY PLACE AT THE SAME
TIME.+
    PEREZ DE CUELLAR, ACCOMPANIED BY HIS WIFE, MRS. MARCELA TEMPLE,
WERE MET AT THE AIRPORT BY PRESIDENT PATRICIO AYLWIN AND HIS WIFE AND
MEMBERS OF THE CABINET.
    THE SECRETARY GENERAL IS TO RECEIVE AN HONORARY DOCTORATE AT THE
UNIVERSITY OF CHILE AND MEET WITH GOVERNMENT OFFICIALS BEFORE
DEPARTING WEDNESDAY. DD-D
    JAB-EKMI
UPI 02:06 GMT

=08200213
NNNN

10

0166

외 무 부

종 별 :

번 호 : UNW-1565   일 시 : 90 0820 1700

수 신 : 장 관(국연,중근동,봉일,기정)

발 신 : 주 유엔 대사

제 목 : 안보리(이라크 사태)

1. 8.18 표제건 관련 안보리가 속개되어 아래 요지의 결의안 664 호가 만장일치의 찬성으로 채택됨.

2. 결의안 요지 (전문은 별전 FAX 로 송부)

0 헌장 7조하의 조치로 (1) 이라크가 이라크 및 쿠웨이트내 제 3국 국민들의 즉각적인 출국을 허용하고 촉진할것, (2) 이들의 안전과 건강을 해치는 어떠한 행동도 취하지 말것을 요구하며, (3)이라크가 쿠웨이트내 외국 공관을 폐쇄토록한 명령을 취소할것을 요구함.

0 유엔 사무총장에게 동 결의안의 이행상태를 조속히 안보리에 보고토록 요청

3. 한편 유엔 사무총장은 8.19 연호 관련국 요청에 따라 자신의 개인특사 2명을 이라크로 파견, 외국인의 출국허용을 촉구토록 하였음.끝

(대사 현홍주-국장)

국기국	1차보	2차보	중아국	통상국	안기부	대책반	차관	장관실

PAGE 1   90.08.21   09:07 WG

외신 1과 통제관

0167

UNITED
NATIONS

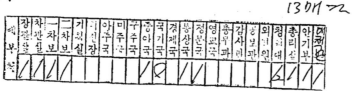

 Security Council

664(1990)

Distr.
GENERAL

13매 72

S/21562
18 August 1990

ORIGINAL: ENGLISH

Draft resolution

The Security Council,

Recalling the Iraqi invasion and purported annexation of Kuwait and resolutions 660, 661 and 662,

Deeply concerned for the safety and well being of third state nationals in Iraq and Kuwait,

Recalling the obligations of Iraq in this regard under international law,

Welcoming the efforts of the Secretary-General to pursue urgent consultations with the Government of Iraq following the concern and anxiety expressed by the members of the Council on 17 August 1990,

Acting under Chapter VII of the United Nations Charter:

1. Demands that Iraq permit and facilitate the immediate departure from Kuwait and Iraq of the nationals of third countries and grant immediate and continuing access of consular officials to such nationals;

2. Further demands that Iraq take no action to jeopardize the safety, security or health of such nationals;

3. Reaffirms its decision in resolution 662 (1990) that annexation of Kuwait by Iraq is null and void, and therefore demands that the government of Iraq rescind its orders for the closure of diplomatic and consular missions in Kuwait and the withdrawal of the immunity of their personnel, and refrain from any such actions in the future;

4. Requests the Secretary-General to report to the Council on compliance with this resolution at the earliest possible time.

90-19672 2402Z (E)

0168

이라크·쿠웨이트사태속보 (28)
(8. 21.   15:00)

중동아프리카국
중 근 동 과

---

1. 군사적 대결 위기 고조

o 미국은 걸프지역에 군사력 배치 증강 계속

 - Stealth 전투기 20대 사우디 배치

 - 공격 병력을 쿠웨이트 국경지대로 전진 배치

 - UAE 에 군 수송기와 공군 병력 배치

o 부시 대통령은 처음으로 억류 미국인들을 '인질' 이라 칭하고, 이들의
  안전에 대해 이라크가 책임을 저야 할 것이라 말함.

o 또한 부시 대통령은 사태 해결을 위한 미국의 비타협적 입장을 재확인
  하고, 사태 종식을 위해 미국은 희생을 감수해야 할 것이라 경고함.

o 미국 언론과 여론도 부시 대통령이 사태 해결을 위해서 인질 문제에
  지나치게 구애되어서는 안된다는 견해를 나타내고 있음.

o 사 우 디 : 국민들의 군입대 촉구

o 이스라엘 : 방독면 배포 여부 금주중 결정

---

2. 미국, 무력 사용 승인을 위한 긴급 안보리 회의 소집

o 미국은 효과적인 대이라크 경제 제재 이행을 위해 "필요한 최소한의
  무력 사용"을 허용하는 결의안을 긴급 소집된 안보리에 제출

o 동 결의안에는 해상봉쇄, 유엔군 파견등에 관한 내용은 없음.

o 미국은 동 결의안 체택 여부에 관계 없이, 쿠웨이트의 요청과 U.N.
  헌장에 명시된 자위권에 의거, 일방적으로 대이라크 제재조치를 강행
  하겠다고 발표한 바 있음.

0169

3. 주쿠웨이트 공관 폐쇄 관련 각국 입장

o 네덜란드 : EC 국가들과 협의후 결정

o 벨 지 움 :

- 주벨지움 이라크대사 소환, 항의

- 쿠웨이트내에 벨지움 국민이 있는 한 외교관 1명 잔류 지시

- 토요일부터 외교관 특권 박탈 위협에 대해 "생각할 수도 없는 일"이라

  평가

o 일   본 : 대사관에 피신중인 일본인 교민 보호 위해 24일 이후에도

                개속 유지

4. 기   타

o 이라크 부총리 소련 방문

- 소련인의 안전 출국 약속

- 소련은 어타 억류 외국인의 석방을 요청

o 유엔 사무차장 2명, 이라크 방문

- 후세인 대통령의 유엔 사무총장앞 서한 접수후 억류 외국인 문제

  협의차 방문

o 리 비 아

- 이라크의 외국인 대우를 비난하면서, 아울러 유엔이 미국의 대이라크

  봉쇄 조치를 비난하지 않을시 유엔 탈퇴 하겠다고 위협

0170

분류번호	보존기간

발 신 전 보

번   호 :   WUN-1081   900822 1547 DY   종별 :

수   신 : 주   유엔   대사.총영사

발   신 : 장 관 (국연)

제   목 : 이락.쿠웨이트 사태

　　　　미국은 효과적인 대이락 경제제재 이행을 위해 필요한 최소한의 무력
사용을 허용하는 결의안을 안보리에 제출하였다고 하는 바, 동 결의안 FAX
송부바라며 관련 안보리 동향 파악 보고바람.　　　　　　　끝.

(국기국장　　문동석)

1990.12.31. 새 고문에
의거 민반문서로 ..됨

앙고재	90년8월22일 N과	기안자	과 장	국 장	차 관	장 관	보안통제	외신과통제
		송영일						

0171

발 신 전 보

번 호 : WUN-1086   900822 1924 DY   종별 :

수 신 : 주   유엔   대사. ☘☘☘☘

발 신 : 장 관   (국연)

제 목 : 대이락 제재조치 통보문제

대 : UNW-1548(1), 1500

주국련 20313671

대호(1) 본직명의의 서한 발송과 관련, ~~일응 8.10자 귀직와 사무총장앞~~ ^{참고로라시써}
~~서한으로 우리정부가 안보리 결의 661호에 따라 취하어야 할 조치를 유엔에 가~~
~~통보한 것으로 간주되는 바, 대호(2)~~ 이번 조치에 참가한 44개국중 제재조치
이행을 위하여 국내법적 초치를 취하고 이를 별도로 통보한 국가명 ~~및~~ 동 별도 ^{가능하면}
통보 내용~~을~~ 지급 조사 보고바람.   끝. ^{동안}

(국제기구조약국장   문동석)

1990. 12. 31 ... 고문에
의거 ... 문서로 분됨 ...

	90 년 8 월 22 일	N 과	기안자 송영민	과장 (서명)	국장 (서명)	차관	장관 (서명)	보안통제 (서명)	외신과통제

0172

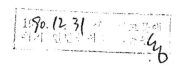

외 무 부

종 별 :

번 호 : UNW-1580

일 시 : 90 0822 1400

수 신 : 장관(국연,중근동,통일,기정)

발 신 : 주 유엔 대사

제 목 : 대이락 제재 조치통보

대:WUN-1086

1. 표제 제재조치를 위한 국제법적조치를 유엔사무총장에 통보한 국가는 현재까지 아래국가로 파악됨.

-뉴질랜드, 아이스랄랜드, 이태리, 룩셈불그, 아르헨티나, 노르웨이, 서독, 일본, 미국, 영국, 핀랜드, 호주, 스페인, 카나다, 스웨덴, 브라질, 루마니아,프랑스

2. 상기 조치의 예시로서 루마니아, 브라질, 스웨덴, 일본, 핀랜드, 아이스랜드의 통고내용을 별전 송부함.

첨부:UNW(F)-142

끝

(대사 현홍주-국장)

예고:90.12.31 까지

국기국 안기부	장관 대책반	차관	1차보	2차보	미주국	중아국	통상국	정와대

PAGE 1

90.08.23 08:50

외신 2과 통제관 BN

0173

UNITED NATIONS

첨부 UNw(F)-142 008221#10
(종연, 중라등, 통이, 기라)

S

Security Council

Distr.
GENERAL

S/21549
17 August 1990

ORIGINAL: ENGLISH

NOTE VERBALE DATED 17 AUGUST 1990 FROM THE CHARGE D'AFFAIRES A.I.
OF THE PERMANENT MISSION OF ICELAND TO THE UNITED NATIONS
ADDRESSED TO THE SECRETARY-GENERAL

The Acting Permanent Representative of Iceland to the United Nations presents his compliments to the Secretary-General of the United Nations and, with reference to the latter's note SCPC/7/90(1) dated 8 August 1990, has the honour to enclose herewith an English translation of announcement No. 49 of 9 August 1990 on measures to implement resolution 661 (1990) of the United Nations Security Council on the Iraqi invasion of Kuwait.

90-19519 1873j (E)

/...

18-1

0174

Annex

Announcement No. 49 of 9 August 1990 on measures to implement resolution 661 (1990) of the United Nations Security Council on the Iraqi invasion of Kuwait

In accordance with article 3 of Law No. 5/1969 on the Implementation of Decisions of the United Nations Security Council the Government has decided to apply the Law in order to implement resolution 661 (1990) of the United Nations Security Council adopted on 6 August 1990 on account of the Iraqi invasion of Kuwait, and issues herewith the following orders:

1. The import into Iceland of all goods originating in Iraq or Kuwait exported therefrom after 6 August 1990 is prohibited.

2. Any activities by Icelandic nationals or in Iceland which are calculated to promote the export or transshipment of any goods from Iraq or Kuwait are prohibited. Furthermore, any dealings by Icelandic nationals or in Iceland in any goods originating in Iraq or Kuwait and exported therefrom after 6 August 1990 are prohibited, as well as the use of Icelandic ships in such dealings.

3. The sale or supply by Icelandic nationals of any goods to any party in Iraq or Kuwait and the sale or supply of any goods for the purposes of any business carried on in or operated from Iraq or Kuwait are prohibited. Furthermore, it is prohibited to sell or supply such goods from Iceland or use for such purpose Icelandic ships. Activities by Icelandic nationals or in Iceland which are calculated to promote such sale or supply are also prohibited.

4. Icelandic nationals and any party in Iceland are prohibited from making funds or any other financial or economic resources available to the Government of Iraq or to any undertaking in Iraq or Kuwait and from remitting any funds to any other party within Iraq or Kuwait.

5. Medical supplies and foodstuffs used for humanitarian purposes are exempt from the provisions of paragraph 3. Furthermore, payments for medical purposes, payments for humanitarian purposes and foodstuffs used for humanitarian purposes are exempt from the provisions of paragraph 4.

Any person who violates the orders set out above shall be subject to the penalties under article 2 of Law No. 5/1969, unless heavier penalties apply under other Laws.

This Announcement shall enter into force immediately.

Ministry for Foreign Affairs
9 August 1990

2

0175

UNITED NATIONS

Security Council

S

Distr.
GENERAL

S/21511
14 August 1990

ORIGINAL: ENGLISH

NOTE VERBALE DATED 14 AUGUST 1990 FROM THE CHARGE D'AFFAIRES OF
THE PERMANENT MISSION OF FINLAND TO THE UNITED NATIONS ADDRESSED
TO THE SECRETARY-GENERAL

The Acting Permanent Representative of Finland to the United Nations presents
her compliments to His Excellency the Secretary-General of the United Nations and,
in response to the Secretary-General's note SCPC/7/90(1), dated 8 August 1990, has
the honour to inform him that a Decree on the Enforcement of Obligations Arising
from the Resolution on Iraq and Kuwait adopted by the Security Council of the
United Nations was issued in Helsinki on 9 August 1990. The Act was adopted
pursuant to Articles 1 and 5 of the Act (659/67) of 29 December 1967 on the
Enforcement of Certain Obligations on Finland as a Member of the United Nations.
Enclosed is an English translation of the text of Act of 9 August 1990.

It is requested that this note together with the attached translation be
circulated as a document of the Security Council.

90-19052   1574c (E)

/...

3

0176

Annex

DECREE

On the Enforcement of Obligations Arising from the Resolution on Iraq and Kuwait adopted by the Security Council of the United Nations.

Issued in Helsinki on 9 August 1990.

Upon presentation by the Minister for Foreign Affairs the following is enacted by virtue of articles 1 and 5 of the Act (659/67) of 29 December 1967 on the Enforcement of Certain Obligations on Finland as a Member of the United Nations.

1 Para

In order to enforce the obligations arising from resolution 661 (1990) of the Security Council of the United Nations, Finland restricts her economic relations with Iraq and Kuwait according to the provisions in this Decree.

2 Para

The import into Finland of commodities or products originating in Iraq or Kuwait is prohibited. Any activities by Finnish nationals or in the Finnish territory which would promote or are calculated to promote the export of transshipment of commodities or products from Iraq or Kuwait, and dealings by Finnish nationals and vessels flying the Finnish flag or in the Finnish territory in commodities or products originating in Iraq or Kuwait and exported therefrom after the date of the resolution is also prohibited. The same applies to the transfer of funds to Iraq or Kuwait for the purposes of such activities or dealings.

The sale or supply by Finnish nationals or from the Finnish territory or using vessels flying the Finnish flag of commodities or products, including weapons or other military equipment, whether or not originating in the Finnish territory, to any person or body in Iraq or Kuwait or for the purposes of business carried on from these countries, is prohibited. Any activities by Finnish nationals or in the Finnish territory which promote or are calculated to promote such sale or supply of commodities or products, are also prohibited.

It is prohibited to transfer funds or grant other economic resources to the Government of Iraq, or to a commercial industrial or public utility undertaking or to a natural person in Iraq or Kuwait. The same applies to the transfer of funds from Finland by Finnish nationals or other persons in the Finnish territory.

The provisions above concerning the sale or supply of commodities or products or the transfer of funds do not include supplies intended stricty for medical purposes, and in special humanitarian circumstances, food supplies or payment for the purposes of these supplies.

4

/...

0177

3 Para

The provisions of Article 2 shall also apply to contracts entered into prior to the date of this Decree.

4 Para

Regarding violations of this Decree or Directives issued by virtue thereof, Article 4 of the Act on the Enforcement of Certain Obligations on Finland as a Member of the United Nations shall apply.

5 Para

The Council of Ministers shall, if necessary, issue more detailed directives on the application of this Decree.

6 Para

This Decree will enter into force on 10 August 1990.

President of the Republic
    Mauno Koivisto

Minister for Foreign Affairs
    Pertti Paasio

6

0178

UNITED NATIONS

Security Council

Distr.
GENERAL

S/21535
15 August 1990

ORIGINAL: ENGLISH

NOTE VERBALE DATED 15 AUGUST 1990 FROM THE PERMANENT MISSION OF
JAPAN TO THE UNITED NATIONS ADDRESSED TO THE SECRETARY-GENERAL

The Permanent Representative of Japan to the United Nations presents his
compliments to the Secretary-General of the United Nations and has the honour to
notify him, in response to his note Ref. SCPC/7/90(1) dated 8 August 1990, of the
details of the measures that Japan has taken to date. Please note that this is a
provisional communication, made in anticipation of the meeting of the Committee of
the Security Council to be convened on 17 August 1990; it will be followed by a
formal communication shortly.

90-19288   1675i (E)

/...

6

0179

Annex

Measures taken by the Government of Japan

As indicated in its statement issued on 5 August 1990 (circulated as document A/45/386-S/21449 dated 6 August), the Government of Japan has decided as follows:

1.   To embargo oil imports from Iraq and Kuwait;

2.   To embargo exports to Iraq and Kuwait;

3.   To take appropriate measures to suspend investments, loans and other capital transactions with Iraq and Kuwait;

4.   To freeze economic co-operation to Iraq.

The Government of Japan will faithfully implement Security Council resolution 661 (1990).

Supplementary to the above, the Government of Japan has undertaken the following:

I.   Measures prohibiting imports from Iraq and Kuwait

On 7 August, Japan issued administrative guidelines requesting entities under its jurisdiction to refrain from engaging in import transactions with Iraq and Kuwait.

The procedures for prohibiting the import of all goods - but particularly oil - produced in or shipped from Iraq or Kuwait were finalized and became effective on 9 August (revising the Ministry of International Trade and Industry (MITI) Import Control Order, relevant imports approved by MITI will not be approved, with the exception of those loaded prior to 8 August.

II.   Measures prohibiting exports to and services in Iraq and Kuwait, as well as trade with any third country acting as agent of Iraq or Kuwait

On 7 August, Japan issued administrative guidelines requesting entities under its jurisdiction to refrain from engaging in export and service transactions with Iraq and Kuwait.

A.   Includes exports of all goods to Iraq and Kuwait subject to approval by MITI (medical supplies and food for humanitarian purposes will be approved). For this purpose, the Export Control Order (hereinafter "the Order"), based on the Foreign Exchange and Foreign Control Act (hereinafter "the Act"), (Article 25, para. 3), is partially amended.

B.   Service transactions with Iraq and Kuwait (with the exception of medical and related services) are subject to approval. In this regard, the Order, based on the Act (Article 3, para. 3) is partially amended.

/...

7

0180

C.   The intermediary trade of cargo produced in, shipped from, or destined for Iraq or Kuwait is prohibited in principle.   For this purpose, the Order was partially amended.

(The amendments to the Foreign Exchange and Foreign Control Act and the Export Trade Control Order become effective 22 August.)

III. Measures prohibiting capital transactions

A.   Japanese banks and securities companies have been requested, as of 3 August, to confirm that all transactions of the Kuwaiti Government and other entities are duly authorized by responsible personnel.

On 7 August, Japan issued administrative guidelines requesting entities under its jurisdiction to refrain from engaging in capital transactions with Iraq and Kuwait.

(The Order was partially amended, effective 10 August, with respect to the following measures.)

B.   Payments to Iraq and Kuwait became subject to approval, based on the Act, and payments to Iraq and Kuwait are frozen.

C.   Japanese entities are requested/ordered to suspend new loans to Iraq and Kuwait, in accordance with the Act.

D.   Japanese entities are requested to refrain from making direct investments in Iraq and Kuwait.

IV. Transportation

On 7 August administrative guidelines were issued to marine and air shipping companies to prohibit Japanese nationals and vessels under Japanese flag from engaging in cargo transactions originating in or destined for Iraq or Kuwait.

V.   Transitional regulations (to be implemented in accordance with the Act and the Order)

A.   All previously approved exports will be subject to reapproval, in accordance with administrative guidelines.

B.   Service contracts previously authorized but not yet in effect will require re-authorization.

0181

UNITED NATIONS

S

 Security Council

Distr.
GENERAL

S/21518
14 August 1990

ORIGINAL: ENGLISH

NOTE VERBALE DATED 14 AUGUST 1990 FROM THE PERMANENT MISSION OF
SWEDEN TO THE UNITED NATIONS ADDRESSED TO THE SECRETARY-GENERAL

    The Chargé d'affaires a.i. of the Permanent Mission of Sweden to the United
Nations presents his compliments to the Secretary-General of the United Nations and
has the honour to communicate to him, in response to his note SCPC/7/90(1), the
text in English translation of the two ordinances issued by the Government of
Sweden on 7 August 1990 in accordance with the provisions of Security Council
resolution 661 (1990).

90-19131 1821b (E)

/...

9

0182

<u>Annex</u>

1.   Ordinance
on the implementation with regard to Iraq and Kuwait of the act on certain
international sanctions (1971:176)

issued on 7 August 1990.

The Government provides that sections 3-5, 6 and 7 of the act on certain
international sanctions (1971:176) shall apply with regard to Iraq and Kuwait in
view of resolution No. 661 (1990) which the United Nations Security Council adopted
on 6 August 1990.

This ordinance enters into force on 7 August 1990.

2.   Ordinance
on certain sanctions against Iraq and Kuwait

issued on 7 August 1990.

The Government hereby ordains as follows.

<u>Section 1</u> Within the meaning of this ordinance commodities are material objects
having the nature of movable property with the exception of

1.   Publications and news-matter,

2.   Commodities which are intended for humanitarian purposes,

3.   Commodities which are intended for strictly medical purposes.

<u>Section 2</u> Commodities may not be imported to Sweden if they originated in Iraq or
Kuwait and were exported from those countries on 7 August 1990 or later.

<u>Section 3</u> Commodities may not be exported from Sweden if their destination is Iraq
or Kuwait.

<u>Section 4</u> Commodities may not be imported to or exported from Iraq or Kuwait.

<u>Section 5</u> Commodities may not be supplied for business activities within Iraq or
Kuwait.

Nor may commodities be supplied outside Iraq or Kuwait if the commodities are
intended for business activities which are operated from Iraq or Kuwait.

<u>Section 6</u> Measures may not be taken which would promote or are calculated to
promote the acts mentioned in sections 2-5 and which entail

1.   The manufacture, processing, assembly, installation, maintenance or repair of
commodities or provision of technical assistance for such measures,

/...

10

2.   The loading, unloading, transport or receiving for storage of commodities or the supply of transport facilities or of equipment or necessities for transport,

3.   The transfer or acquisition of commodities, grant of acquisition of special rights thereto or the issue of insurance thereon or legal transactions relating to the measures mentioned in sub-section 1 or 2 with regard to a commodity,

4.   The transfer or acquisition of any invention or the granting or acquisition of special rights thereto or

5.   The granting or negotiation of mandates for the measures specified in sub-sections 1-4.

<u>Section 7</u> The measures referred to in section 6 sub-sections 1-3 and mandates for such measures may not be granted or negotiated as regards commodities which have been exported from Iraq or Kuwait on 7 August 1990 or later.

<u>Section 8</u> Payment from outside Iraq or Kuwait may not be effected or credit granted to the Government of Iraq or to any other recipient in Iraq or Kuwait. Nor may payment be effected or credit granted to any person outside Iraq or Kuwait if the payment or credit is intended for any person or body in Iraq or Kuwait or for any business activities which are carried on in or operated from Iraq or Kuwait.

Nor may mandates be granted or negotiated for such measures as are prohibited in accordance with the first paragraph.

The prohibitions in the first and second paragraphs do not comprehend payments exclusively for strictly medical or humanitarian purposes.

//

0184

UNITED NATIONS

Security Council

Distr.
GENERAL

S/21522
14 August 1990

ORIGINAL: ENGLISH

LETTER DATED 14 AUGUST 1990 FROM THE CHARGE D'AFFAIRES A.I.
OF THE PERMANENT MISSION OF BRAZIL TO THE UNITED NATIONS
ADDRESSED TO THE SECRETARY-GENERAL

Further to my notes No. 204, of 8 August 1990, and 208 of 10 August 1990, I have the honour to transmit herewith the unofficial translation of the text of Communiqué No. 2.159, approved on 8 August 1990 and published on 10 August 1990 in the Official Register, by which the Department of Foreign Capital of the Central Bank of Brazil suspended the validity of any Certificate related to external loans and foreign investments, for purposes of remittances abroad to persons, entities or enterprises in Iraq or in Kuwait, or which have as beneficiaries, in any other territories, the Government of Iraq or enterprises located in Iraq or in Kuwait.

I should be grateful if you would transmit the text of the present letter and its annex to the Committee established in accordance with operative paragraph 6 of Security Council resolution 661 (1990).

(Signed) Alvaro Gurgel de ALENCAR
Ambassador
Acting Permanent Representative of Brazil
to the United Nations

Annex

CENTRAL BANK OF BRAZIL

DIRECTORATE OF FOREIGN EXCHANGE AND INTERNATIONAL AFFAIRS

Department of Foreign Capital

Circular-letter No. 2.107 of 8 August 1990. Informs of the temporary suspension of the utilization of the special mechanism for payments of the external debt with deposits linked to the Brazilian Financing Plan.

We inform all interested parties that, until further notice, the utilization of the special mechanism for the payment of the external debt with deposits linked to the Brazilian Financing Plan, referred in Circular No. 1.577, of 9 February 1990, and in Resolution No. 1.726, of 27 June 1990, is suspended.

Antonio Carlos MONTEIRO
Head of Department

Communiqué No. 2.159 of 8 August 1990

Foreign exchange restrictions. Iraq-Kuwait conflict

We inform that:

I. Bearing in mind Decree No. 99.441 of 7 August 1990, which determined compliance with resolution 661 (1990) of the United Nations Security Council, the validity, for remittance abroad, of the following Certificates related to external loans and foreign investments, are henceforth suspended:

Number	Date	Beneficiary/Investor
141/25057	02/27/89	KUWAIT FOREIGN TRADE CO.
841/00018	03/26/84	KUWAIT FOREIGN TRADE CO.
260/10573-29667	05/25/84	GOVERNMENT OF KUWAIT
260/13496-41024	08/24/89	GOVERNMENT OF KUWAIT
360/07016-05993	05/18/79	KUWAIT FOREIGN TRADE CO.
360/07017-05994	05/18/79	KUWAIT INTL. INVESTMENT CO.
360/07018-05995	05/18/79	KUWAIT INVESTMENT CO.
360/12507-14627	06/04/87	RAFIDAIN BANK
360/13352-14208	09/30/86	FAISAL YOUSUF AL-MARZOOK

/...

0186

II. The validity of any other Certificate issued by this Central Bank supporting the following remittances is likewise suspended:

(a) destined to persons, entities or enterprises in Iraq or in Kuwait;

(b) having as beneficiaries, in any other territory, the Government of Iraq or enterprises located in Iraq or in Kuwait.

III. The suspension indicated in this Communiqué does not apply to the external credit Certificates subject to the provisions of Resolutions Nos. 1.525 of 26 October 1988, 1.541 of 30 November 1988 and 1.564 of 16 January 1989.

Antonio Carlos MONTEIRO
Head of Department

(Of. No. 612/90)

14

0187

2.   The loading, unloading, transport or receiving for storage of commodities or the supply of transport facilities or of equipment or necessities for transport,

3.   The transfer or acquisition of commodities, grant of acquisition of special rights thereto or the issue of insurance thereon or legal transactions relating to the measures mentioned in sub-section 1 or 2 with regard to a commodity,

4.   The transfer or acquisition of any invention or the granting or acquisition of special rights thereto or

5.   The granting or negotiation of mandates for the measures specified in sub-sections 1-4.

<u>Section 7</u> The measures referred to in section 6 sub-sections 1-3 and mandates for such measures may not be granted or negotiated as regards commodities which have been exported from Iraq or Kuwait on 7 August 1990 or later.

<u>Section 8</u> Payment from outside Iraq or Kuwait may not be effected or credit granted to the Government of Iraq or to any other recipient in Iraq or Kuwait. Nor may payment be effected or credit granted to any person outside Iraq or Kuwait if the payment or credit is intended for any person or body in Iraq or Kuwait or for any business activities which are carried on in or operated from Iraq or Kuwait.

Nor may mandates be granted or negotiated for such measures as are prohibited in accordance with the first paragraph.

The prohibitions in the first and second paragraphs do not comprehend payments exclusively for strictly medical or humanitarian purposes.

/5

0188

UNITED
NATIONS

S

Security Council

Distr.
GENERAL

S/21507
14 August 1990
ENGLISH
ORIGINAL: FRENCH

LETTER DATED 13 AUGUST 1990 FROM THE PERMANENT REPRESENTATIVE OF
ROMANIA TO THE UNITED NATIONS ADDRESSED TO THE SECRETARY-GENERAL

Upon instructions from my Government, I have the honour to transmit herewith
the text of decision No. 935 of the Government of Romania concerning the
implementation of Security Council resolution 661 (1990).

I should be grateful if you would kindly have this letter and its annex
circulated as a document of the Security Council.

(Signed) Aurel-Dragoş MUNTEANU
Ambassador
Permanent Representative

90-19014   1744e (E)

/...

16

S/21507
English
Page 2

<u>Annex</u>

DECISION

concerning the implementation by Romania of United Nations
Security Council resolution 661 (1990)

The Government of Romania,

Bearing in mind the provisions of United Nations Security Council resolution
661 (1990), adopted on 6 August 1990,

Taking account of the obligation of States Members of the United Nations to
implement Security Council resolutions, in accordance with the provisions of
Chapter VII of the Charter of the United Nations,

DECIDES AS FOLLOWS:

<u>Article 1</u> - State organs and institutions and Romanian persons and bodies, as
well as foreign persons and bodies carrying out economic and financial activities
within Romanian territory, shall not:

(a) Import into Romania goods and products originating in Iraq or Kuwait
exported therefrom after 6 August 1990;

(b) Carry out activities which would promote or are calculated to promote the
export or trans-shipment of any goods or products originating in Iraq or Kuwait or
conduct any dealings in goods or products originating in Iraq or Kuwait exported
therefrom after 6 August 1990, including any transfer of funds to Iraq or Kuwait
for the purposes of such activities or dealings;

(c) Sell or supply from Romania or using Romanian flag vessels any goods or
products, including weapons or any other military equipment, whether or not
originating in Romanian territory (with the exception of supplies intended for
medical purposes and, in special humanitarian cases, foodstuffs), to any person or
body in Iraq or Kuwait or to any person or body for the purposes of any business
carried on in or operated from those countries, or carry out any activity which
promotes or is calculated to promote the sale of such goods and products.

<u>Article 2</u> - No funds or other financial or economic resources shall be made
available to the Government of Iraq or to any other commercial, industrial or
public utility undertaking in Iraq or Kuwait.

Romanian citizens and other persons present in Romanian territory shall not
remove such funds or resources from Romania or otherwise make them available to the
Government of Iraq or to any such undertaking, or remit any other funds to persons
or bodies within Iraq or Kuwait, except payments exclusively for medical or
humanitarian purposes and, in special humanitarian circumstances, foodstuffs.

/...

0190

S/21507
English
Page 3

<u>Article 3</u> - The aforementioned provisions shall not affect payments made through Romanian banking institutions by the Embassy of Iraq at Bucharest for public services used by the Embassy or for other normal activities carried out in accordance with the Vienna Conventions on diplomatic and consular relations.

<u>Article 4</u> - The Ministry of Finance, the Ministry of Trade and Tourism, the Ministry of Resources and Industry, the Ministry of Defence and other State organs shall, according to their competence, take the measures required for the implementation of the provisions of this decision.

<u>Article 5</u> - Any violation of the provisions of this decision shall incur administrative liability or liability for contraventions or crimes, as appropriate, on the part of the guilty parties, in accordance with the provisions of the legal regulations in force.

Petre ROMAN
Prime Minister

0191

/8

관리 90
번호 -1563

외 무 부

종 별 :

번 호 : UNW-1586

일 시 : 90 0822 1900

수 신 : 장관(국연)

발 신 : 주 유엔 대사

제 목 : 이락.쿠웨이트 사태

대:WUN-1081

대호 관련 안보리내 동향을 아래 보고함.

1. 미국은 안보리 결의안 661 호의 대이락 경제제재 조치를 위반하는 선박에 대해 무력사용을 허용하는 내용의 안보리 결의안 채택을 위하여 동 초안을 안보리 상임이사국과 비공식 협의중임. 상금 동 결의안 초안은 정식으로 안보리에제출되거나 안보리문서로 배포되지는 않았음.

2. 금 8.22 현재 상임이사국간 의견일치를 보지 못하여 협의를 진행중인바, 현 싯점에서의 동 결의안 채택에 반대의견을 제시하고 있는 소련측은 대이락 경제제재 조치에 명백한 위반 사례가 나타난 후에 유사 결의안을 채택하여도 늦지 않을 것이라는 입장을 표명하고 있는것으로 알려짐.

3. 8.21 카나다 대사등 일부 안보리 회원국들은 미.소간에 동건에 관한 이견이 조정되어 금일중 안보리 공식회의가 소집될 것으로 전망한바 있었음. 끝

(대사 현홍주-국장)

예고:90.12.31 까지

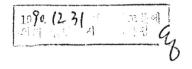

국기국	장관	차관	1차보	2차보	미주국	중아국	통상국	정와대
안기부	대책반							

PAGE 1

90.08.23   08:57

외신 2과 통제관 BN

0192

분류번호	보존기간

발 신 전 보

번　　호 :　WUN-1091　　900823 1912 DY　종별 :

수　　신 :　주　　유엔　　대사 . 총◆◆◆◆◆

발　　신 :　장　관　　　（국연）

제　　목 :　대이락 제재조치

　　　대 :　UNW-1580, 1548

　　1.　대호, 아국이 취한 조치 내용을 별첨 타전하니 귀직명의 공한으로 첨부, 사무총장에 전달바람.

　　2.　아국의 대이락 제재조치와 관련, 상공부의 별도고시는 없으며 대외무역법 규정에 의거, 특별조치(EL/IL 발급금지조치)를 8.22.자부터 취하고 있으며 또한 건설수주 금지는 건설부의 도급업무 처리 지침에 따라 이락의 쿠웨이트 침공사태 발발즉시 도급허가를 중단토록 해외건설협회에 지시 하였음을 참고바람.

　　　　　　　　　　-　아　　래　-

（별 도）

1990. 12. 31 　　고문에
의서 인반문서로 재분됨

（차관 유종하）

통상국장:　　　　대책반장:

앙 고 재	90 년 8 월 23 일	UN 과	기안자	과 장	국 장	1차보	차 관	장 관
			홍영표					

보안통제	외신과통제

0193

<u>ANNEX</u>

<u>Measures taken by the Government of</u>

<u>the Republic of Korea to implement</u>

<u>resolution 661 (1990) of the United Nations</u>

<u>Security Council</u>

Further to the decisions taken on 9 August 1990 and circulated as document S/21487, the Government of the Republic of Korea has taken the following supplementary measures on 20 August, which are to take effect immediately :

1. Suspension of issuance of the import licence(IL) for all commodities and products originating in Iraq or Kuwait.

   - The Government of the Republic of Korea issued <u>special</u> <u>guidelines</u> to suspend issuance of the IL for all commodities and products originating in Iraq and Kuwait.

   - The special guidelines issued in accordance with the provisions of the Foreign Trade Act(hereinafter "the Act"), are to prohibit the import of all goods, including crude oil, produced in or shipped from Iraq and Kuwait.

2. Suspension of issuance of the export licence(EL) for all commodities and products to Iraq and Kuwait.

   - The Government of the Republic of Korea announced, <u>based</u> <u>on the Act,</u> special guidelines to suspend issuance of the EL for the sale or supply by Korean nationals or Korean flag vessels of all commodities and products to any party in Iraq and Kuwait.

0194

- The Ministry of Commerce may approve issuance of the EL only for the export of items for medical and humanitarian purposes.

3. Suspension of procurement of construction contracts in Iraq and Kuwait.

   - On 2 August, the Government of the Republic of Korea issued, based on relevant ordinance, administrative guidelines prohibiting the procurement of construction contracts in Iraq and Kuwait.

   - The inter-ministrial meeting held on 9 August confirmed the administrative guidelines.

4. Protection of assets of the legitimate Government of Kuwait

   - As previously announced by the Government of the Republic of Korea in documnet S/21487, it has been confirmed that there are no such assets in the Repulic of Korea.

5. Penal provisions

   - Any person who violates the special/administrative guidelines set out above shall be subject to the penalties under article 67 of the Act, unless heavier penalties apply under other Laws.

6. The Special Inter-Ministerial Task Force to monitor implementation of the measures taken by the Government of the Republic of Korea in pursuance of the resolution 661(1990) has not found, since its establishment on 9 August, any violation of the above-mentioned special/administrative guidelines by person or body under the jurisdiction of the Government of the Republic of Korea.

Ministry of Foreign
Affairs
Republic of Korea

0195

송

이라크-쿠웨이트 事態 綜合対策

1990. 8. 23

外 務 部

0196

目 次

1. 事態展望

가. 現 況

1) 이라크의 挑發

  ○ 8. 2   쿠웨이트 侵攻
  ○ 8. 8   쿠웨이트 合併 宣言
  ○ 8.20   西方 外國人 人質化 宣言

2) 美國의 대응

  ○ 8. 8   사우디에 軍隊派遣
  ○ 8.13   海上봉쇄 開始
  ○ 8.20   UAE에 軍隊派遣

3) UN 安保理의 조치

  ○ 平和維持 決議(添附1)
   - 決議 660 : 이라크의 쿠웨이트 侵攻 비난, 撤軍 促求 決議
   - 決議 661 : 이라크.쿠웨이트와의 交易 및 經濟支援 全面禁止 決議
   - 決議 662 : 쿠웨이트 合併 無効 및 쿠웨이트 新政府 承認禁止 決議
   - 決議 664 : 外国人 即時 出国許容 및 공관폐쇄 명령 撤回 促求 決議

  ○ 이라크의 外國人 人質化 宣言(8.20)後 憲章
    第42條의 軍事的 制裁 措置 협의중

4) 아랍圈의 動向

  ○ 아랍연합군 結成(20個國中 8個國 参加)

   * 詳細는 이라크와 美國等의 立場 및 對應表 参照
   * 이라크-쿠웨이트事態 關聯 各國 主要 軍事措置
     現況(別添2)

0198

이라크와 미국등의 입장 및 대응표

(조   정)

③ 요르단의 대응
1. 후세인 국왕 방미 (8.14~16)
2. 이라크군에의 간섭 회피를 위해 사우디, 이집트, 시리아, 카타르, 바레인, 예멘과 조정
3. 미국측 방답한 반응

① 이라크의 요구	④ 미국의 대응
요구 1. 원유가격의 인상 (17→25$) 2. 불법 도굴 (24억 $) 배상 3. 채무 (GCC 예 약350억불) 변제 4. 경제구제조직의 조직화 5. 루마일라 유전의 영유 6. 부비안섬 등 2개 도서의 대여 7. 쿠웨이트에 종합적 정부의 수립	1. 이라크군의 즉시 무조건 전면철수 2. 쿠웨이트 합법정권의 회복 3. 석유의 안정 공급 확보 4. 페르시아만의 안전 유지 5. 미국민의 보호 (8.8. 부시 연설 등) 6. 해상 봉쇄 (8.13~) 7. 사우디, UAE 파병
교섭조건 1. 외국군의 사우디 철수 2. 이스라엘 점령지, 시리아의 철수 3. 대이라크 경제제재 철지 4. 미군사력의 등결. 국제회의 참가. 사우디 회의 불가침 약속	⑤ 아랍제국 (이라크 우호국 제외)의 대응 1. 이라크의 즉시 합법정권의 회복 2. 쿠웨이트 등의 여망하는... 3. 사우디 아랍의 제국의 파견 (8.10. 긴급 아랍정상회의) 4. 아랍군의 파견 합의. 이집트, 모로코, 시리아, 쿠웨이트

② 이라크 우호국등의 대응	⑥ 국제연합 (안보리)의 대응
1. 이라크 비난 결의 (8.3. 아랍 긴급 외상 회의) 리비아(결석), PLO(기권) 2. 미국의 이합에 대한 군사행동을 지지 (8.10. 리비아, PLO 등) 3. 팔레스아라팟 하기와 다른 중동 분쟁 해결을 결부시킨 이라크 대통령의 연설 (8.12) 지지 (8.13. PLO)	1. 대이라크 비난 결의 · 8.1. 당시 국경선까지 철수 · 고성에 의한 해결등 2. 대이라크 제재 결의 · 쿠웨이트, 이라크의 생산품 · 수입의 금지 · 무기등의 판매, 공급, 수송 금지 · 금융거래등 전면정지등 3. 방한 무효, 쿠웨이트 신정부 불승인 4. 외국인 출국 촉구, 공관폐쇄 요구 철회 촉구

나. 美國과 이라크의 立場(目標와 戰略)

1) 이라크

ㅇ 短期的:
- 域內 壓倒的인 軍事的 優位를 이용, 쿠웨이트
合倂, 기정 사실화
- 石油價 引上 및 이. 이戰 負債 輕減
- 西方人質(2만명 이상) 利用, 外部威脅 牽制

ㅇ 長期的:
- 이라크와 쿠웨이트産 原油(O P E C 産油量의
2 0 %) 로 主導的 發言權 強化
- 이라크의 主導下에 統一 아랍圈 成就

2) 美國

ㅇ 短期的:
- 사우디 侵攻 예방
- U N, 아랍支持國, 西方, 蘇聯等 國際的 壓力
으로 이라크 孤立化
- 쿠웨이트의 원상 回復
- 후세인 除去 또는 이라크 軍事力의 縮小로
아랍圈內 勢力 均衡 回復
- 但, 上記目標는 中東에 P A N A R A B I S M이
擴散되기 前 또는 1 1月 美 中間選擧 以前까지
相當部分 達成 希望

0200

ㅇ 長期的

- 美國이 主導하는 새시대의 平和 維持 秩序
  確立
- 脫冷戰 새시대의 첫 侵略者를 斷乎히 응징,
  先例化
- 美. 蘇가 協力(美國의 主導에 蘇聯이 順應)
- UN 中心의 집단적 平和維持 體制 活性化
- 아랍의 均衡 통한 石油價 適正維持로 世界
  經濟 安定化
- 이스라엘의 存立保存 및 中東平和에 寄與하는
  雰圍氣 維持
- 脫 冷戰時에도 美軍事力 維持 必要性을
  國內外에 誇示

다. 展 望

1) 槪觀

ㅇ 이라크의 쿠웨이트 永久合倂 合理化는 國際
  輿論으로 보아 저지 可能

ㅇ 여러가지 狀況의 變化要因이 있어 短期 解決과
  長期化 可能性이 共히 存在

0201

2) 想定可能 시나리오

 * 시나리오I : 후세인 失脚으로 事態 수습
  - 이라크內部 反후세인파에 의한 후세인 除去로
   現이라크 政府顚覆, 이경우 短期間內 事態解決
   可能

 * 시나리오II : 局地的 軍事的 응징
  - 美國, 國內政治的 理由에서 교착사태 長期化
   불원
  - 이라크 挑發時 UN憲章 第42條에 의한
   UN 기치하의 集團的 軍事的 制裁 措置
   加速 豫想

 * 시나리오III : 經濟制裁와 軍事的 봉쇄에 의한
        壓力
  - 海上봉쇄등을 통한 強力한 對이라크 질식戰略
  - 經濟制裁 效果는 3個月 以後 發生

 * 시나리오IV : 軍事的 外交的 壓迫을 통한
        이라크와의 妥協에 의한 解決
  - 이라크의 굴복을 얻어내기 위해, 強力한
   軍事的.外交的 壓迫 加速化
  - 이라크의 立場이 弱化된 時点에서 西方側
   條件 受諾線에서 協商 妥結(사실상의 원상회복)

0202

2. 우리의 對處方案 檢討

가. 基本的 考慮事項

第1: 我國人 安全. 迅速 撤收

第2: 유엔原則 遵守, 國際社會의 平和維持 活動
    參與 및 美國等 友邦과의 友好協力關係 尊重

第3: 我國의 쿠웨이트, 이라크 所在 經濟利益 保全

나. 對應 方向

1) 最優先的으로 我國人의 安全撤收 도모, 人命
    犧牲 極小化

2) 我國人 撤收를 대체로 마친 後, 國際社會의
    制裁措置에 보다 적극자세로 참여
    - 可及的이면 UN의 決議와 關係當事國의 要請에
      따라 행함.
    - 이를 위해 國內 輿論 支持確保 努力 傾注

3) 上記 2個 目標를 優先 推進하면서, 我國의 經濟
    利益 保全 위한 努力 傾注

4) 事態와 並行, 我國의 安保. 統一. 經濟 等 관련
    綜合對策 樹立

0203

3.　當面問題　對處方案

　　가.　現地　僑民　撤收

　　　1)　僑民撤收　現況

　　　　　　　　　　　　　　　　　(90.8.23.12:00　現在)

区分 国別	僑民総数	歸国 및 사우디等 安全国 待避	요르단으로 移動中	요르단 滯在	殘留者
쿠웨이트	605	331	69	192	13
이라크	712	86	79	65	482
計	1,317	417	148	257	495

　　　　* 쿠웨이트　僑民은　必須要員　및　撤收不願者　除外
　　　　　全員　出國　完了,　이라크　僑民　撤收에　注力

　　　　* 요르단　政府　이라크와의　國境폐쇄(8.22.24:00)

　　　2)　撤收　計劃

　　　　ㅇ　可及的　全　僑民의　安全.迅速　撤收
　　　　　　- 최소　必須人員　및　一部　公舘員만　殘留

　　나.　쿠웨이트　駐在公舘　活動　中斷

　　　1)　이라크　外務省의　要求(8.9　회람　公翰)

　　　　ㅇ　쿠웨이트　合併을　理由로　쿠웨이트駐在　外國公舘을
　　　　　　8.24.24:00限　폐쇄토록　要求

　　　　ㅇ　業務　및　公舘員　駐이라크　大使舘으로　移管　要求

　　　　ㅇ　8.24까지　미폐쇄시　公舘員　外交特權　不認定

　　　　　　　　　　　　　　　　　　　　　　0204

2) 對策

    ○ 原則

        - 名分을 살리고 犧牲을 最小化
          (他國家의 措置에 맞추어 對應)

        - 유엔결의 呼應(이라크의 쿠웨이트 合倂 不認定)

    ○ 措置計劃

        - 一次的으로 폐쇄에 不應하되, 物理的으로
          不可避할 경우, 他國公舘의 對應을 관망후
          8.24後 大使舘 活動의 一時的 中斷
          (Temporary Suspension of
           Function)

        - 同 措置時 聲明을 통해 不可避한 狀況에서 취한
          暫定 措置라는 立場 表明(文案 添附3)

    ○ 關聯 措置

        - 公舘員 撤收前 필수요원을 제외한 僑民 全員撤收
          (旣措置)

        - 大使舘 施設 保護

          . 現地 職員이 臨時 管理
          . 長期化時 駐이라크 大使舘에서 최소인원 파견

        - 友邦과 事前 協議

0205

다. 유엔의 對이라크 制裁措置 參與

1) 經濟制裁措置 參與問題

ㅇ 8.9 總理主宰 關係部處長官會議, 유엔 安保理
決議(661號)에 따라 對이라크 經濟制裁措置 決定

- 이라크 및 쿠웨이트로부터의 原油 輸入 禁止
- 商品(醫藥品等 人道的 物品은 除外) 交易禁止
  및 武器 等 軍需物資 輸出禁止
- 新規 建設受注 禁止

ㅇ 商工部, 8.22字로 對外貿易法 規定에 의한
特別措置(輸出入承認 禁止) 實施

ㅇ 建設部, 事態發生 즉시 新規都給 許可 中斷 指示

ㅇ 8.24까지 我國 措置事項 UN에 通報(-豫定)

2) 軍事的 制裁措置 支援

ㅇ 쿠웨이트 國王의 大統領閣下앞 8.13字 書翰,
軍事的. 經濟的 支援 公式 요청

ㅇ 美國 政府의 要請 內容

- 韓國의 軍事力에 의한 기여는 아니더라도
  積極的인 物質的. 財政的 支援 要請
- 韓國의 船舶 및 航空機에 의한 軍兵力 및
  物資 輸送

0206

ㅇ　考慮事項

- 軍事的　制裁　不參時는　韓美關係에　直間接　影響
可能

- 國際的　制裁가　가져올　北韓에　대한　警告　効果

- 國際　社會에서　我國의　役割　수행으로　太平洋
時代의　我國　位相　提高

ㅇ　對處　方案

＊　美國의　要請에　可能한　最大　誠意表示,　協調

- 直接的인　軍事支援은　困難,
- 非軍事分野　支援　檢討

(1)　醫藥品, 醫療裝備, 醫療支援團　派遣
(2)　海上運送　民間船舶等　輸送支援
(3)　民間　航空機에　의한　輸送　支援

- 具體的인　事項은　美側과　協議

라.　我國의　經濟的　利益保護問題

1)　이번　事態로　인한　我國의　經濟的　損害는　初年度
15億-30億弗로　推定

ㅇ　油價引上:　1弗　引上時,　年間　3.3億弗　追加負擔
ㅇ　建設　未收金　:　約10億弗
ㅇ　商品　輸出　차질:　約　2億弗

0207

2) 油價 및 GNP 展望

　o　油價

　　- 事態 最長期化되지 않는한 原油需給에 큰
　　　차질 없을 것으로 展望
　　　. 이라크. 쿠웨이트 供給 減少分: 400만B／D
　　　. 사우디等 余他國 增産可能量 : 350만B／D

　　- 專門家, 25弗 前後에서 油價 安定 展望

　　o　韓國 GNP에 미칠 影響(油價 25弗 基準)

　　- 91年度 GNP 低下 : 2.5%
　　- 都売物價 上昇 　　: 3.70%
　　- 消費者物價 上昇 　: 0.59%

3) 具體 分野別 對策

　o　原油 需給

　　- 原油의 安定的 確保위한 原油 도입선 다변화
　　　(中南美等 轉換으로 中東依存度 縮小), 代替
　　　에너지 開發 및 에너지 節約等 綜合對策 推進
　　- 石油依存 縮小, 天然가스 導入 促進

0208

ㅇ 建設關係

  - 事態 惡化로 現場撤收時, 不可抗力에 의한
    것임을 文書通報 하는등 분쟁소지 可及的 除去

  - 未收金 回收 問題는 발주처와 協議, 극소화

  - 紛爭地域 以外 産油國(例: 리비아)의 原油所得
    增大 活用, 建設受注 擴大

  - 長期的으로는 建設市場 다변화(先進國, 東歐等)
    및 技術集約型 建設로 轉換 推進

ㅇ 一般交易

  - 他地域에 대한 積極 輸出로 克服

  - 事態 解決後의 域内 需要에 對備

0209

4. 關聯問題 對應策

가. 脫冷戰期의 韓半島 安保體制 再点檢

   ㅇ 이라크 侵略行爲의 ·效果的인 抑制 失敗時는 北韓의
      軍事的 모험 衝動 可能性

      - 이라크와 北韓의 類似性(高度의 軍事力,   内部
        不滿等)
      - 美國의 太平洋 및 韓半島 周邊戰力의 部分的
        移動 可能性

   ㅇ 이라크 侵略 저지는 北韓의 潛在的 挑發慾에 대한
      抑制 要因

      - 美國의 即刻的인 軍事介入이 北韓에 주는
        心理的 效果
      - UN에 의한 集團的 制裁措置의 對北 警告 效果
      - 美. 蘇間 地域紛爭 防止 協力의 可視的 先例

   ㅇ 北韓의 挑發 可能性과 我國의 對備體制 再点檢

나. 對美 協調體制 構築

   ㅇ 脫冷戰期 美國의 主導役割 强化 認識

      - 美國 主導의 새로운 秩序 形成中
      - 美國은 · 새시대의 第1號 侵略者를 응징하는
        새로운 모델과 先例를 세운다는 姿勢
        . 美國의 軍事力과 友邦國의 軍事的. 財政的 參與 促求

0210

ㅇ 我國의 積極的 協助 姿勢 誇示

- 韓. 美間 安保體制에 대한 影響을 考慮 我國의
  確固한 對美 協力 姿勢 堅持

- 단, 對外的으로는 UN과 當事國의 要請을
  내세워 大義名分 세움

다. 美蘇關係와 蘇聯의 軍部動向 銳意 注視

ㅇ 금번 事態解決 方向과 關聯된 美蘇 立場 推移

ㅇ 蘇聯이 消極的 立場을 堅持할 경우, 고르바초프
  統治力에 대한 蘇軍部勢力의 對應 姿勢 注目

라. 對UN 關係 對策

ㅇ 我國의 UN加入 努力 維持

ㅇ 韓半島 平和定着을 위한 UN의 寄與 確保

ㅇ UN의 결의와 行動에 積極 參與

마. 對아랍 對策

ㅇ 아랍版圖 再編成을 銳意 注視

ㅇ 새 版圖에 부응하는 對策樹立 推進

ㅇ 油價引上으로 發生한 새 所得源을 建設, 輸出
  機會로 活用
  - 對사우디 等

ㅇ 에너지協力 體制, 調整 再整備

0211

바. 殘餘 僑民撤收, 保護對策

ㅇ 軍事的 支援 參與 不可避時에 對備한 最大限
迅速한 撤收를 계속 促求. 推進

ㅇ 殘餘僑民은 이라크 政府의 最大 身邊安全 보호를
받도록 事前保障 講究

ㅇ 緊急撤收 一部 僑民에 대한 人道的 支援 檢討

사. 弘報對策

ㅇ 國際社會의 責任있는 一員으로서 我國의 制裁 參加를
의연히 弘報

ㅇ 脫冷戰期 韓半島 安保의 死角地帶 可能性에 만반
對備, 경각심 고취
- 50年代 冷戰初期 北韓의 南侵과 80년대 脫冷戰期
벽두 이라크의 侵略과의 相互 연관성 浮刻

0212

이라크, 쿠웨이트 사태 속보 <31>
(8.23. 07:00)

중동아프리카국
중근동과

1. 상 황

o 요르단 정부, 이라크와의 국경 폐쇄
  - 철수 외국인 과다
  - 90. 8. 22. 24:00 부터 실시
  - 외국인 철수 불능
  - 주 요르단 대사관 보고(8.23. 08:00)

o 부쉬 미 대통령 예비군 소집령 시달 (8.22)
  - 이라크 공격 대비, 사우디 방어 미군 지원의 일환

o 유엔 안보리 5개 상임이사국, 미국이 제출한 결의안 검토 개시
  - 걸프만에서 제한적 무력사용 허용 여부
  - 소련, 중국은 제동 움직임

o 미.일본 주 쿠웨이트 대사관 8.24 이후도 유지 표명

o 유엔 사절 2명, 이라크 외무장관 면담 (8.22)
  - 비렌드라 데이 알 (인도), 코피 안난 (가나) 유엔 사무차장
    이라크 억류 외국인 출국 협의

o 이라크, 서방 6개국 국민 출국 허용 (8.22)
  - 이태리, 벨기에, 덴마크, 네덜란드, 그리스, 스페인등
  - 이라크 경유, 요르단이나 터키로 출국 가능
  - 미, 영, 불등 국민에 대해서는 언급 회피

o 미테랑 불 대통령, 걸프만 적대국 선박에 발포 가능성 시사
  - 기자회견시, "이라크 상대로 벗어나기 어려운 전의에 돌입했다.
    실행이 없는 봉쇄는 술수에 불과"

o 4번째 미항모 걸프 도착
  - 미항모 사라토가호 및 미사일 적재함 비눌 필리핀 C호등 미함
    3척 스웨즈운하 통과 걸프만 도착

0213

o 사우디 화드국왕 특사, 소련 방문 (8.22)

- 반다르 빈 술탄 주미 사우디 대사 모스크바 도착

o 이라크, 이란 포로 석방

- 8.22 까지 이란포로 총 35,000 석방

2. 교민 철수 현황

o 쿠웨이트 잔류 교민중(현대소속) 44명 육로 요르단 철수

- 쿠웨이트 (한양소속) 3명 항공편 요르단 철수

o 본인 잔류 고집 9명과 공관원 4명등 총 13명 잔류

o 요르단 정부, 국경 폐쇄로 8.22. 24:00 부터 교민 철수 완전 중단

3. 조 치 사 항

o 대한항공 특별기 2진 출발

- 8.22. 22:00 요르단 향발

o 철수교민 위문품등 특별기편 발송

- 외무장관 명의 라면, 김등 비상식품 100상자

o 피난 철수교민 사후 대책 강구

- 노동부, 보사부, 적십자사등에 협조 요청

- 직장 알선, 융자등 생활 대책

0214

이라크.쿠웨이트사태속보 (32)
(8. 23. 15:00)

중동아프리카국
중 근 동 과

---
1. 전쟁 위기 고조
---

o 미국, 대이라크 강경 입장 고수

  - 예비군 동원령 승인

  - 인질에 대한 위험에도 불구하고 대이라크 제재를 단행할 것임을 재천명

  - 주쿠웨이트 대사관 폐쇄 거부

  - 무력 사용을 위한 U.N. 안보리의 승인을 위해 계속 노력할 것이나,
    필요시에는 독자적으로 감행할 근거도 마련되었음을 발표

o 키신저 전국무장관은 U.N. 이 결의한 대이라크 제재의 이행을 위해,

   i) 미국은 인질문제를 과대 평가해서는 안되며,

   ii) 이라크는 미국이 이미 "돌이킬 수 없는 단계 (beyond the point
       of no return)" 에 이르렀음을 알아야 할 것이며,

   iii) 현 상황이 장기화되면 사태의 본질이 변질되어 미국에 불리할
        것이라고 경고함.

o 이스라엘 언론 : 향후 수일내 전투 발발 가능성 보도

  - 이라크가 이스라엘 공격 위해 미사일을 이동 배치

  - 이라크가 이스라엘을 공격시 막대한 댓가를 치를 것임을 경고

  - 후세인 이라크 대통령이 이스라엘을 금번 사태에 끌어 들이러 하고
    있으나, 이스라엘은 미국의 요청에 따라 Low Profile 을 유지하고 있음.

0215

○ 이라크는 외국인 즉각 석방을 요청한 U.N. 특사에게 외국인의 운명은
  미국의 행동에 달려 있다고 답변함으로써 조기 석방 가능성을 배제함.

○ 터어키 : 사우디 요청시 군대파견 검토 가능 발표

2. 유엔 안보리 동정

○ 상임이사국은 대이라크 제재 위해 필요한 경우 무력 사용한다는 원칙
  에는 동의한듯 보이나, 무력 사용 절차와 시기에 대한 이견 노정,
  콘센서스 도출 노력중

○ 미국, 영국, 볼란서 : 자국 군대에 대한 어떠한 U.N. 통제에도 반대
                      입장

○ 중   국 : 어떠한 무력 사용에도 반대하나, 안보리 표결시 기권 암시

○ 소   련 :

 - 무력이 "적절한 시기에 몹시 주의 깊게 (Very carefully and at due
   time)" 사용되어야 한다는 원칙하에 유엔이 통제를 해야 한다는 입장

 - 아울러 헌장 47조에 의거, "U.N. Military Staff Committee"를 활성화
   하여, 안보리의 조정하에 무력 사용할 것을 주장

○ 유엔 사무총장

 - 유엔은 현재의 다국적군의 활동을 지지한 바 없으며, 대이라크 봉쇄를
   선언한 바도 없음.

3. 기   타

○ 요르단, 쿠웨이트.이라크 국경 폐쇄

 - 후세인 요르단 왕은 요르단에 기입국한 난민들이 출국될 때까지 국경
   폐쇄 발표

○ 미주국가기구 (OAS)

 - 이라크의 쿠웨이트 병합, 외국인 억류 비난

0216

관리 번호	90 -1577

외 무 부

종 별 :

번 호 : UNW-1591

일 시 : 90 0823 1730

수 신 : 장관(국연,중근동,통일,기정)

발 신 : 주 유엔 대사

제 목 : 대이락 제재조치

대: WUN-1091

대호 조치내용을 금 8.23 자 유엔사무총장앞 당관 구상서로 통보하였음. 동서한은 금명간 안보리 문서로 배포될 예정임.끝

(대사 현홍주-국장)

예고:90.12.31 까지

1990.12.31. ~ ~~~~~
~~~~ ~~~~ ~~~~

국기국   중아국   통상국   안기부

90.08.24   07:39
외신 2과 통제관 EZ

0217

관리 번호	90 -1593

외 무 부

종 별 :

번 호 : UNW-1595

일 시 : 90 0823 1830

수 신 : 장관(국연, 서구일,중근동,기정)

발 신 : 주 유엔 대사

제 목 : 이태리대사 면담

1. 본직은 금 8.23 TRAXLER 이태리대사를 예방한바, 동인의 주요 언급사항을 아래보고함.

2. 이라크 사태관련

0. 금일 EC 회원국은 쿠웨이트내 외국공관을 8.24 까지 철수하라는 이라크 정부의 명령을 거부키로 결의함.

금일중 재회합하여 12 개 EC 회원국이 공동으로 안보리 소집을 요청코자함.

0. 661 호 이행을 위한 해상봉쇄및 필요시 무력사용을 승인하는 새로운 안보리 결의안 채택동향과 관련 그간 유보적 입장을 취해오던 소련도 거의 동의 단계에와 있는것으로 알고있음. 소련이 1-2 일간 더 시간을 요청하고 있는것은 현재 이락부봉령이 모스코바를 방문하고 있는 사실과관련 있는것으로 알려짐.

0. 금주말(토요일경)에 동취지의 결의안이 공식 채택될 가능성이 큰 것으로보임. 동 결의안 채택시 안보리가 만장일치의 단합력을 보여 줄지는 미지수임. 강대국에 의한 무력사용에 중국이 유보적인 입장을 표명했기 때문임. 중국의 기권, 큐바의 반대가 예상됨.

0. 금일 안보리는 전체 비공식 회합을 갖고 요르단, 불가리아의 661 호 제재조치 이행에 따르는 경제적 곤궁 지원요청에 대해 논의함. 이들나라에 의한 제재조치 이행완화는 승인키 곤란한 것으로 의견이 집약됨. 단, 요르단에 대한 경제적 지원에 대해서는 의견일치가 있었으나 대 불가리아 지원에 대해서는 합의를 보지 못한 것으로 알려짐.

3. 본직이 금차 유엔총회 기조연설시 이태리가 EC 의 의장국으로서 아국가입 입장을 지지한다는 점을 표명해줄것을 요청한바 , 동대사는 전통적인 입장에 비추어 어려움이 없을 것으로 보나 아측 요청을 본국에 보고하겠다고 말하였음.

국기국   미주국   구주국   중아국   안기부

PAGE 1

90.08.24   08:52

외신 2과 통제관 EZ

0218

4. 유엔총회기간중 한.이태리 외무장관 회담개최 당관의 제의에 대해서는 이미 본국에 보고했다함. 끝

5. 당관 참고로 주 쿠웨이트 아국 대사관의 철수 여부에 대한 본부 방침을 회시바람.

(대사 현홍주-국장)

예고:90.12.31. 일반

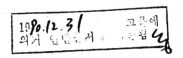

PAGE 2

0219

	분류번호	보존기간

발 신 전 보

번   호 : WUN-1107   900824 1850 DY   종별 :

수   신 : 주 유엔 대사 .(총영사)

발   신 : 장 관 (국연, 중근동)

제   목 : 이락.쿠웨이트 사태 (공관철수 문제)

대 : UNW-1595

1. 대호 주쿠웨이트 아국공관 철수문제와 관련, 국제적 연대노력에의
동참이라는 정부방침에 따라 8.24. 이후 공관 철수를 추진 할것임. 있구 있음.
계속

2. 그러나 8.24.이후 이라크 정부가 물리적으로 쿠웨이트 주재 외국
공관을 폐쇄할 경우, 미.일등 동지역 주재 우방국 공관과 협조 공동 대처하되
주쿠웨이트 대사 판단으로 공관원 신변안전상 계속 잔류가 불가능할시 본부
보고후 철수토록 지시한 바 있음. 끝.
지시하였는바, 이는 기관참고로만 하기바람. 끝.

예 고 : 1990.12.31. 일반

(국기국장   문동석)

1990.12.31 새 예고문에
의거 일반문서로 재분류됨

		대책반장 :		아중동국장 :		보 안 통 제	

앙 고 재	90 년 8 월 24 일	기안자 성명	과 장	국 장	차 관	장 관	외신과통제
		중근동과					

0220

이라크.쿠웨이트사태속보 (34)
(8. 24. 15:00)

중동아프리카국
중 근 동 과

---

1. 주쿠웨이트 외국 공관 패쇄 상황

o 주쿠웨이트 외국 공관 패쇄 시한인 8.25. 0시 (한국시간 25일 06:00)가
  임박함에 따라 현재까지 대사관 패쇄에 불응키로 결정한 국가는 아래와
  같음.

 - 미국, EC 국가, 소련, 오스트리아, 폴랜드, 채코, 스웨덴, 핀란드,
   노르웨이, 카나다, 일본, 방글라데시, 불가리아, 필리핀, 태국

o 미   국 : 대사관 필수요원만 유지, 미국인이 있는 한 대사관 유지할
             것임.

o· E   C : EC 국가 대사들이 한곳에 집결해서 대응

o 일   본 : 직원 2명만 잔류

o 타   이 : 이라크가 강재 패쇄시까지 유지

---

2. 유엔 안보리 동정

o 유엔 안보리 상임이사국은 대이라크 경제 재재 이행을 위해 "걸프만
  출입 선박을 정선시켜 국적, 화물, 목적지등을 확인하는데 필요한
  최소한의 무력 사용"을 허용하는 결의안을 마련하는대 합의를 본 것으로
  알려짐.

o 동 결의안을 금주중 안보리 본회의에 상정하기에 앞서, 본국 정부에
  조회중

0221

o 미국은 동 결의안 채택에 낙관적 견해를 나타내고 있으나, 소련은

　헌재까지 경제 재재 이행을 위한 충분한 시간이 경과하지 않았으며,

　위반된 사례도 없다는 점을 들어 조속한 시일내에 표결에 부치는데

　대해 조심스런 반응

o 미.소 외무장관간 전화를 통한 협의가 있었음이 확인됨.

---

3. 기   타

o 이스라엘의 태도

　- 현재 사태는 최고의 위기에 달해 있다고 평가

　- 이스라엘이 불가피하게 개입하게 될시에는 강경 대응할 것이라고 경고

o 이라크, 사우디 국경 배치 이라크 정예군 5만 교체

　- 전쟁 발발시 작전 투입용으로 후방 배치 하였거나, 또는 이라크 내부

　　반란에 대비, 정예부대를 후세인 대통령 측근에 배치한 것으로 추측됨.

o 일본 외무장관, 터키 방문

　- 터키가 경제 재재 이행으로 입은 경제적 손실을 일본이 보상해 주는

　　방안 협의

0222

외 무 부

종   별 : 지 급

번   호 : UNW-1606   일   시 : 90 0825 1100

수   신 : 장관(국연,중근동,통일,기정)

발   신 : 주유엔대사

제   목 : 안보리(아랍사태)

1. 안보리는 철야협의를 거쳐 금 8.25 06:00 안보리결의 <u>665호를 찬 13,반 0,</u> <u>기권2(쿠바,예멘)로 채택함.</u> 동 결의안은 <u>대이락 경제제재조치(결의안 661호)를</u> 위반하는 선박에 대해 필요한 조치를 취할수있는 권한을 부여하는 내용임.

2. 동결의안 요지는 아래와 같음.

가. 선박들의 화물과 목적지를 조사, 검색하고 정선등 특정상황에 따라 필요한 조치를 취할수 있도록 함.

나. 동조치관련 모든 회원국들의 지원제공 요청

다. 상기 이행관련 조사참모위원회와 같은 적절한 기구의 활용, 결의안 661호에 의거 설치된 산하위원회에의 보고등 관련국들의 상호 행동조정 촉구

3. 결의안 전문은 입수되는대로 추보위계임.끝

(대사 현홍주-국장)

국기국 안기부	장관 대책반	차관	1차보	2차보	중아국	통상국	정문국	정와대

PAGE 1

이라크, 쿠웨이트 사태 속보 <37>

(8.27. 07:00)

연 동

중동아프리카국
중 근 동 과

1. 상　　황

o 후세인 이라크 대통령, 걸프 위기사태 해결을 위해 발트하임 오스트리아 대통령에게 중재를 요청 (8.26)

o 케야르 UN 사무총장, 걸프사태 해결 위해 후세인 이라크 대통령과의 회담 제의

- 개인 자격으로 내주중 뉴욕 또는 제네바에서 개최 제의
- 후세인 동 회담 제의 환영 표시
- 미국도 이러한 UN 중재 노력에 반대하지 않음을 표명

o 고르바쵸프 소련 대통령, 걸프사태 해결은 UN 구도하에 해결되야 할 것임을 시사 (프랑스 외상과의 회담시)

o 부시 미국 대통령, 아래 사항이 이라크와의 협상 전제 조건임을 표명

- 이라크의 쿠웨이트로 부터 무조건 철수
- 전 쿠웨이트 정부 복귀
- 이라크 및 쿠웨이트 억류 외국인 석방
- 걸프지역 안전 보장

o 이라크, 식품 및 의약품 부족에 직면하고 있다면서, 미국이 대 이라크 경제 제재로 인한 인류의 범죄를 저지르고 있음을 비난

o 이라크, 대 이라크 제재 조치에 의해 자국 선박이 손해 및 침몰을 당할 경우, 가해군함에 대해 공격할 것임을 경고

0224

o 소련 외상, 소련은 걸프내 무력사용 및 대 이라크 제재 행동에 동참할
  계획이 없음을 표명
  - UN 결의아래 여타국가들은 행동을 취할 수 있을 것임을 부언
  - 또한 이라크에게 외국인 석방 및 쿠웨이트 주재 각국 공관 재개 허용을
    촉구

o 캘리 미국무차관보, 쿠웨이트 주재 미 대사관 주변에 대한 이라크군 포위
  불구, 미국대사 포함 직원 신변은 안전하다고 발표

o 미 국무성, 55명의 미국 외교관 가족이 터어키 국경 이라크 출국을 허용
  받았다고 발표

o 미국, UN의 대 이라크 경제 제재 조치에 협력하는 이라크 유조선 승무원애게
  망명처 제공 용의 있음을 시사

o 영국 수상, 후세인 이라크 대통령과의 협상 거절 (8.26)
  - 후세인과 같은 폭군과의 대화는 있을 수 없음을 표명

o 이태리, EC 국가가 UN 안보리 긴급 소집을 요구할 것을 희망
  - 쿠웨이트 주재 EC 국가 대사관의 외교 면책 특권 침해 관련

o 일본, 이라크내 억류 일본인 인질의 소재 불명 장소이동 관련, 걸프위기
  확산 대응책 준비중

o 이란 외상, 인도적 고려로서 이라크와 쿠웨이트내 외국인 출국 위해 서부
  국경선 개방(8.26 부터), 발표

o 쿠웨이트 망명 정부 수상, 쿠웨이트 주재 미국 대사와 최근 걸프사태 진전과
  관련 협의

o 아라파트 PLO 의장, 걸프지역으로 부터 서방병력 철수 및 아랍 연맹에서의
  쿠웨이트 장래 해결을 원칙으로 하는 아랍 평화안 지지

o 하쌍 요르단 국왕, 평화적 방법에 의한 걸프사태 종식을 위해 새로운
  아랍 외교 전개 모색
  - 리비아, 수단등 여타 아랍국가 순방차 출국

2. 교민 철수 현황 (90.8.27. 07:00 현재)

- o 이 라 크 : 294 명
- o 쿠웨이트 : 592 명
- o 총 철수인원 : 886 명
- o 잔류인원 : 431 명

  ※ 교민 104명(쿠웨이트 공관원 및 가족 27명 포함), KE 802편 8.26.
     17:40 서울 착

3. 조 치 사 항

- o 요르단 국경 재개방에 따라, 이라크 잔류 교민의 요르단 경유 철수 추진을
  지시 (주 이라크 대사관 8.26)

- o 이라크 잔류 교민의 요르단 국경 경유 철수 추진에 따른 재반 사전 필요
  조치 강구 지시 (주 요르단 대사관, 8.26)

0226

외 무 부

종 별 :

번 호 : UNW-1611
일 시 : 90 0827 1700

수 신 : 장 관(국연)

발 신 : 주 유엔 대사

제 목 : 이락.쿠웨이트 사태

1. 유엔 사무총장은 중남미 방문을 마치고 지난주말 당지에 귀임하였는바, 8.25. 콜롬비아 방문중 발표한 표제사태 중재를 위해 8.29 당지출발, 8.30(목) 요르단 암만에서 TARIQ AZIZ 이락 외무장관과 회담예정으로 있음.

2. 금번 방문중 사무총장과 사담 후세인 이락 대통령과의 면담은 현재 주선하고 있지 않다고 사무국측은 밝히고 있음.끝.

(대사 현 홍주-국장)

국기국   1차보   정문국   안기부   미주국 통상국 대책반 2차신

공　　　　　란

공   란

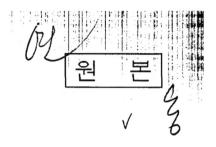

외 무 부

종 별 :

번 호 : UNW-1618   일 시 : 90 0827 1800

수 신 : 장 관(국연,통일,중근동,기정)

발 신 : 주 유엔 대사

제 목 : 대이락 제재조치

　　1.요르단은 8.20자 외무장관의 안보리 의장앞 서한에서 안보리결의 661 에 따른 대이라크 경제제재조치 이행시 요르단이 봉착할 '특별한 경제적 문제'점에 관한 해결책을 강구하기 위하여 헌장 제50조에 따른 안보리와의 협의를 요청한바 있음.(UNW-1595 보고와 같이 안보리는 공식 협의회를 통해 요르단의 경제적 손실을 보전할 필요에 대해 합의한바 있음.)

　　2.요르단은 661호 이행시 요르단에 대한 직접적인 재정적 손실은 매년 미불 15억불, 간접적 손실은 5억불로 추산하고 있음.

　　3.동요르단측 서한 및 동서한에 첨부된 경제적 손실내역을 별첨(FAX) 송부함.

　　첨부:상기 요르단 서한 (UNW(F)-0146)) 끝

　　(대사 현홍주-국장)

국기국　　1차보　　중아국　　통상국　　안기부　　외무국 강문극 대책반 차관 장관

PAGE 1

90.08.28　　09:35 WG

외신 1과 통제관

0230

UN(F)-0146 00827 1820 총 6매
(국연, 통일, 중근동, 기정)

S

UNITED NATIONS

Security Council

Distr.
GENERAL

S/21620
24 August 1990

ORIGINAL: ENGLISH

LETTER DATED 20 AUGUST 1990 FROM THE PERMANENT REPRESENTATIVE OF
JORDAN TO THE UNITED NATIONS ADDRESSED TO THE PRESIDENT OF THE
SECURITY COUNCIL

    I have the honour of enclosing herewith the text of a letter addressed to
Your Excellency from His Excellency Mr. Marwan Kasim, Deputy Prime Minister and
Foreign Minister of Jordan, relating to Jordan's request to enter into
consultations with the Security Council under article 50 of the Charter, concerning
the effects of the carrying out of resolution 661 of 1990 on Jordan.

    I should be grateful if this letter and its enclosure would be given urgent
consideration by the Council in view of the magnitude of the problem and its
pressing nature.

(Signed)   Abdullah SALAH
Ambassador

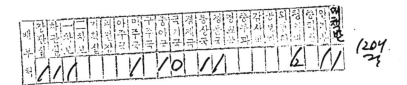

90-20438 16981 (E)   6-1   /...

0231

S/21620
English
Page 2

<u>Annex</u>

<u>Text of a letter dated 20 August 1990 from the Deputy Prime Minister
and Foreign Minister of Jordan addressed to the President of the
Security Council</u>

I have the honour of bringing to your attention the following:

1.   The Government of the Hashemite Kingdom of Jordan has taken note of the
Security Council's adoption of resolution 661 on 6 August 1990. Cognizant of its
obligations under the Charter, and the resolution's mandatory nature, Jordan shall
comply with its provisions.

2.   The competent Jordanian authorities have, after careful studies and analysis,
determined that compliance with the resolution will lead to extreme economic
hardships to Jordan and its population, which constitute "special economic
problems" within the meaning of Article 50 of the Charter.

In this respect, may I draw Your Excellency's attention to Jordan's geographic
location and the degree of interdependence between, on the one hand, Jordan's
economy and on the other, those of Iraq and Kuwait. The extent of this
interdependence can be gleaned from the attached memorandum. You will recall also
that Jordan is currently passing through an economic crisis unprecedented in its
history.

Motivated on the one hand by their wish to carry out their Charter obligations
in good faith, and conscious at the same time of the excessive onerousness for
Jordan arising from compliance with resolution 661, my Government hereby officially
requests to enter into consultations, on an urgent basis, with the Security Council
with regard to finding a solution to the problems that will arise from the carrying
out of measures under Chapter VII.

(Signed) Marwan S. KASIM

6-2   /...

0232

Enclosure

A memorandum on the economic and financial impact on Jordan resulting from the imposition of restrictions on its economic relations with Iraq and Kuwait

This memorandum explains the economic losses that would affect Jordan as a result of the imposition of restrictions on exchange of trade, services and financial transactions with Iraq and Kuwait.

These losses could be classified under the following topics:

(1)   Exports of goods

(2)   Transport to Iraq

(3)   Import of crude oil and fuel oil

(4)   Grants to the budget

(5)   Iraq's debt to Jordan

(6)   Remittances from Jordanians working in Kuwait

(7)   Dismissal of Jordanian expatriates in Kuwait

(8)   Burden resulting from the massive outflow of expatriates from Kuwait through Jordan

(1)   Exports of goods to Iraq and Kuwait

Jordan's exports to Kuwait in 1989 amounted to about $US 65 million. Most of these exports consist of vegetables and foodstuffs. It was expected that total exports in 1990 will be around $US 80 million. Jordan's exports to Iraq are expected to exceed $US 200 million this year, of which $US 180 million is to be settled under the bilateral payment arrangement and the balance by convertible currencies. The restrictions on Jordan's exports to both countries will result in a loss exceeding $US 280 million annually. The magnitude of this burden amounts to 30 per cent of Jordan's national exports, or over 60 per cent of Jordan's non-commodity exports.

This sharp drop in exports of goods would affect the balance of trade as well as the economic activity of the country and will further accentuate the already high unemployment level in Jordan.

(2)   Transport to Iraq

Goods in transit from Aqaba port in Jordan and destined to Iraq is a major activity in the Jordanian economy. The total income generated from port charges

6-3   /...

0233

S/21620
English
Page 4

transformation and packing activities as well as inland freight is estimated to exceed $US 250 million annually.

The elimination of these activities would also have a sharp adverse effect on the current account of the balance of payments, GDP and employment in the country.

(3) Import of crude oil and fuel oil

Jordan imports about 22 million barrels of oil and oil derivatives annually. About 90 per cent of this is imported from Iraq and Kuwait. Kuwait provides crude oil and fuel oil as grants to Jordan amounting to $US 60 million annually, while the balance is imported from Iraq and is financed from Jordan's outstanding debt to Iraq as well as through the bilateral trade arrangements. One fourth of Jordan's total import bill consists of fuel oil. Fuel oil is being purchased from Iraq at concessionary prices not exceeding 60 per cent of crude oil international price. Shifting to new sources of oil and fuel oil will subject Jordan to serious difficulties with regard to the loss of concessionary oil supplies, obtaining the necessary finance, as well as finding new sources of fuel oil at competitive prices.

(4) Grants to the budget

Kuwait made a commitment to pay Jordan an amount of $US 135 million in the form of grants for the fiscal year 1990-1991 whereas Iraq made a commitment for an amount of $US 50 million during 1990 in grants. The total amount committed by both countries is $US 185 million.

This amount is crucial for the budget and the balance of payments and without the receipt of these grants Jordan's budget as well as the balance of payments would be subjected to strong pressures.

(5) Iraq's debt to Jordan

Iraq's total outstanding direct debt to Jordan at the beginning of 1990 stood at $US 310 million and the Iraqi Government has agreed to reduce this debt during 1990 by about $US 240 million through paying $US 144 million in cash and exporting crude oil and oil derivatives for the balance. However, $US 72 million only has been paid in cash so far, and the balance therefore shall not be met under present circumstances.

In addition, the Jordanian Government has incurred an additional obligation, the balance of which at present is $US 2.6 billion, on behalf of the Iraqi Government to guarantee debt to a third party which the latter has been repaying regularly. This amount is not included in Jordan's outstanding foreign debt for the purposes of rescheduling. The imposition of financial and trade restrictions on Iraq shall necessarily force Iraq to stop repayment and consequently the burden of servicing this amount, (i.e. $US 2.6 billion), shall be transferred to Jordan's Treasury.

6-4

/...

0234

(6) Remittances from Jordanians working in Kuwait

Jordan estimates that during 1990 remittances from Jordanians working abroad will exceed $US 800 million, 40 per cent of which were expected to come from Kuwait.

Imposing restrictions on Iraq will jeopardize the transfer of such remittances to Jordan and will further widen the gap in the balance of payments of Jordan.

(7) Dismissal of Jordanian expatriates in Kuwait

It is estimated that Jordan has around 330,000 expatriates working abroad, out of which a minimum of 100,000 work in Kuwait. The imposition of the embargo could result in sudden and massive dismissal of these expatriates and the immediate return of a large percentage of them along with their families to Jordan. (Jordanians working in Kuwait together with their families are estimated to number over 350,000.)

This imminent inflow of returning migrants will further aggravate the unemployment situation in the country which currently stands at around 15 per cent of the labour force. What will make the situation more difficult is the recent erosion of their savings in Kuwait, a fact which will impose a heavier social burden on the Government.

(8) Burden from the massive outflow of expatriates from Iraq and Kuwait through Jordan

Jordan is the only country through which expatriates working in Kuwait and Iraq can pass on their way to their home countries. Since the beginning of the crisis the through-flow of those expatriates has increased substantially. Jordan will face tremendous difficulties if it were to handle this flow.

CONCLUSION

Jordan is at present passing through a crucial economic situation which is characterized by rising unemployment, high rates of inflation and serious difficulties in servicing its foreign debt. It is already implementing an adjustment programme with the IMF in order to resume growth and address internal and external imbalances.

The success of this programme is largely dependent on the ability of Jordan to increase exports, and to obtain additional financial inflows from abroad in the form of grants and remittances.

The imposition of the embargo will certainly result in a complete reversal in these objectives and will destroy the fundamentals of this effort and hence subject the economy to total collapse. It is imperative that arrangements are made to provide Jordan with the following:

6-5

/...

0235

S/21620
English
Page 6

    (1) Grants to compensate for the reduction in grants from Iraq and Kuwait, the reduction in expatriate remittances, and to compensate Jordan for the increase in public expenditures resulting from imposing the embargo.

    (2) Oil and oil derivatives with concessionary conditions and with long-term financing at most favourable terms.

    (3) Long-term soft loans to enable Jordan to revitalize the economy and to overcome the sharp drop expected in economic activity, employment and exports.

    It has been demonstrated that the direct financial loss that Jordan will incur as a result of implementing the embargo decision will not be less than $US 1.5 billion a year and Jordan would require further funding in the magnitude of half a billion dollars to cover the indirect consequences and repercussions of reduced economic activity and external imbalances.

————

6 - 6

0236

외 무 부

종 별 :

번 호 : UNW-1619

일 시 : 90 0827 1820

수 신 : 장 관(국연,통일,중근동,기정)

발 신 : 주 유엔 대사

제 목 : 대이락 제재조치 이행

연: UNW-1548

1. 표제조치 이행에 관한 유엔사무 총장의 보고서에 의하면 연호 국가에 추가하여 90.8.24. 현재 새로이 56개국으로 부터 61건의 추가통보를 받았다고함.

2. 이로 써 8.24. 현재까지 총88개국으로부터 안보리결의 661호 이행관련 100건의 회신이 있었다고함.

3. 북한으로부터는 상금 회신이없는 것으로 확인됨.

4. 동사무총장 보고서는 별전(FAX) 과 같음.

첨부:사무총장보고서 ((UNW(F)-0147)) 끝

(대사 현홍주-국장)

국기국	1차보	2차보	중아국	통상국	안기부	대책반		

PAGE 1

'90.08.28   09:37 WG

외신 1과 통제관

0237

걸프사태 관련 유엔안전보장이사회 동향, 1990-91. 전5권 (V.1 1990.8월) 243

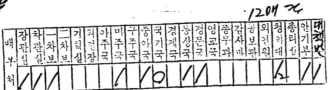

**UNITED
NATIONS**

S

Security Council

Distr.
GENERAL

S/21641
25 August 1990

ORIGINAL: ENGLISH

FURTHER REPORT OF THE SECRETARY-GENERAL ON THE IMPLEMENTATION
OF SECURITY COUNCIL RESOLUTION 661 (1990)

1.   Pursuant to paragraph 10 of resolution 661 (1990), adopted by the Security Council at its 2933rd meeting, on 6 August 1990, the Secretary-General submitted an interim report to the Council on the implementation of the resolution on 15 August 1990 (S/21536 and Corr.1).

2.   It will be recalled that by a telegram dated 6 August 1990, the Secretary-General transmitted the text of resolution 661 (1990) to the Ministers for Foreign Affairs of all States 1/ and that in a note dated 8 August 1990 addressed to Ministers for Foreign Affairs of all States, the Secretary-General drew attention to paragraphs 6, 7 and 10 of the resolution. In the light of his reporting responsibility under paragraph 10 of the resolution, the Secretary-General indicated that he would appreciate receiving as early as possible, but no later than 24 August 1990, information on the measures taken by Governments in accordance with the provisions of the resolution (S/21536 and Corr.1, paras. 2 and 3).

3.   Since the issuance of the Secretary-General's interim report on 15 August 1990 (S/21536 and Corr.1), as of 24 August 1990, 61 additional replies were received from 56 States, which are listed in alphabetical order in the annex to the present report, with an indication of the symbols of the documents in which the texts are reproduced in full. Taking into account the additional replies reflected in the present report, a total of 100 replies have been received to date from 88 States.

4.   It is the intention of the Secretary-General, pursuant to paragraph 10 of resolution 661 (1990), to address a further request for information on the measures taken by Governments in accordance with the provisions of the resolution to those States that have not yet responded.

Notes

1/   In accordance with the established practice of the Secretariat, the term "all States" refers to States Members of the United Nations or members of specialized agencies or of the International Atomic Energy Agency or parties to the Statute of the International Court of Justice.

90-20444 1760e (E)   /...

3—1

Annex

List of States that have replied to the note dated 8 August 1990 from the Secretary-General

	Symbol of the document in which the text of the reply is reproduced
Austria	S/21593
Bahrain	S/21575
Belgium	S/21583
Bolivia	S/21550
Bulgaria	S/21573 and S/21576
Burundi	S/21633
China	S/21594
Colombia	S/21570
Costa Rica	S/21521
Cuba	S/21580 and S/21626
Cyprus	S/21542
Czechoslovakia	S/21598
Denmark	S/21604
Dominican Republic	S/21600
Egypt	S/21629
Ethiopia	S/21584
Greece	S/21613
Guatemala	S/21533
Iceland	S/21549
India	S/21602
Indonesia	S/21578
Iran (Islamic Republic of)	S/21557
Ireland	S/21609
Israel	S/21552
Italy	S/21551 and S/21612*

---

*   On behalf of the States members of the European Community.

3-2

/...

0239

	Symbol of the document in which the text of the reply is reproduced
Jordan	S/21614
Lebanon	S/21588
Lesotho	S/21587
Luxembourg	S/21543
Mali	S/21622
Malta	S/21601 and S/21628
Mexico	S/21605
Myanmar	S/21597
Netherlands	S/21611
New Zealand	S/21538 and S/21547
Oman	S/21567
Paraguay	S/21579
Peru	S/21623
Philippines	S/21630
Poland	S/21607
Portugal	S/21632
Qatar	S/21582
Republic of Korea	S/21617
Saudi Arabia	S/21596
Senegal	S/21624
Singapore	S/21619
South Africa	S/21610
Sri Lanka	S/21627
Switzerland	S/21585
Syrian Arab Republic	S/21595
Turkey	S/21577
Union of Soviet Socialist Republics	S/21599
United Arab Emirates	S/21581
Uruguay	S/21606
Yemen	S/21615
Yugoslavia	S/21618

-----

3 - 3

0240

외 무 부

종 별 :

번 호 : UNW-1620   일 시 : 90 0827 1820

수 신 : 장 관(국연,중근동,통일,기정)

발 신 : 주 유엔 대사

제 목 : 대이락 제재조치

연:1) UNW-1591, 2)UNW-1606

1. 연호(2) 결의안 전문은 별첨과 같음.

2. 연호(1) 당관의 8.23.자유엔 사무총장앞 구상서가 8.24.자 안보리문서 (S/21617) 로 금 8.27 배포되었음.

첨부:1. 안보리결의안 665

2. 당관의 8.23.자 구상서 ((UNW(F)-0148)) 끝.

(대사 현홍주-국장)

국기국	1차보	2차보	중아국	통상국	안기부				

장관
PAGE 1

90.08.28   09:38 WG

외신 1과 통제관

0241

**UNITED
NATIONS**

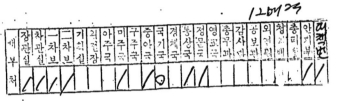

UNW(F)-0148 00827 1820 총 6매
(국연, 중근동, 통일, 기정)

Security Council

Distr.
GENERAL

S/RES/665 (1990)
25 August 1990

RESOLUTION 665 (1990)

Adopted by the Security Council at its 2938th meeting,
on 25 August 1990

The Security Council,

Recalling its resolutions 660 (1990), 661 (1990), 662 (1990) and 664 (1990) and demanding their full and immediate implementation,

Having decided in resolution 661 (1990) to impose economic sanctions under Chapter VII of the Charter of the United Nations,

Determined to bring an end to the occupation of Kuwait by Iraq which imperils the existence of a Member State and to restore the legitimate authority, and the sovereignty, independence and territorial integrity of Kuwait which requires the speedy implementation of the above resolutions,

Deploring the loss of innocent life stemming from the Iraqi invasion of Kuwait and determined to prevent further such losses,

Gravely alarmed that Iraq continues to refuse to comply with resolutions 660 (1990), 661 (1990), 662 (1990) and 664 (1990) and in particular at the conduct of the Government of Iraq in using Iraqi flag vessels to export oil,

1.   Calls upon those Member States co-operating with the Government of Kuwait which are deploying maritime forces to the area to use such measures commensurate to the specific circumstances as may be necessary under the authority of the Security Council to halt all inward and outward maritime shipping in order to inspect and verify their cargoes and destinations and to ensure strict implementation of the provisions related to such shipping laid down in resolution 661 (1990);

2.   Invites Member States accordingly to co-operate as may be necessary to ensure compliance with the provisions of resolution 661 (1990) with maximum use of political and diplomatic measures, in accordance with paragraph 1 above;

90-20562 2408Z (E)   /...

6-1

S/RES/665 (1990)
Page 2

   3.   Requests all States to provide in accordance with the Charter such
assistance as may be required by the States referred to in paragraph 1 of this
resolution;

   4.   Further requests the States concerned to co-ordinate their actions in
pursuit of the above paragraphs of this resolution using as appropriate mechanisms
of the Military Staff Committee and after consultation with the Secretary-General
to submit reports to the Security Council and its Committee established under
resolution 661 (1990) to facilitate the monitoring of the implementation of this
resolution;

   5.   Decides to remain actively seized of the matter.

6-2

0243

UNITED NATIONS

 Security Council

Distr.
GENERAL

S/21617
24 August 1990

ORIGINAL: ENGLISH

S

NOTE BY THE SECRETARY-GENERAL

The attached note verbale dated 23 August 1990 from the Permanent Observer of the Republic of Korea to the United Nations has been addressed to the Secretary-General.

90-20379 1898j (E)   6-3   /...

0244

<u>Annex</u>

<u>Note verbale dated 23 August 1990 from the Permanent Observer of
the Republic of Korea to the United Nations addressed to the
Secretary-General</u>

The Permanent Observer of the Republic of Korea to the United Nations presents
his compliments to the Secretary-General of the United Nations and, with reference
to the latter's note SCPC/7/90 (1) dated 8 August 1990, has the honour to enclose
herewith the memorandum of 20 August 1990 by the Ministry of Foreign Affairs on
supplementary measures, further to the decisions taken on 9 August 1990 and
circulated as Security Council document S/21487, to implement United Nations
Security Council resolution 661 (1990) on the Iraqi invasion of Kuwait.

/...

6-4

S/21617
English
Page 3

Enclosure

Memorandum dated 20 August 1990 from the Ministry of Foreign Affairs of the Republic of Korea on measures taken by the Government of the Republic of Korea to implement Security Council resolution 661 (1990)

Further to the decisions taken on 9 August 1990 and circulated as document S/21487, the Government of the Republic of Korea has taken the following supplementary measures with immediate effect.

1.   Suspension of issuance of the Import License for all commodities and products originating in Iraq and Kuwait:

-   The Government of the Republic of Korea has issued special guidelines to suspend issuance of the Import License for all commodities and products originating in Iraq and Kuwait;

-   The special guidelines issued in accordance with the provisions of the Foreign Trade Act (hereinafter "the Act"), are to prohibit the import of all goods, including crude oil, produced in or shipped from Iraq and Kuwait.

2.   Suspension of issuance of the Export License for all commodities and products to Iraq and Kuwait:

-   The Government of the Republic of Korea announced, based on the Act, special guidelines to suspend issuance of the Export License for the sale or supply by Korean nationals or Korean flag vessels of all commodities and products to any party in Iraq and Kuwait;

-   The Ministry of Commerce may approve issuance of the Export License only for the export of items designated for medical and humanitarian purposes.

3.   Suspension of the procurement of construction contracts in Iraq and Kuwait:

-   On 2 August, the Government of the Republic of Korea issued, based on relevant ordinance, administrative guidelines prohibiting the procurement of construction contracts in Iraq and Kuwait;

-   The inter-ministerial meeting held on 9 August confirmed the administrative guidelines.

4.   Protection of assets of the legitimate Government of Kuwait:

-   As previously announced by the Government of the Republic of Korea in document S/21487, it has been confirmed that there exist no such assets in the Republic of Korea.

6—5

/...

0246

S/21617
English
Page 4

5.   Penal provisions:

     -   Any person who violates the special/administrative guidelines set out
         above shall, in the absence of stricter penalties under other laws, be
         subject to the penalties under article 67 of the Act.

6.   The special inter-ministerial task force monitoring implementation of the
measures taken by the Government of the Republic of Korea in pursuance of the
resolution 661 (1990) has not found, since its establishment on 9 August, any
violation of the above-mentioned special/administrative guidelines by persons or
bodies under the jurisdiction of the Government of the Republic of Korea.

6-6

0247

외 무 부

종 별 :

번 호 : UNW-1642   일 시 : 90 0829 1830

수 신 : 장관(국연,서구일,기정)

발 신 : 주 유엔 대사

제 목 : 핀랜드대사와 오찬

1. 금 8.29 TORNUDD 핀랜드 대사의 초청으로 본직은 동인과 오찬면담함. 동인 금번 방한이 자신으로서는 동아시아지역 최초방문으로 매우 유익하였다고 하고 방한시 한국정부의 환대에 사의를 표명하였음.

2. 이락사태와 관련, 안보리결의 665 호(제재조치 위반선박에 대한 무력사용) 채택과정관련, 아래내용을 언급하였음.

0. 당초 미국은 "MINIMUM USE OF FORCE" 를 승인한다는 어귀를 포함시키고자 하였으나, 소련의 주장으로 "무력사용" 의 직접 언급은 삭제되고 그대신 쏘련이 제안한 "MEASURES COMMENSURATE TO " 로 대체되었음.

0. 중국이 찬성부표한것은 혼자서 "UNPOPULAR " 한 입장을 취하기 곤란하였으며, 첫번째 결의안 660 호를 찬성하였기 때문에 그후 여타 후속 결의안에 대해서도 부정적인 입장을 취하기 어려웠던 점에 기인한다고 봄.

0. 안보리 661 호 결의안 이행과관련 문제가 되고있는 것은 요르단의 경우이며, 그밖에 제재위원회에서 크게 문제가 제기되고 있는 나라는 없음.

3. 동인은 유엔사무총장의 요르단 방문에 대해 회원국들은 성과를 기대치 않고 있다고 언급하고, 다만 사무총장이 빈손으로 귀환하드라도 금후 UN 의 조치에 대해 안보리 회원국을 결속하는 효과는 있다고 본다함.

4. 북한이 단일의석 가입안등 문제로 핀랜드를 접촉해온 사실은 없다고 함.

5. 유엔총회기조연설시 아국입장지지 요청에 대해 본국에 보고하겠다고 대답하였음. 끝

(대사 현홍주-국장)

예고:90.12.31. 일반

국기국   미주국   구주국   안기부

90.08.30   08:52

외신 2과 통제관 EZ

0248

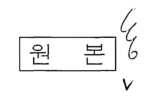

외 무 부

종 별 :

번 호 : UNW-1667 일 시 : 90 0830 2300

수 신 : 장 관(국연,동구이,기정)

발 신 : 주 유엔 대사

제 목 : 이락사태

　　요르단, 불가리아에 이어 유고, 루마니아도 8.27자 유엔안보리 의장앞 서한을 통해 안보리결의 661호상 제재조치 이행으로 인하여 자국이 경제적으로 부담할 어려움을 해결할 수 있도록 안보리가 도와줄 것을 요청하였음. 끝

　　(대사 현홍주-국장)

국기국　　1차보　　구주국　　정문국　　안기부

PAGE 1

외신 1과 통제관

0249

↑ WOIMUBU K24651

↓ IIX2508101-1651(UNNY:WUCB1651)
TXJ952 78724651
WUCB1651 NYKT227 UNNY:WUCB1651
TLXCAB
78724651 24651//78724652 24652

WUCB1651 MCX0966

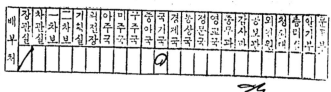

SS CABKS
.NEWYORK (UNNY) 1915 GMT 08/30/90
ETATPRIORITE
HIS EXCELLENCY
THE MINISTER FOR FOREIGN AFFAIRS
OF THE REPUBLIC OF KOREA
MINISTRY OF FOREIGN AFFAIRS
SEOUL (KOREA)
BT
40696-08 I HAVE THE HONOUR TO TRANSMIT HEREWITH THE TEXT
OF RESOLUTION 665 (1990) ADOPTED BY THE SECURITY COUNCIL AT
ITS 2938TH MEETING ON 25 AUGUST 1990.
QUOTE
    THE SECURITY COUNCIL,
RECALLING ITS RESOLUTIONS 660 (1990),661 (1990), 662
(1990), AND 664 (1990) AND DEMANDING THEIR FULL AND
IMMEDIATE IMPLEMENTATION.
    HAVING DECIDED IN RESOLUTION 661 (1990) TO IMPOSE
ECONOMIC SANCTIONS UNDER CHAPTER VII OF THE CHARTER OF THE
UNITED NATIONS.
    DETERMINED TO BRING AN END TO THE OCCUPATION OF KUWAIT
BY IRAQ WHICH EMPERILS THE EXISTENCE OF A MEMBER STATE AND
TO RESTORE THE LEGITIMATE AUTHORITY, AND THE SOVEREIGNTY,
INDEPENDENCE AND TERRITORIAL INTEGRITY OF KUWAIT WHICH
REQUIRES THE SPEEDY IMPLEMENTATION OF THE ABOVE
RESULUTIONS.
    DEPLORING THE LOSS OF INNOCENT LIFE STEMMING FROM THE

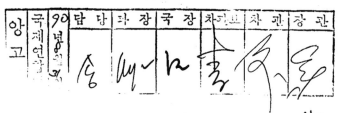

0250

SUCH LOSSES.

. . . GRAVELY ALARMED ≡ IRAQ CONTINUES TO REFUSE TO COMPLY
WITH RESOLUTIONS 660 (1990), 661 (1990), 662 (1990) AND 664
(1990) AND IN PARTICULAR AT THE CONDUCT OF THE GOVERNMENT
OF IRAQ IN USING IRAQI FLAG VESSELS TO EXPORT OIL.

     1. CALLS UPON THOSE MEMBER STATES CO-OPERATING WITH THE
GOVERNMENT OF KUWAIT WHICH ARE DEPLOYING MARITIME FORCES TO
THE AREA TO USE SUCH MEASURES COMMENSURATE TO THE SPECIFIC
CIRCUMSTANCES AS MAY BE NECESSARY UNDER THE AUTHORITY OF
THE SECURITY COUNCIL TO HALT ALL INWARD AND OUTWARD
MARITIME SHIPPING IN ORDER TO INSPECT AND VERIFY THEIR
CARGOES AND DESTINATIONS AND TO ENSURE STRICT IMPLEMENTTION
OF THE PROVISIONS RELATED TO SUCH SHIPPING LAID DOWN IN
RESOLUTION 661 (1990):

     2. INVITES MEMBER STATES ACCORDINGLY TO CO-OPERATE AS
MAY BE NECESSARY TO ENSURE COMPLIANCE WITH THE PROVISIONS
OF RESOLUTION 661 (1990) WITH MAXIMUM USE OF POLITICAL AND
DIPLOMATIC MEASURES, IN ACCORDANCE WITH PARAGRAPH 1 ABOVE:

     3. REQUESTS ALL STATES TO PROVIDE IN ACCORDANCE WITH
CHARTER SUCH ASSISTANCE AS MAY BE REQUIRED BY THE STATES
REFERRED TO IN PARAGRAPH 1 OF THIS RESOLUTION:

     4. FURHTER REQUESTS THE STATES CONCERNED TO CO-ORDINATE
THEIR ACTIONS IN PURSUIT OF THE ABOVE PARAGRAPHS OF THIS
RESOLUTION USING AS APPROPRIATE MECHANISMS OF THE MILITARY
STAFF COMMITTEE AND AFTER CONSULATIONS WITH THE
SECRETARY-GENERAL TO SUBMIT REPORTS TO THE SECURITY COUNCIL
AND ITS COMMITTEE ESTABLISHED UNDER RESOLUTION 661 (1990)
TO FACILITATE THE MONITORING OF THE IMPLEMENTATION OF THIS
RESOLUTION:

     5 DECIDES TO REMAIN ACTIVELY SEIZED OF THE MATTER
UNQUOTE

     HIGHEST CONSIDERATION.

     JAVIER PEREZ DE CUELLAR
          SECRETARY-GENERAL
GBS S3520 PAD M2581
COL CKD

議案番號	第　1　號
會議次回	'90年度　第 1 次

報告事項

페르시아灣事態 展開狀況에 따른 我國의 對應策

報 告 機 關	外　　務　　部
報 告 年 月 日	1990. 8. 31

가. 韓·美 安保協力體制 鞏固化

○ 美國 主導의 新平和秩序維持體制가 形成中이며
  南·北韓 信賴關係 및 東北亞 平和構圖가 樹立될 때 까지는
  美國과의 堅實한 安保協力關係 維持가 緊要함을 認識,
  ― 我國의 積極的인 對美協調 姿勢를 誇示함으로써
  ― 韓·美 安保協力體制를 鞏固化하고

○ 나아가, 東北亞 平和 및 安保協議體制 構築을 위한 努力을
  並行하면서
  ― 韓·美協調下에 內實있는 北方外交를 推進함.

나. 對유엔 對策 强化

○ 平和 維持機構로서 유엔의 機能이 過去보다 增大함에 따라,

○ 國力에 相應하게 유엔 中心의 國際協力에 積極 參與해야 함.

○ 유엔 加入問題는 關聯問題들을 愼重히 檢討하여 對處코저 함.

다. 主導的인 南·北對話 努力

○ 短期的으로는, 北韓이 中東事態에 鼓舞되어 對南策動 衝動을
  느낄수도 있으나,
  ― 結局은 國際的 制裁雰圍氣로 萎縮이 豫想됨

13 ― 12

0253

정 리 보 존 문 서 목 록					
기록물종류	일반공문서철	등록번호	2017060004	등록일자	2017-06-05
분류번호	731.33	국가코드	XF	보존기간	30년
명 칭	걸프사태 관련 유엔안전보장이사회 동향, 1990-91. 전5권				
생 산 과	국제연합과/중동1과	생산년도	1990~1991	담당그룹	
권 차 명	V.2 1990.9-12월				
내용목차	* 1990.9.13 인도적 목적의 대이라크 식품 수출 허용에 관한 결의안 (안보리 결의 666호) 채택 　　　9.16 이라크군대의 쿠웨이트 내 외교공관 침범 행위 규탄 결의안(안보리 결의 667호) 채택 　　　9.24 결의안 661호 이행 관련 조치 안보리 의장 앞 보고 위임 결의안(669호) 채택 　　　9.25 대이라크 경제 제재 조치의 항공편 운송 적용 결의안(안보리 결의 670호) 채택 　　　10.11 유엔사무총장, 한국의 결의 661호 이행 상황 관련 질문서 송부(10.8자) 　　　10.29 이라크 국가책임 및 배상청구 관련 결의안 (안보리 결의 674호) 채택 　　　11.1　안보리 결의 661호 이항 관련 한국 답변서 제출 　　　11.29 대이라크 무력 사용 승인 결의안(안보리 결의 678호) 채택				

0001

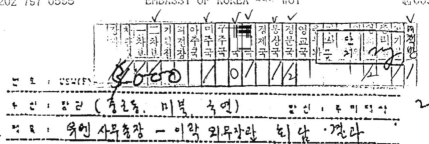

The New York Times
U.N. CHIEF SAYS HIS TALKS FAILED
AND LOOKS TO U.S.-SOVIET EFFOR

IRAQIS UNYIELDING

Pérez de Cuéllar, Calling Situation Explosive, Urges Fast Action

By JOHN F. BURNS
Special to The New York Times

AMMAN, Jordan, Sept. 2 — The United Nations Secretary General, Javier Pérez de Cuéllar, said today that two days of talks here with the Iraqi Foreign Minister had failed to produce any concessions from Baghdad on its occupation of Kuwait or on the policy of holding an estimated 10,000 Westerners as hostages.

After his seeming failure here, Mr. Pérez de Cuéllar said that hopes for a peaceful settlement should be directed to the meeting in Helsinki next Sunday between President Bush and the Soviet President, Mikhail S. Gorbachev.

"I am being very honest," Mr. Pérez de Cuéllar said at a news conference here. "I am not playing diplomacy with you. I have been disappointed."

Situation Called Explosive

The meetings with the Iraqi Foreign Minister, Tariq Aziz, on Friday and Saturday were the only direct talks with the Iraqi leadership since the earliest days of the monthlong crisis, when Iraq stormed out of an Arab summit meeting in Cairo.

Mr. Pérez de Cuéllar, in what aides described as a despondent mood, called the situation in the region explosive.

He questioned Mr. Aziz's suggestion before leaving for Baghdad on Saturday night that the crisis would yield to patience and "quiet diplomacy." The Secretary General said the Iraqi's comments reflected a failure to recognize the urgency of the situation.

"You cannot say 'quiet diplomacy,' and then spend months and years dealing with the problem," he said. "The situation is extremely serious. We cannot wait indefinitely for the crisis to be solved step by step."

[In Paris, Mr. Pérez de Cuéllar told French television that Iraq had agreed to consider dropping its decision to close embassies in Kuwait. "The Iraqi Foreign Minister told me he would see what he could do regarding the embassies, show some flexibility, not expel the diplomats, let them play their role," he said.]

Speaking at the Basman Palace here, one of a complex of hilltop residences

Continued on Page 4, Column 1.

Continued From Page 1

built for the family of King Hussein of Jordan, Mr. Pérez de Cuéllar said that his six and a half hours of talks with Mr. Aziz had failed to produce "a clear-cut determination to withdraw from Kuwait."

He added, "As far as I am concerned, I haven't heard any indication of what is the final decision of the Iraqi Government on the question of their presence in Kuwait."

The Secretary General said the talks had been similarly unavailing on the issue of the hostages. Several hundred Western men are believed to have been rounded up for use as human shields at military and strategic installations in Iraq and Kuwait.

When he invited Mr. Aziz to meet him here, Mr. Pérez de Cuéllar said that his purpose was to persuade Iraq to bow to Security Council resolutions, unanimously approved, that demanded Baghdad's immediate and uncondi-

'I am not playing diplomacy with you. I have been disappointed.'

tional withdrawal from Kuwait and the release of all foreigners who have been refused permission to leave Iraq.

Iraq's Position 'Unyielding'

Iraq's position "on the humanitarian aspects of the problem" had been unyielding, Mr. Pérez de Cuéllar said, apart from the announced decision last week to release all women and children.

He said one concession made by Mr. Aziz was the pledge, repeated by the Iraqi official to reporters outside the talks, that Iraq would, as Mr. Pérez de Cuéllar put it, "never be the first now to initiate military operations." When he spoke to reporters on Friday, Mr. Aziz coupled the pledge with a proposal that all male hostages would be released if the United States gave "guarantees" that it would not attack Iraq.

Mr. Pérez de Cuéllar's remark that "now there is some hope with the meeting that will take place between President Bush and President Gorbachev" left unclear what he expected Mr. Bush and Mr. Gorbachev to accomplish in the face of Iraq's seeming intransigence. Diplomats here said the Secretary General may have been signaling

In Amman, diplomatic efforts failed to gain ground.

The New York Times

Iraq's suggestion of 'quiet diplomacy' is questioned.

that he felt his own influence, for now, was insufficient to promote a settlement and that the Helsinki meeting might make a difference by convincing the Iraqi leadership of the common resolve of the two superpowers.

The diplomats said there had been suggestions in Mr. Aziz's remarks here that Baghdad was hoping that the Kremlin, after supporting Security Council resolutions against Iraq, might be shifting to a more neutral stance. The diplomats said Mr. Aziz during his talks with Mr. Pérez de Cuéllar had noted statements by senior Soviet officials late last week that challenged the American military deployments in the region and suggested that they might be intended as a permanent foothold there.

'A Certain Disappointment'

The seeming failure of Mr. Pérez de Cuéllar's mission appeared to have been deeply discouraging to the Secretary General, whose eight-year tenure in his post has been highlighted by successful mediation in the Iran-Iraq war and in persuading the Soviet Union to withdraw its troops from Afghanistan. He told reporters at his news conference that what occurred here was "not a rebuff," since Mr. Aziz had said before leaving here that he was prepared to continue contacts with the United Nations chief. But otherwise he made no effort to disguise his feelings.

"As I leave Amman, I must acknowledge a certain disappointment because I had hoped for more in my discussions with Foreign Minister Tariq Aziz," he said in a prepared statement read to reporters. Saying that he would be briefing the Security Council on the talks in New York, the Secretary General said, "I would have liked to inform the Council that real progress had been made during the discussions here in Amman, but in all honesty I cannot do so at present."

While blaming Baghdad for the lack of progress in the talks, Mr. Pérez de Cuéllar appeared to go part of the way toward identifying himself with one of Baghdad's charges, that there has been a "double standard" in the United States' willingness to deploy military force to drive Iraq out of Kuwait while failing to use its power to force Israel into acceptance of United Nations resolutions calling for withdrawal from occupied Arab lands. While averring that "a sin doesn't justify another sin," the United Nations chief said he understood Arab frustrations.

"I totally agree, as I have said before, that all resolutions of the Security Council should be implemented," he told an Arab reporter who pressed the issue.

At another point, Mr. Pérez de Cuéllar appeared to suggest that the Kuwait crisis was in part an outgrowth of Arab frustrations over Israel. Saying that he, too, hoped for a "complete solution of Middle East problems" that would avoid similar crises in the future, he added, "I hope that what is happening now will open the eyes of those who are against attacking frontally this problem of Palestine."

4000-2

(END) (END)

0003

외 무 부

종 별 :

번 호 : UNW-1723 　　　　　　　　　　일 시 : 90 0906 1700

수 신 : 장관 (국연,중근동,정이,기정)

발 신 : 주유엔대사

제 목 : 이락사태

　1. 대 이락 경제제재조치 관련 안보리 결의 (661)의이행을 촉구하는 유엔사무총장의 8.8.자 서한에대한 답신으로 북한의 김영남 외교부장이 동사무총장에게 보낸 9.1.자전문이 9.5.자 안보리문서(S/21704) 로 배포됨.

　2. 동 전문은 북한과 이락의 국가관계가 오래전부터 동결되었음을 상기시킨다고 언급함. 동 FULL TEXT 는 별첨 과 같음. 끝

　(대사현홍주-국장)

　첨부: FAX (UNW(F)-0157)

국기국 　　중아국 　　정문국 　　안기부 　　미주국 통상국 대책반 1정보 2차보

PAGE 1 　　　　　　　　　　　　　　　　　　90.09.07 　08:35 CT

UNW(F)-0157   0090061700   총 2매   **S**

UNITED NATIONS

Security Council

(국연. 중간동. 전여. 가정)

Distr.
GENERAL

S/21704
5 September 1990

ORIGINAL: ENGLISH

NOTE BY THE SECRETARY-GENERAL

The attached telegram dated 1 September 1990 from the Vice Premier and Minister for Foreign Affairs of the Democratic People's Republic of Korea has been addressed to the Secretary-General.

2-1

90-21466 1764g (E)

/...

S/21704
English
Page 2

<u>Annex</u>

<u>Telegram dated 1 September 1990 from the Vice Premier and
Minister for Foreign Affairs of the Democratic People's
Republic of Korea addressed to the Secretary-General</u>

I acknowledge the receipt of your letter dated 8 August 1990. Referring to your letter I would like to remind you of the fact that the State relations between the Democratic People's Republic of Korea and Iraq have long been frozen.

The Democratic People's Republic of Korea Government is following with deep concern the tense situation created in the Gulf area and is opposed to use of armed forces in settlement of disputes in any case. In this context we oppose not only the aggression of Kuwait by Iraq but also the military intervention of external forces in the Gulf area which might cause a new armed conflict and we hold that the regional situation should be settled peacefully at an earliest possible date.

I avail myself of this opportunity to express my expectation that Your Excellency as United Nations Secretary-General will continue to strive for peaceful solution of the dispute in the Gulf area.

Kim Yong Nam
Vice-Premier and Minister of
Foreign Affairs
Democratic People's Republic of Korea

2-2

0006

원 본

외 무 부

종 별 :

번 호 : UNW-1744　　　　　　　　　　　　일 시 : 90 0907 1930

수 신 : 장관(국연,통일,중근동,기정)

발 신 : 주 유엔 대사

제 목 : 이락사태관련 안보리 동향

　　금 9.7. 권종락참사관은 유엔사무국 CHAN 안보리 담당관과 면담하는 기회에이락사태 관련 최근 안보리 동향을 문의한바 동인언급사항 아래보고함.

　　1. 안보리 5 개상임 이사국간 이락의 쿠웨이트내 외국공관 폐쇄령과 관련한결의안 초안이 이미 합의되었으며, 이들은 미.소간 헬싱키 회담결과를 기다리고 있는상태임.

　　2. 미국은상기와 별도로 이락크의 쿠웨이트내 비인도적 행위(인큐베이터등 쿠웨이트내 중요 의료시설과 의료장비의 반출등) 를 규탄하는 내용의 결의안을 추진코자하나, 안보리내 분위기는 안보리 의장 성명채택쪽으로 기울려지고 있다함. 동 성명도 미.소 정상회담이후 채택될 것으로 전망됨.

　　3. 안보리의 제재위원회는 9.10 경 회합, 요르단에 대한 경제적 보전(661 결의 이행에 따른 경제적 어려움을 해소해 주기위한 보전) 관련 결의안 채택을 검토할 예정임.동 결의안이 제재위원회에서 채택되면 안보리 회의가 내주중 속개될수 있음.

　　4. 안보리 661 호 결의안이 규정한 대이락 경재제재 조치가 이락내 "준설공사, (DREDGING SERVICES)," 컨턴턴시(CONSULTANCY)" 도 금지하는지 여부에 대하여 최근 화란은 안보리 제재위에 유권해석을 요청한바 있음. 안보리 제재위는 이를 유엔법률국에 문의한바 법률국은 별첨과같은 법률의견을 제재위 의장에게 제출하였음. 동문서는 배포치 않는 내부문서이므로 귀하의 참고로만 하기 바람.

　　5. 유엔법률국의 법률의견서(FAX)끝

　　(대사 현홍주-국장)

　　첨부:UNW(F)-159

　　예고:90.12.31. 일반

일반문서로 재분류(90.12.31)

국기국	장관	차관	1차보	2차보	중아국	통상국	정와대	안기부

UNITED NATIONS ☮ NATIONS UNIES

(국연, 통일, 중근동, 기정)

POSTAL ADDRESS—ADRESSE POSTALE· UNITED NATIONS, N.Y. 10017

CABLE ADDRESS—ADRESSE TELEGRAPHIQUE· UNATIONS NEWYORK

REFERENCE:

27 August 1990

Dear Madam Chairman,

I wish to refer to your letter dated 20 August 1990 addressed to Mr. Fleischhauer requesting, on behalf of the Security Council Committee established by resolution 661(1990), the advice of the Legal Counsel on the matter contained in the letter dated 16 August 1990 addressed to you by the Permanent Representative of the Netherlands to the United Nations (S/AC.25/1990/COMM.1).

In his letter, the Permanent Representative of the Netherlands raised the following question:

"In absence of any reference to "services" in operative paragraphs 1 to 6 of resolution 661(1990), I would be grateful for the opinion of the Committee as to whether services procured by contractors in Iraq and Kuwait including consultancy and dredging services- are covered by resolution 661 and thus, in the view of the Security Council Committee, should be affected by the measures to be applied according to this resolution."

In subsequent communications between the Permanent Representative and yourself as well as between the Permanent Representative and this Office, the question was clarified to mean "services rendered by foreign contractors in Iraq and Kuwait". It is this question, therefore, which is addressed in the present letter.

Ms. Marjatta Rasi
Chairman
Security Council Committee established
 by resolution 661(1990) concerning the
 situation between Iraq and Kuwait

5 - 1

0008

- 2 -

In international economics and in international economic law
there exists no established definition of the term "services";
the definition of services is an important item in the current
Uruguay Round of multilateral trade negotiations. The issue of
services is also under consideration in the context of the work
of various organs of the United Nations, such as the United
Nations Conference on Trade and Development and the United
Nations Commission on Transnational Corporations. The common
element in the wide variety of definitions in the literature is
the intangible and invisible nature of services and the fact that
they determine a change in the condition of the beneficiary.[1]

The provisions of resolution 661(1990) which relate
specifically to the question raised by the Permanent
Representative of the Netherlands are paragraphs 3(b) and (c), 4
and 5, which provide as follows:

"[The Security Council...
    3.   **Decides** that all States shall prevent...]
    (b) Any activities by their nationals or in their
territories which would promote or are calculated to
promote the export or trans-shipment of any commodities
or products from Iraq or Kuwait; and any dealings by
their nationals or their flag vessels or in their
territories in any commodities or products originating
in Iraq or Kuwait and exported therefrom after the date
of the present resolution, including in particular any
transfer of funds to Iraq or Kuwait for the purposes of
such activities or dealings;

    (c) The sale or supply by their nationals or from
their territories or using their flag vessels of any
commodities or products, including weapons or any other
military equipment, whether or not originating in their
territories but not including supplies intended
strictly for medical purposes, and, in humanitarian
circumstances, foodstuffs, to any person or body in
Iraq or Kuwait or to any person or body for the
purposes of any business carried on in or operated from
Iraq or Kuwait, and any activities by their nationals
or their territories which promote or are calculated to
promote such sale or supply of such commodities or
products;

    4.   **Decides** that all States shall not make
available to the Government of Iraq or to any
commercial, industrial or public utility undertaking in
Iraq or Kuwait, any funds or any other financial or

5-2

0009

- 3 -

economic resources and shall prevent their nationals
and any persons within their territories from removing
from their territories ⁻or otherwise making available
to that Government or to any such undertaking any such
funds or resources and from remitting any other funds
to persons or bodies within Iraq or Kuwait, except
payments exclusively for strictly medical or
humanitarian purposes and, in humanitarian
circumstances, foodstuffs;

    5.   Calls upon all States, including States non-
members of the United Nations, to act strictly in
accordance with the provisions of the present
resolution notwithstanding any contract entered into or
licence granted before the date of the present
resolution;"

The terms used in paragraphs 3 and 4 of resolution 661(1990)
have a broad scope and are obviously intended to cover a wide
variety of economic activities and dealings. Reference may be
made in particular to the following phrases: "Any activities by
their nationals...which would promote or are calculated to
promote the export or trans-shipment of any commodities and
products from Iraq or Kuwait"; "any dealings by their nationals
or their flag vessels...in any commodities or products
originating in Iraq or Kuwait"; "any activities by their
nationals...which promote or are calculated to promote such sale
or supply of such commodities or products"; and "not make
available...any funds or any other financial or economic
resources". Thus, although the term "services" is not expressly
used in resolution 661(1990), the ordinary meaning of such terms
as "activities", "dealings" and "make available...resources"
would certainly encompass a range of economic activities broad
enough to include services instrumental in promoting the import
and the export of goods and the transfer of funds or other
financial or economic resources.

    Furthermore, in considering whether services are affected by
the measures to be applied pursuant to resolution 661(1990), it
is important to take into account the purpose and object of the
resolution which is to prevent exports and imports of commodities
and products from and to Iraq or Kuwait, and the direct or
indirect availability of financial and economic resources to the
Government of Iraq. Taking into account the broad scope of the
terms of the resolution and its purpose and object, the Office of
Legal Affairs is of the view that services rendered by foreign
contractors in Iraq or Kuwait which would result in activities,

5-3

0010

- 4 -

dealings or transfer of funds or other financial or economic
resources proscribed under resolution 661(1990) are prohibited.

It should, however, be noted that not all services rendered
by foreign contractors in Iraq or Kuwait are prohibited under
resolution 661(1990), but only those services which promote or
are calculated to promote the import from or the export to Iraq
and Kuwait of products and commodities and which make available
funds or other financial or economic resources. Whether specific
services fall into this category must be determined on a case-by-
case basis, having particular regard to the use which can be made
of the output of the service.

In his letter of 16 August 1990 (S/AC.25/1990/Comm. 1), the
Permanent Representative of the Netherlands specifically refers
to dredging and consultancy services. Dredging services would,
by their very nature, appear prima facie to fall within the
purview of resolution 661(1990). However, in the absence of more
detailed information on the specific nature of the dredging
services being carried out, the Office of Legal Affairs is unable
to go beyond this general statement at the present time. As far
as other services such as consultancy are concerned, those which
result in activities, dealings or transfer of funds or any other
financial or economic resources proscribed under paragraphs 3 and
4 of resolution 661(1990) would be affected.

In addition to paragraphs 3 and 4 of the resolution,
paragraph 5 is particularly relevant to the question under
consideration since this calls upon all States "...to act
strictly in accordance with the provisions of the present
resolution notwithstanding any contract entered into or licence
granted before the date of the present resolution".

Finally, Madam Chairman, I would note that the general
approach to the question of services expressed above appears to
be confirmed by a number of communications received from Member
States in reply to the Secretary-General's note SPC/7/90(1) dated
8 August 1990. In describing the measures adopted in compliance
with resolution 661(1990), a number of States either explicitly
refer to "services" or implicitly include economic activities
which clearly constitute economic services and which they have
prohibited in regard to Iraq and Kuwait. For example, the note
verbale dated 15 August 1990 from the Permanent Representative of
Japan (S/21535) states, inter alia, that Japan has undertaken
"measures prohibiting...services in Iraq and Kuwait..." and has
"...issued administrative guidelines requesting entities under
its jurisdiction to refrain from engaging in export and service
transactions with Iraq and Kuwait". In a note verbale dated 14
August 1990 (S/21518), the Permanent Representative of Sweden
communicated the text of an ordinance issued on 7 August 1990,

5 - 4

- 5 -

which prohibits, <u>inter alia</u>: "The...processing, assembly, installation, maintenance or repair of commodities or provision of technical assistance for such measures". In a note verbale dated 16 August 1990 (S/21543), the Permanent Representative of Luxembourg informed the Secretary-General that Luxembourg had prohibited, among others, "any provision of services for the benefit of residents of Iraq or Kuwait".

I trust that you will find the advice set out in this letter to be helpful to the work of the Committee.

Yours sincerely,

Ralph Zacklin
Director and Deputy
to the Under-Secretary-General
in charge of the Office of Legal Affairs

1. See United Nations Conference on Trade and Development, <u>Trade and Development Report, 1988</u>, especially Part Two on "Services in the World Economy", United Nations, New York, 1988; ibid., <u>Trade in Services: Sectoral Issues</u>, United Nations, New York, 1989; United Nations Centre on Transnational Corporations, <u>Transnational Corporations, Services and the Uruguay Round</u>, ST/CTC/103, United Nations, New York, 1990; T.P. Hill, 'On Goods and Services', <u>Review of Income and Wealth</u>, 23 (1977), p.318.

5 - 5

0012

이라크, 쿠웨이트 사태 일보 〈55〉
(9.13. 16:00)

중동아프리카국
근동과

1. 상   황

〈이 라 크〉

o 부쉬 미 대통령 의회 연설 논평 (9.12. 이라크 관영통신)
- 부쉬 대통령이 악마에 사로잡혀 있음
- 부쉬 대통령은 이라크가 위협, 협박에 결코 굴하지 않을것임을
  알아야 함

o 이라크군, 쿠웨이트내 게릴라 및 외국인 색출 노력 강화
- 게릴라 지도자, 이라크군 2,000명 살상 주장 (외부 관측통, 사상자
  숫자가 다분히 과장된 것으로 평가)

o 쿠웨이트 주재 이집트 대사관 철수 (일자 미상)

〈미   국〉

o 미 하원, 일본의 아시아지역 미군주둔 비용 전액 부담 축구 결의
  압도적으로 채택
- 일본이 걸프사태 관련 비용 분담에 소극적인데 대한 보복

o 부쉬 대통령, 이라크 TV 방영용 메시지(8분) 녹화 (9.12)
- 이라크측에서 5일내 방영 안할 경우 동 메시지를 전세계에 공개 예정

o 사우디, 쿠웨이트등 지원 예정 120억불은 미국 전비 60억불, 이집트,
  터키등 인근국 지원 60억불로 나누어 사용 예정
  (9.11. Baker 국무장관 기자회견)
- 90년말 까지의 미국 전비 대부분 보전 가능

0013

〈유　엔〉

○ 유엔 안보리 토의, 인도적 견지에서의 대이라크 식량, 의약품 공급
　문제를 놓고 교착상태
　　- 서방측은 외국인 및 아동에 대해서만 식량 공급 허용 주장
　　- 반면, 예멘.쿠바는 모든 민간인을 대상으로 하자는 주장
　　- 유엔 사무총장, 유엔이 이라크, 쿠웨이트내 식량사정을 파악할
　　　능력이 없다고 언급 (대이라크 제재 위원회 보고)
　　- 주 유엔 이라크 대사, 국제기구의 이라크내 식량 배급 활동 허용
　　　가능성 부인

〈이　란〉

○ Khamenei 최고 지도자, 걸프주둔 미군에 대한 성전 촉구 (9.12)
　　- 테헤란 외교 소식통, 베이커 미국무장관의 사태 해결 이후에도
　　　미군 주둔 가능성 언급이 이란 태도 변화의 계기가 되었다고 분석

○ Rafsanjani 대통령, 이란에 대피한 쿠웨이트인들 환대 호소 (9.12. Teheran Radio)

○ 이란, 대이라크 식량 의약품 공급 검토(9.12. Teheran Times)

〈기　타〉

○ '가지야마' 일본 신임 법무장관, 비전투요원 해외 파견이 가능토록 헌법
　개정 검토 예정임을 언급 (9.13)

○ '전기침' 중국 외무장관, 걸프사태 중재 용의 시사 (9.12)

○ 파키스탄, 자국민 구호를 위한 식량 의약품 암만으로 공수, 외교화물로
　바그다드 수송 예정임을 발표 (9.12)

○ 소련, 스리랑카 난민 본국 귀환용 항공기 2대 지원

2. 교민 철수 현황 (9.13. 08:00 현재)

○ 이라크 : 총 교민 722명중 457명 철수, 265명 잔류

※ 9.11. 이라크 현대건설 근로자 80명 및 남광 근로자 1명, 요르단 향발
　(도착 보고 미정)

첨　부 : 각국의 이라크.쿠웨이트 교민 철수 현황

0014

각국의 이라크·쿠웨이트 교민 철수 현황

(90.9.12. AP 추계)

90.9.13
홍보용화

국 별	당초인원	철수인원	잔류인원
(서 방)			
미 국	3,500	1,700	1,800
서 독	1,000	290	710
영 국	4,000	1,800	2,200
불 란 서	미 상	수십명	430
일 본	수백명	미 상	216
카 나 다	800	500	300
화 란	180	50	130
놀 웨 이	46	11	35
폴 투 갈	53	9	44
스 페 인	150	120	30
스 웨 덴	165	162	103
스 위 스	168	118	70
터 키	4,000	3,775	225
유 고	7,000	6,000	1,000
오 지 리	140	136	4
벨 기 에	59	13	46
덴 마 크	100	24	76
핀 랜 드	42	20	22
희 랍	121	21	100
이 태 리	540	180	360
소 계	약23,000	약15,000	7,901
(기 타)			
파 키 스 탄	130,000	30,000	100,000
필 리 핀	93,000	6,000	87,000
스 리 랑 카	150,000	50,000	100,000
방 글 라 데 시	110,000	80,000	30,000
인 도	190,000	90,000	100,000
		(65,000은 난민캠프 체류중)	
레 바 논	60,000	5,000	55,000
이 집 트	1,400,000	236,000	1,164,000
* 한 국	1,327	1,049	278
계	약2,200,000	약600,000	1,644,179

0015

외 무 부

관리번호 90-2096

종 별 :

번 호 : UNW-1837

일 시 : 90 0914 1800

수 신 : 장관(국연,중근동,통일,기정)

발 신 : 주 유엔 대사

제 목 : 안보리(이락사태)

1. 9. 13. 밤 안보리가 속개되어 인도적 목적의 대이락 식품수출허용에 관한 기본지침을 규정한 결의안 666 호를 <u>찬 13, 반 2 (큐바, 예멘)</u> 로 가결함. 동 결의안은 미, 소, 영, 불및 카나다가 공동제안하였음.

2. 동결의안 요지

0. 이락및 쿠웨이트내 인도적 목적의 식량공급 허용문제는 안보리만이 결정할수 있음.

0. 유엔사무총장이 이락및 쿠웨이트내 식품의 가용(AVAILABILITY) 상태에 관한 정보를 제재위에 정기적으로 보고토록 요청함.

0. 유엔사무총장의 보고에 기초하여 제재위가 이락, 쿠웨이트에 인도적 목적상 식품을 긴급히 공급할 필요성이 발생하였다고 인정할경우 안보리에 동대처 방안을 보고토록함.

0. 동 식품 공급시 이들 식품이 의도된 수혜자에게 도달하도록 보장하기 위해 국제적십자사 또는 유관 인도적 기관과 협력하여 유엔을 통하여 제공되고 배급되어야함.

0. 엄격히 의료목적의 공급품은 결의 661 호의 적용대상이 아니나 동 공급도 공급국 또는 적절한 인도적 기관의 엄격한 감독하에 제공되어야 함을 권고

3. 큐바는 기본식품의 공급과 적절한 의료지원은 어떠한 상황에서도 보호되어야 할 기본적 인권이라고 규정한 요지의 결의안을 제출하였으나 표결에 회부되지 못하였음. 끝

(대사 현홍주-국장)

첨부:결의안 666 호전문(FAX): UNW(F)-168

예고:90.12.31. 일반

일반문서로 재분류(90.12.31)

국기국	차관	1차보	중아국	통상국	청와대	안기부	대책반
미주국	2차보						

90.09.15   07:41

외신 2과 통제관 FE

0016

ㅂㅗ(주)-168 00914 1800

(국연, 중근동, 통킬, 기정)

총2매

연 S

UNITED NATIONS

Security Council (B-5)

Distr.
GENERAL

S/RES/666 (1990)
13 September 1990

안보리결의 666호

90. 9. 13.

RESOLUTION 666 (1990)

Adopted by the Security Council at its 2939th meeting
on 13 September 1990

The Security Council,

Recalling its resolution 661 (1990), paragraphs 3 (c) and 4 of which apply, except in humanitarian circumstances, to foodstuffs,

Recognizing that circumstances may arise in which it will be necessary for foodstuffs to be supplied to the civilian population in Iraq or Kuwait in order to relieve human suffering,

Noting that in this respect the Committee established under paragraph 6 of that resolution has received communications from several Member States,

Emphasizing that it is for the Security Council, alone or acting through the Committee, to determine whether humanitarian circumstances have arisen,

Deeply concerned that Iraq has failed to comply with its obligations under Security Council resolution 664 (1990) in respect of the safety and well-being of third State nationals, and reaffirming that Iraq retains full responsibility in this regard under international humanitarian law including, where applicable, the Fourth Geneva Convention,

Acting under Chapter VII of the Charter of the United Nations,

1. Decides that in order to make the necessary determination whether or not for the purposes of paragraph 3 (c) and paragraph 4 of resolution 661 (1990) humanitarian circumstances have arisen, the Committee shall keep the situation regarding foodstuffs in Iraq and Kuwait under constant review;

2. Expects Iraq to comply with its obligations under Security Council resolution 664 (1990) in respect of third State nationals and reaffirms that Iraq remains fully responsible for their safety and well-being in accordance with international humanitarian law including, where applicable, the Fourth Geneva Convention;

90-22562 2423Z (E)

2 -1

S/RES/666 (1990)
Page 2

    3.   <u>Requests</u>, for the purposes of paragraphs 1 and 2 of this resolution, that the Secretary-General seek urgently, and on a continuing basis, information from relevant United Nations and other appropriate humanitarian agencies and all other sources on the availability of food in Iraq and Kuwait, such information to be communicated by the Secretary-General to the Committee regularly;

    4.   <u>Requests further</u> that in seeking and supplying such information particular attention will be paid to such categories of persons who might suffer specially, such as children under 15 years of age, expectant mothers, maternity cases, the sick and the elderly;

    5.   <u>Decides</u> that if the Committee, after receiving the reports from the Secretary-General, determines that circumstances have arisen in which there is an urgent humanitarian need to supply foodstuffs to Iraq or Kuwait in order to relieve human suffering, it will report promptly to the Council its decision as to how such need should be met;

    6.   <u>Directs</u> the Committee that in formulating its decisions it should bear in mind that foodstuffs should be provided through the United Nations in co-operation with the International Committee of the Red Cross or other appropriate humanitarian agencies and distributed by them or under their supervision in order to ensure that they reach the intended beneficiaries;

    7.   <u>Requests</u> the Secretary-General to use his good offices to facilitate the delivery and distribution of foodstuffs to Kuwait and Iraq in accordance with the provisions of this and other relevant resolutions;

    8.   <u>Recalls</u> that resolution 661 (1990) does not apply to supplies intended strictly for medical purposes, but in this connection recommends that medical supplies should be exported under the strict supervision of the Government of the exporting State or by appropriate humanitarian agencies.

-----

2 - 2

0018

외　무　부

종　별 :

번　호 : UNW-1861　　　　　　　　　　　일　시 : 90 0917 1800

수　신 : 장 관(국연,중근동,통일,기정)

발　신 : 주 유엔 대사

제　목 : 이락사태(안보리)

　　1.9.16 안보리가 속개되어 이락군대의 쿠웨이트내 일부 외교공관 침범행위를 규탄하는 결의안 (667호)을 만장일치로 채택함

　　2.동건 토의를 위한 안보리는 프랑스, 이태리, 화란등 18개국의 요청에 따라 소집되었음.

　　3.동결의안 전문은 아래와같음.

　　첨부:결의안 텍스트 (FAX)((UNW(F)-169))

　　끝

　　(대사 현홍주-국장)

국기국　　2차보　　중아국　　통상국　　안기부

외신 1과 통제관

0019

UNITED
NATIONS

Security Council

Distr.
GENERAL

S/21774
16 September
ENGLISH
ORIGINAL: FR

**Canada, Côte d'Ivoire, Finland, France, United Kingdom of Great
Britain and Northern Ireland and Zaire: draft resolution**

The Security Council,

Reaffirming its resolutions 660 (1990), 661 (1990), 662 (1990), 664 (1990
665 (1990) and 666 (1990),

Recalling the Vienna Conventions of 18 April 1961 on diplomatic relations
of 24 April 1963 on consular relations, to both of which Iraq is a party,

Considering that the decision of Iraq to order the closure of diplomatic
consular missions in Kuwait and to withdraw the immunity and privileges of the
missions and their personnel is contrary to the decisions of the Security Coun
the international Conventions mentioned above and international law,

Deeply concerned that Iraq, notwithstanding the decisions of the Security
Council and the provisions of the Conventions mentioned above, has committed a
of violence against diplomatic missions and their personnel in Kuwait,

Outraged at recent violations by Iraq of diplomatic premises in Kuwait an
the abduction of personnel enjoying diplomatic immunity and foreign nationals
were present in these premises,

Considering that the above actions by Iraq constitute aggressive acts and
flagrant violation of its international obligations which strike at the root o
conduct of international relations in accordance with the Charter of the Unite
Nations,

Recalling that Iraq is fully responsible for any use of violence against
foreign nationals or against any diplomatic or consular mission in Kuwait or i
personnel,

Determined to ensure respect for its decisions and for Article 25 of the
Charter of the United Nations,

90-22795 2428Z (E)

S/21774
English
Page 2

Further considering that the grave nature of Iraq's actions, which const
a new escalation of its violations of international law, obliges the Council
only to express its immediate reaction but also to consult urgently to take f
concrete measures to ensure Iraq's compliance with the Council's resolutions,

Acting under Chapter VII of the Charter of the United Nations,

1.   Strongly condemns aggressive acts perpetrated by Iraq against diplc
premises and personnel in Kuwait, including the abduction of foreign national
were present in those premises;

2.   Demands the immediate release of those foreign nationals as well as
nationals mentioned in resolution 664 (1990);

3.   Further demands that Iraq immediately and fully comply with its
international obligations under resolutions 660 (1990), 662 (1990) and 664 (1
of the Security Council, the Vienna Conventions on diplomatic and consular
relations and international law;

4.   Further demands that Iraq immediately protect the safety and well-b
of diplomatic and consular personnel and premises in Kuwait and in Iraq and t
action to hinder the diplomatic and consular missions in the performance of t
functions, including access to their nationals and the protection of their pe
and interests;

5.   Reminds all States that they are obliged to observe strictly resolu
661 (1990), 662 (1990), 664 (1990), 665 (1990) and 666 (1990);

6.   Decides to consult urgently to take further concrete measures as sc
possible, under Chapter VII of the Charter, in response to Iraq's continued
violation of the Charter, of resolutions of the Council and of international

-----

2-2

외 무 부

종 별 :

번 호 : UNW-2023   일 시 : 90 0925 1800

수 신 : 장관(국연,중근동,통일,기정)

발 신 : 주유엔대사

제 목 : 안보리(이락사태)

    9.24. 안보리가 속개되어 안보리내 제재위로 하여금 결의안 661호 이행으로 인하여 경제적 곤궁을 받고있는 국가들의 헌장 50조상의 지원요청을 검토하여 필요한 조치를 안보리의장에게 보고토록 위임하는 결의안 669호 를 만장일치로 채택함.끝

    첨부:동결의안(FAX):UNW(F)-194

    (대사 현홍주-국장대리)

국기국   1차보   2차보   중아국   통상국   안기부

PAGE 1   90.09.26   07:57 BX

0022

UNN(FR) -194 00925 1900
(국연, 천동, 통일, 기정)   최대 **S**

UNITED NATIONS

Security Council

Distr.
GENERAL

S/RES/669 (1990)
24 September 1990

RESOLUTION 669 (1990)

Adopted by the Security Council at its 2942nd meeting,
on 24 September 1990

The Security Council,

Recalling its resolution 661 (1990) of 6 August 1990, ~~~ ~~~~ ~~ ~ ~~~~~ ~~~~,

Recalling also Article 50 of the Charter of the United Nations,

Conscious of the fact that an increasing number of requests for assistance have been received under the provisions of Article 50 of the Charter of the United Nations,

Entrusts the Committee established under resolution 661 (1990) concerning the situation between Iraq and Kuwait with the task of examining requests for assistance under the provisions of Article 50 of the Charter of the United Nations and making recommendations to the President of the Security Council for appropriate action.

90-23771 2444Z (E)

| — |

0023

외 무 부

```
종  별 :
번  호 : UNW-2028                              일  시 : 90 0925 2100
수  신 : 장 관대리(국연,중근동,통일,기정)
발  신 : 주 유엔 대사
제  목 : 안보리(이락사태)
```

1. 금 9.25. 저녁 안보리가 속개되어 결의 661에 의한 대이락 경제제재 조치가 항공편에 의한 운송에도 적용됨을 규정한 결의 670 호를 찬 14, 반 1(큐바) 로 채택함.

2. 동일 안보리는 쉐바르드나제 소련외무장관의 주재로 13개국 외무장관 참석하에 개최 (코트디브와르, 큐바는 주유엔대사가 참석)되었는바, 동 외무장관 수준 안보리가 개최된것은 유엔창설이후 3번째임.

3. 동 결의안 요지

0 모든 국가들은 661호 결의를 위반한 화물을 적재하지 않았음을 검색하기 위해 특정비행장에 착륙하는 경우를 제외하고는 이락.쿠웨이트에 착륙할 목적의 어떠한 항공기에 대해서도 자국 영공봉과 허가를 거부할것.

0. 자국등록 항공기가 661 호를 준수토록 모든국가들은 필요한 조치를 취할것.

0. 모든 국가는 661호를 위반한 이락선적 선박이 자국 항구에 입항시 억류할것.

4. 동 결의안 전문은 별전(FAX) 과 같음.끝

첨부:상기문서(FAX):UNW(F)-196

(대사 현홍주-국장대리)

```
국기국     1차보     2차보     중아국     통상국     정문국     안기부
```

TW(F)-196 00925 2/00

(국연, 중근동.통일, 기정)

총3매

UNITED NATIONS

SECURITY

COUNCIL

PROVISIONAL*

S/21816
25 September 1990

ORIGINAL: ENGLISH

~~Canada, Côte d'Ivoire~~, Finland, France, Romania, Union of Soviet
Ireland, United States of America and Zaire: draft resolution

The Security Council,

Reaffirming its resolutions 660 (1990), 661 (1990), 662 (1990), 664 (1990),
665 (1990), 666 (1990), and 667 (1990),

Condemning Iraq's continued occupation of Kuwait, its failure to rescind its
actions and end its purported annexation and its holding of third State nationals
against their will, in flagrant violation of resolutions 660 (1990), 662 (1990),
664 (1990) and 667 (1990) and of international humanitarian law;

Condemning further the treatment by Iraqi forces of Kuwaiti nationals,
including measures to force them to leave their own country and mistreatment of
persons and property in Kuwait in violation of international law,

Noting with grave concern the persistent attempts to evade the measures laid
down in resolution 661 (1990);

Further noting that a number of States have limited the number of Iraqi
diplomatic and consular officials in their countries and that others are planning
to do so,

Determined to ensure by all necessary means the strict and complete
application of the measures laid down in resolution 661 (1990),

Determined to ensure respect for its decisions and the provisions of
Articles 25 and 48 of the Charter of the United Nations,

Affirming that any acts of the Government of Iraq which are contrary to the
above-mentioned resolutions or to Articles 25 or 48 of the Charter of the United
Nations, such as Decree No. 377 of the Revolution Command Council of Iraq of
16 September 1990, are null and void.

Reaffirming its determination to ensure compliance with Security Council
resolutions by maximum use of political and diplomatic means,

1851E

/....

3 — 1

0025

S/21816
English
Page 2

    Welcoming the Secretary-General's use of his good offices to advance a peaceful solution based on the relevant Security Council resolutions and noting with appreciation his continuing efforts to this end,

    Underlining to the Government of Iraq that its continued failure to comply with the terms of resolutions 660 (1990), 661 (1990); 662 (1990), 664 (1990), 666 (1990) and 667 (1990) could lead to further serious action by the Council under the Charter of the United Nations, including under Chapter VII;

    Recalling the provisions of Article 103 of the Charter of the United Nations,

    Acting under Chapter VII of the Charter of the United Nations, .

    1.   Calls upon all States to carry out their obligations to ensure strict and complete compliance with resolution 661 (1990) and in particular paragraphs 3, 4 and 5 thereof;

    2.   Confirms that resolution 661 (1990) applies to all means of transport, including aircraft;

    3.   Decides that all States, notwithstanding the existence of any rights or obligations conferred or imposed by any international agreement or any contract entered into or any licence or permit granted before the date of the present resolution, shall deny permission to any aircraft to take off from their territory if the aircraft would carry any cargo to or from Iraq or Kuwait other than food in humanitarian circumstances, subject to authorization by the Council or the Committee established by resolution 661 (1990) and in accordance with resolution 666 (1990), or supplies intended strictly for medical purposes or solely for UNIIMOG;

    4.   Decides further that all States shall deny permission to any aircraft destined to land in Iraq or Kuwait, whatever its State of registration, to overfly its territory unless:

    (a) The aircraft lands at an airfield designated by that State outside Iraq or Kuwait in order to permit its inspection to ensure that there is no cargo on board in violation of resolution 661 (1990) or the present resolution, and for this purpose the aircraft may be detained for as long as necessary; or

    (b) The particular flight has been approved by the Committee established by resolution 661 (1990); or

    (c) ...., ... for the purposes

/...

3-2

0026

5.   Decides that each State shall take all necessary measures to ensure that any aircraft registered in its territory or operated by an operator who has his principal place of business or permanent residence in its territory complies with the provisions of resolution 661 (1990) and the present resolution;

6.   Decides further that all States shall notify in a timely fashion the Committee established by resolution 661 (1990) of any flight between its territory and Iraq or Kuwait to which the requirement to land in paragraph 4 above does not apply, and the purpose for such a flight;

7.   Calls upon all States to co-operate in taking such measures as may be necessary, consistent with international law, including the Chicago Convention, to ensure the effective implementation of the provisions of resolution 661 (1990) or the present resolution;

8.   Calls upon all States to detain any ships of Iraqi registry which enter their ports and which are being or have been used in violation of resolution 661 (1990), or to deny such ships entrance to their ports except in circumstances recognized under international law as necessary to safeguard human life;

9.   Reminds all States of their obligations under resolution 661 (1990) with regard to the freezing of Iraqi assets, and the protection of the assets of the legitimate Government of Kuwait and its agencies, located within their territory and to report to the Committee established under resolution 661 (1990) regarding those assets;

10.   Calls upon all States to provide to the Committee established by resolution 661 (1990) information regarding the action taken by them to implement the provisions laid down in the present resolution;

11.   Affirms that the United Nations Organization, the specialized agencies and other international organizations in the United Nations system are required to take such measures as may be necessary to give effect to the terms of resolution 661 (1990) and this resolution;

12.   Decides to consider, in the event of evasion of the provisions of resolution 661 (1990) or of the present resolution by a State or its nationals or through its territory, measures directed at the State in question to prevent such evasion;

13.   Reaffirms that the Fourth Geneva Convention applies to Kuwait and that as a High Contracting Party to the Convention Iraq is bound to comply fully with all its terms and in particular is liable under the Convention in respect of the grave breaches committed by it, as are individuals who commit or order the commission of grave breaches.

3-3

0027

WUCA5819 MCX4515
SS CABKS
.NEWYORK (UNNY) 0612 GMT 09/26/90
ETATPRIORITE
HIS EXCELLENCY
THE MINISTER FOR FOREIGN AFFAIRS
OF THE REPUBLIC OF KOREA
MINISTRY OF FOREIGN AFFAIRS
SEOUL (REPUBLIC OF KOREA)
BT
45322-09
    I HAVE THE HONOUR TO TRANSMIT HEREWITH THE TEXT OF RESOLUTION
670 (1990) ADOPTED BY THE SECURITY COUNCIL AT ITS 2943RD MEETING
ON 25 SEPTEMBER 1990. -QUOTE-
    ''THE SECURITY COUNCIL,
    REAFFIRMING ITS RESOLUTIONS 660 (1990), 661 (1990), 662 (1990),
664 (1990), 665 (1990), 666 (1990), AND 667 (1990),
    CONDEMNING IRAQ'S CONTINUED OCCUPATION OF KUWAIT, ITS FAILURE TO
RESCIND ITS ACTIONS AND END ITS PURPORTED ANNEXATION AND ITS HOLDING
OF THIRD STATE NATIONALS AGAINST THEIR WILL, IN FLAGRANT VIOLATION
OF RESOLUTIONS 660 (1990), 662 (1990), 664 (1990) AND 667 (1990)
AND OF INTERNATIONAL HUMANITARIAN LAW,
    CONDEMNING FURTHER THE TREATMENT BY IRAQI FORCES OF KUWAITI
NATIONALS, INCLUDING MEASURES TO FORCE THEM TO LEAVE THEIR OWN
COUNTRY AND MISTREATMENT OF PERSONS AND PROPERTY IN KUWAIT IN
VIOLATION OF INTERNATIONAL LAW,
    NOTING WITH GRAVE CONCERN THE PERSISTENT ATTEMPTS TO EVADE THE
MEASURES LAID DOWN IN RESOLUTION 661 (1990),
    FURTHER NOTING THAT A NUMBER OF STATES HAVE LIMITED THE NUMBER
OF IRAQI DIPLOMATIC AND CONSULAR OFFICIALS IN THEIR COUNTRIES AND
THAT OTHERS ARE PLANNING TO DO SO,
    DETERMINED TO ENSURE BY ALL NECESSARY MEANS THE STRICT AND
COMPLETE APPLICATION OF THE MEASURES LAID DOWN IN RESOLUTION 661
(1990),

0028

DETERMINED TO ENSURE RESPECT FOR ITS DECISIONS AND THE PROVISIONS
OF ARTICLES 25 AND 48 OF THE CHARTER OF THE UNITED NATIONS,

AFFIRMING THAT ANY ACTS OF THE GOVERNMENT OF IRAQ WHICH ARE
CONTRARY TO THE ABOVE-MENTIONED RESOLUTIONS OR TO ARTICLES 25 OR
48 OF THE CHARTER OF THE UNITED NATIONS, SUCH AS DECREE NO. 377 OF
THE REVOLUTION COMMAND COUNCIL OF IRAQ OF 16 SEPTEMBER 1990, ARE
NULL AND VOID,

REAFFIRMING ITS DETERMINATION TO ENSURE COMPLIANCE WITH SECURITY
COUNCIL RESOLUTIONS BY MAXIMUM USE OF POLITICAL AND DIPLOMATIC MEANS,

WELCOMING THE SECRETARY-GENERAL'S USE OF HIS GOOD OFFICES TO
ADVANCE A PEACEFUL SOLUTION BASED ON THE RELEVANT SECURITY COUNCIL
RESOLUTIONS AND NOTING WITH APPECIATION HIS CONTINUING EFFORTS TO
THIS END,

UNDERLINING TO THE GOVERNMENT OF IRAQ THAT ITS CONTINUED FAILURE
TO COMPLY WITH THE TERMS OF RESOLUTIONS 660 (1990), 661 (1990), 662
(1990), 664 (1990), 666 (1990) AND 667 (1990) COULD LEAD TO FURTHER
SERIOUS ACTION BY THE COUNCIL UNDER THE CHARTER OF THE UNITED.
NATIONS, INCLUDING UNDER CHAPTER VII,

RECALLING THE PROVISIONS OF ARTICLE 103 OF THE CHARTER OF THE
UNITED NATIONS,

ACTING UNDER CHAPTER VII OF THE CHARTER OF THE UNITED NATIONS,

1.   CALLS UPON ALL STATES TO CARRY OUT THEIR OBLIGATIONS TO
ENSURE STRICT AND COMPLETE COMPLIANCE WITH RESOLUTION 661 (1990)
AND IN PARTICULAR PARAGRAPHS 3, 4 AND 5 THEREOF,

2.   CONFIRMS THAT RESOLUTION 661 (1990) APPLIES TO ALL MEANS
OF TRANSPORT, INCLUDING AIRCRAFT,

3.   DECIDES THAT ALL STATES, NOTWITHSTANDING THE EXISTENCE OF
ANY RIGHTS OR OBLIGATIONS CONFERRED OR IMPOSED BY ANY INTERNATIONAL
AGREEMENT OR ANY CONTRACT ENTERED INTO OR ANY LICENCE OR PERMIT
GRANTED BEFORE THE DATE OF THE PRESENT RESOLUTION, SHALL DENY
PERMISSION TO ANY AIRCRAFT TO TAKE OFF FROM THEIR TERRITORY IF THE

0029

OUTSIDE IRAQ OR KUWAIT IN ORDER TO PERMIT ITS INSPECTION TO ENSURE
THAT THERE IS NO CA[...] ON BOARD IN VIOLATION OF RESOLUTION 661
(1990) OR THE PRESENT RESOLUTION, AND FOR THIS PURPOSE THE AIRCRAFT
MAY BE DETAINED FOR AS LONG AS NECESSARY, OR

(B) THE PARTICULAR FLIGHT HAS BEEN APPROVED BY THE COMMITTEE
ESTABLISHED BY RESOLUTION 661 (1990), OR

(C) THE FLIGHT IS CERTIFIED BY THE UNITED NATIONS AS SOLELY FOR
THE PURPOSES OF UNIIMOG,

5. DECIDES THAT EACH STATE SHALL TAKE ALL NECESSARY MEASURES TO
ENSURE THAT ANY AIRCRAFT REGISTERED IN ITS TERRITORY OR OPERATED BY
AN OPERATOR WHO HAS HIS PRINCIPAL PLACE OF BUSINESS OR PERMANENT
RESIDENCE IN ITS TERRITORY COMPLIES WITH THE PROVISIONS OF
RESOLUTION 661 (1990) AND THE PRESENT RESOLUTION,

6. DECIDES FURTHER THAT ALL STATES SHALL NOTIFY IN A TIMELY
FASHION THE COMMITTEE ESTABLISHED BY RESOLUTION 661 (1990) OF ANY
FLIGHT BETWEEN ITS TERRITORY AND IRAQ OR KUWAIT TO WHICH THE
REQUIREMENT TO LAND IN PARAGRAPH 4 ABOVE DOES NOT APPLY, AND THE
PURPOSE FOR SUCH A FLIGHT,

7. CALLS UPON ALL STATES TO CO-OPERATE IN TAKING SUCH MEASURES
AS MAY BE NECESSARY, CONSISTENT WITH INTERNATIONAL LAW, INCLUDING
THE CHICAGO CONVENTION, TO ENSURE THE EFFECTIVE IMPLEMENTATION OF
THE PROVISIONS OF RESOLUTION 661 (1990) OR THE PRESENT RESOLUTION,

8. CALLS UPON ALL STATES TO DETAIN ANY SHIPS OF IRAQI REGISTRY
WHICH ENTER THEIR PORTS AND WHICH ARE BEING OR HAVE BEEN USED IN
VIOLATION OF RESOLUTION 661 (1990), OR TO DENY SUCH SHIPS ENTRANCE
TO THEIR PORTS EXCEPT IN CIRCUMSTANCES RECOGNIZED UNDER
INTERNATIONAL LAW AS NECESSARY TO SAFEGUARD HUMAN LIFE,

9. REMINDS ALL STATES OF THEIR OBLIGATIONS UNDER RESOLUTION
661 (1990) WITH REGARD TO THE FREEZING OF IRAQI ASSETS, AND THE
PROTECTION OF THE ASSETS OF THE LEGITIMATE GOVERNMENT OF KUWAIT
AND ITS AGENCIES, LOCATED WITHIN THEIR TERRITORY AND TO REPORT TO
THE COMMITTEE ESTABLISHED UNDER RESOLUTION 661 (1990) REGARDING
THOSE ASSETS,

10. CALLS UPON ALL STATES TO PROVIDE TO THE COMMITTEE
ESTABLISHED BY RESOLUTION 661 (1990) INFORMATION REGARDING THE
ACTION TAKEN BY THEM TO IMPLEMENT THE PROVISIONS LAID DOWN IN THE
PRESENT RESOLUTION,

0030

AGENCIES AND OTHER INTERNATIONAL ORGANIZATIONS IN THE UNITED NATIONS
SYSTEM ARE REQUIRED   TAKE SUCH MEASURES AS MA━━E NECESSARY TO
GIVE EFFECT TO THE TERMS OF RESOLUTION 661(1990) AND THIS RESOLUTION,

12.   DECIDES TO CONSIDER, IN THE EVENT OF EVASION OF THE PROVISIONS
OF RESOLUTION 661 (1990) OR OF THE PRESENT RESOLUTION BY A STATE OR
ITS NATIONALS OR THROUGH ITS TERRITORY, MEASURES DIRECTED AT THE
STATE IN QUESTION TO PREVENT SUCH EVASION,

13.   REAFFIRMS THAT THE FOURTH GENEVA CONVENTION APPLIES TO KUWAIT
AND THAT AS A HIGH CONTRACTING PARTY TO THE CONVENTION IRAQ IS BOUND
TO COMPLY FULLY WITH ALL ITS TERMS AND IN PARTICULAR IS LIABLE UNDER
THE CONVENTION IN RESPECT OF THE GRAVE BREACHES COMMITTED BY IT, AS
ARE INDIVIDUALS WHO COMMIT OR ORDER THE COMMISSION OF GRAVE
BREACHES.'' -UNQUOTE-

HIGHEST CONSIDERATION.

JAVIER PEREZ DE CUELLAR
SECRETARY-GENERAL

COL 45322-09
GBS NAV M9614

0031

외 무 부

종 별 :

번 호 : UNW-2152   일 시 : 90 1003 1730

수 신 : 장관대리(국연,중근동,아동,기정,해기)

발 신 : 주 유엔대사

제 목 : 안보리 5개 상임이사국 공동성명

　　1. 9.28 안보리 5개 상임이사국 외무장관과유엔사무총장간 면담후 이들 5개국 외상이 공동발표한 성명문을 별첨(FAX)보고함.(10.2.자 안보리문서로 배포됨.)

　　2. 동 성명은 유엔및 유엔사무총장의 역할을평가하고 국제평화와 안전에 대한 도전에안보리가 신속히 대응할수 있는 능력을 제고하는것이 중요함을 강조하고 있음.

　　첨부:동 성명(FAX):UNW(F)-222

　　끝

　　(대사 현홍주-국장)

국기국	차관	1차보	아주국	중아국	정와대	안기부	공보처

PAGE 1   90.10.04   10:15 DF

외신 1과 통제관

0032

UNITED NATIONS

Security Council

Distr.
GENERAL

S/21835
2 October 1990
ENGLISH
ORIGINAL: FRENCH

LETTER DATED 1 OCTOBER 1990 FROM THE PERMANENT REPRESENTATIVES
OF CHINA, FRANCE, THE UNION OF SOVIET SOCIALIST REPUBLICS, THE
UNITED KINGDOM OF GREAT BRITAIN AND NORTHERN IRELAND AND THE
UNITED STATES OF AMERICA TO THE UNITED NATIONS ADDRESSED TO
THE SECRETARY-GENERAL

We have the honour to transmit to you herewith the statement issued following the meeting which you had on 28 September 1990 with our respective Ministers for Foreign Affairs. We should be grateful if you would have the text of this statement circulated as a document of the Security Council.

(Signed) Pierre-Louis BLANC
Permanent Representative of France
to the United Nations

(Signed) LI Daoyu
Permanent Representative of China
to the United Nations

(Signed) Thomas R. PICKERING
Permanent Representative of the
United States of America to the
United Nations

(Signed) Yuli M. VORONTSOV
Permanent Representative of the
Union of Soviet Socialist Republics
to the United Nations

(Signed) David HANNAY
Permanent Representative of
the United Kingdom of Great
Britain and Northern Ireland
to the United Nations

90-24629 1993j (E)

/...

3-1

Annex

[Original: Chinese, English,
French and Russian]

Statement issued by the Ministers for Foreign Affairs of the
five permanent members of the Security Council following a
meeting with the Secretary-General of the United Nations on
28 September 1990

On 28 September 1990, the Ministers for Foreign Affairs of the five permanent members of the Security Council were the guests at a luncheon given by the Secretary-General of the United Nations, H.E. Mr. Javier Perez de Cuellar. Taking part were the Minister of Foreign Affairs of the People's Republic of China H.E. Mr. Qian Qichen; the Minister of State, Minister of Foreign Affairs of France H.E. Mr. Roland Dumas; the Minister of Foreign Affairs of the Union of Soviet Socialist Republics H.E. Mr. Eduard A. Shevardnadze; the Secretary of State for Foreign and Commonwealth Affairs of the United Kingdom of Great Britain and Northern Ireland H.E. Mr. Douglas Hurd; and the Secretary of State of the United States of America H.E. Mr. James A. Baker III.

The Ministers welcomed the considerable successes achieved by the United Nations over the past year, in particular in Namibia, and the progress made towards settlement of conflicts in Central America, Western Sahara and Afghanistan. They agreed that the United Nations faced important new opportunities and challenges. They stressed the crucial contribution which the United Nations could make in this new era of intensified co-operation and interaction among States.

They paid particular attention to the most serious crisis the international community is facing now, caused by Iraq's invasion of Kuwait.

The Ministers affirmed that this aggressive action must not be tolerated. They condemned the continuing occupation of the State of Kuwait and the increasing persecution of its citizens.

They welcomed, in this regard, the firm and decisive role played by the United Nations and the good offices of the Secretary-General. They reaffirmed their support for the relevant resolutions adopted by the Security Council since the Iraqi invasion of Kuwait and re-emphasized their commitment to seek together, in full compliance with them, a peaceful solution of the crisis.

They demanded that Iraq comply with the will of the international community and withdraw unconditionally and without delay from Kuwait, thus restoring Kuwait's full sovereignty under the authority of its legitimate Government, free all hostages held in Iraq and Kuwait, allow all foreign nationals wishing to leave Iraq or Kuwait to do so and respect the immunity of diplomatic personnel and the inviolability of diplomatic premises in Kuwait.

/...

3-2

0034

They called upon all States to apply strictly the relevant resolutions of the Security Council.

The Ministers expressed their deep concern at the aggravation of tensions in the Near East. They reaffirmed their determination to support an active negotiating process in which all relevant parties would participate, leading to a comprehensive, just and lasting peace. They agreed that such negotiations should be based on resolutions 242 (1967) and 338 (1973) of the Security Council and should take into account the right to security for all States in the region, including Israel, and the legitimate rights of the Palestinian people.

The Ministers also reaffirmed their strong commitment to the sovereignty, independence, unity and territorial integrity of Lebanon and renewed their support for the Taïf agreement as the basis for the resolution of the Lebanese crisis.

Finally, the Ministers welcomed the agreement by the Cambodian parties to form the Supreme National Council as well as their acceptance in its entirety of the framework for a comprehensive settlement of the Cambodia conflict worked out by the five permanent members and the endorsement of that framework by the Security Council. They called on all Cambodians to intensify their efforts to achieve national reconciliation and reiterated, as stated in the framework document, that should Prince Norodom Sihanouk be elected by the Supreme National Council as its President, the five would welcome that decision.

They expressed the view that the Paris International Conference on Cambodia should be reconvened at the earliest possible date to elaborate and adopt a comprehensive political settlement, which will include an important role for the United Nations.

The Ministers stressed the importance of a further development of the ability of the Security Council to respond quickly to challenges to international peace and security. They reaffirmed their determination to continue to work together and with the other members of the Security Council as well as in co-operation with the Secretary-General for the prevention and resolution of international conflicts.

They noted the importance of the meeting of the Security Council at the level of Foreign Ministers on 25 September 1990 and expressed their readiness to participate in such meetings should the need arise.

They expressed again their deep appreciation to the Secretary-General for his untiring efforts with regard to the cause of international peace and security. They thanked him for the invitation to the meeting, which they viewed as a very useful and positive one, and agreed to continue their consultations.

-----

3 - 3

외 무 부

종 별 :

번 호 : UNW-2238   일 시 : 90 1011 1900

수 신 : 장 관 (통일,국연,중근동,기정)

발 신 : 주 유엔 대사

제 목 : 이락사태 관련 유엔 사무총장 서한

  1. 유엔사무총장은 10.8.자 당관앞 구상서에서 대이락 경제제재조치 관련
유엔안보리 결의 661 의 이행상황에 관한 안보리내 제재위원회의 질문서를 송부해
오면서 90.10.31.까지 회신해 줄것을 요청해 왔음.

  2. 동 질문서는 아국이 취한 조치의 법률적 근거, 동 조치 이행부서, 위반자에
대한 강제집행조치등이 포함되어있음. 동 사무총장 서한 및 질문서는 별전(FAX)
송부함.

   첨부: 상기 서한 및 질문서(FAX): UNW(F)-246 끝

   (대사 현홍주-국장)

통상국   1차보   중아국   국기국   정문국   안기부   미주국   대책반   그과반

PAGE 1   90.10.12 · 08:08 FC

P 의 별첨　　UNW(H)-246　이에 1900　　총 3 때 P.1

(통일, 국안, 농건동, 기타)

UNITED NATIONS NATIONS UNIES

POSTAL ADDRESS—ADRESSE POSTALE UNITED NATIONS, N.Y. 10017
CABLE ADDRESS—ADRESSE TELEGRAPHIQUE UNATIONS NEWYORK

REFERENCE: SCPC/7/90(3)

The Secretary-General of the United Nations presents his compliments to the Permanent Observer of the Republic of Korea to the United Nations and, in accordance with the decisions of the Security Council Committee established by resolution 661 (1990) concerning the situation between Iraq and Kuwait, made at its 12th and 14th meetings on 21 and 24 September 1990, has the honour to transmit herewith for the attention of His/Her Excellency's Government the text of the questionnaire which the Committee has decided to address to all States.

In accordance with the decisions of the Committee, the Secretary-General further has the honour to request His/Her Excellency's Government to forward its reply by 31 October 1990.

8 October 1990

S. B.

Annex enclosed

3 —1

0037

SECURITY COUNCIL COMMITTEE ESTABLISHED
BY RESOLUTION 661 (1990) CONCERNING
THE SITUATION BETWEEN IRAQ AND KUWAIT

THE IMPLEMENTATION OF RESOLUTION 661 (1990); A QUESTIONNAIRE CONCERNING NATIONAL MEASURES

Resolution 661 (1990) imposes upon States the obligation to take measures to ensure its full implementation. Much information has already been received pursuant to the request made by the Secretary-General on 8 August 1990 and as reported by him on 15 and 24 August and 6 September 1990 (S/21536 and Corr.1, S/21641 and S/21715). However, the Committee established by resolution 661 (1990) decided that further information was necessary so as to achieve a full picture of the national implementation of resolution 661 (1990). Information is requested from States on the following items to the full extent that they apply to them.

1.   Legislative framework

   a)   What is the legislative basis on which your country has undertaken measures to implement Security Council resolution 661 (1990)?

   b)   Has there been any specific legislation enacted pursuant to Security Council resolution 661 (1990)?

   c)   What types of administrative orders, decrees etc., has your country passed pursuant to the relevant laws?

   Note: Copies of the relevant legislation would be highly appreciated.

2.   Control of Imports or activities which would promote or are calculated to promote imports or transhipment of goods from Iraq and Kuwait

   a)   Which authorities in your country are responsible for implementing the control of imports or activities as required by Security Council resolution 661 (1990)?

   b)   What specific measures has your country established to prevent breaches of Security Council resolution 661 (1990) by imports of items or activities covered by it?

3 - 2

0038

-2-

3.   Control of Exports or activities which would promote or are
      calculated to promote sales or supply of products and
      commodities to Iraq and Kuwait

      a)   Which authorities in your country are responsible for
            implementing the control of exports or activities as
            required by Security Council resolution 661 (1990)?

      b)   What specific measures has your country established to
            prevent breaches of Security Council resolution 661 (1990)
            by exports of items or activities covered by it?

4.   Control of Financial or Economic Resources

      a)   What system of control exists in your country to prevent
            transfers of financial or economic resources covered by
            Security Council resolution 661 (1990)?

      b)   What specific measures has your country taken so as to
            prevent unauthorized movements of funds in contravention
            of Security Council resolution 661 (1990?

5.   Enforcement

      What types of enforcement (penalties, seizures, forfeitures,
      etc.) does your country apply so as to prevent breaches of
      Security Council resolution 661 (1990) by individuals and
      companies in your country?

6.   Other

      a)   What problems has your country confronted in ensuring
            full national implementation of Security Council
            resolution 661 (1990)?

      b)   What legislative or other measures has your country taken
            so as to implement Security Council resolution 661 (1990)
            with regard to contracts entered into or licenses granted
            before the date of the resolution?

      c)   What specific measures has your country taken to protect
            the assets of the legitimate Government of Kuwait and its
            agencies in accordance with paragraph 9 (a) of Security
            Council resolution 661 (1990)?

3-3

0039

기안용지

분류기호 문서번호	통일 2065- 각각	(전화 : 720-2331)	시 행 상 특별취급	
보존기간	영구 : 준영구 10. 5. 3. 1.	장	관	
수 신 처 보존기간				
시행일자	1990. 10. 15			

보조 기관	국 장	전결	협 조 기 관		문서통제 검 열 1990.10.17 담 지 관
	심의관				
	과 장				발 송 인
기안책임자		안 총 기			반송증 1990. 10. 17 외무부

경수 참	유 신 조	수신처 참조	발신명의	

제 목	대이라크 경제제재

1. 유엔 사무총장은 최근 주유엔대사앞 구상서를 통해 아국의 유엔

    안보리 결의 661호(대이라크 경제제재) 이행상황에 관한 별첨

    질의서를 송부하여 왔읍니다.

2. 정부는 지난 8.9 국무총리주재 관계장관 회의에서 UN 안보리 결의를

    존중, 대이라크 경제제재를 결정하고 교역금지 조치등을 실시중인

    바, 이와 관련 별첨 질의서중 귀부(청)소관사항에 대한 회답(국·영문)을

    작성, 90.10.25한 당부로 회보하여 주시기 바랍니다.

1991. 12. 31 .에 예고문에
의거 일반문서로 재분류됨

0040

첨부 : 1. 유엔 사무총장의 주유엔대사앞 구상서

2. 유엔 안보리 대이라크 제재위원회 질의서

3. 상기 질문서 요지. 끝.

예고 : 90.12.31 일반

수신처 : 재무부장관, 국방부장관, 상공부장관, 동력자원부장관,

건설부장관, 교통부장관, 해운항만청장

회행복 3,의 정책관라 정립경 → 보안. 관계국으로이첩

건설부 해외건설과 (fax) 503-7408, 500-2919
Tel. 503-7416. 김영수사무관

동지북. — 상공부와 긴요 백각에서 사식시

상공부 수송1과 이경건 사무관. 8-2374

재무부 종재금융과 ─ ☎ 530☎ 김안영氏 전시기과
추식
8-5383/4
외환2정과
윤액환사무관. ☎☎.

(WooTex
: Woo Young Textile Co.
14-1ρ 신영상사동 남영동 서울시)

0041

UNITED NATIONS NATIONS UNIES

POSTAL ADDRESS—ADRESSE POSTALE UNITED NATIONS, N.Y. 10017
CABLE ADDRESS—ADRESSE TELEGRAPHIQUE UNATIONS NEWYORK

REFERENCE: SCPC/7/90(3)

The Secretary-General of the United Nations presents his
compliments to the Permanent Observer of the Republic of Korea to the
United Nations and, in accordance with the decisions of the Security
Council Committee established by resolution 661 (1990) concerning the
situation between Iraq and Kuwait, made at its 12th and 14th meetings
on 21 and 24 September 1990, has the honour to transmit herewith for
the attention of His/Her Excellency's Government the text of the
questionnaire which the Committee has decided to address to all States.

In accordance with the decisions of the Committee, the
Secretary-General further has the honour to request
His/Her Excellency's Government to forward its reply by
31 October 1990.

8 October 1990

S. B.

Annex enclosed

3 — 1

0042

SECURITY COUNCIL COMMITTEE ESTABLISHED
BY RESOLUTION 661 (1990) CONCERNING
THE SITUATION BETWEEN IRAQ AND KUWAIT

THE IMPLEMENTATION OF RESOLUTION 661 (1990);
A QUESTIONNAIRE CONCERNING NATIONAL MEASURES

Resolution 661 (1990) imposes upon States the obligation to take measures to ensure its full implementation. Much information has already been received pursuant to the request made by the Secretary-General on 8 August 1990 and as reported by him on 15 and 24 August and 6 September 1990 (S/21536 and Corr.1, S/21641 and S/21715). However, the Committee established by resolution 661 (1990) decided that further information was necessary so as to achieve a full picture of the national implementation of resolution 661 (1990). Information is requested from States on the following items to the full extent that they apply to them.

1.   **Legislative framework**

    a)   What is the legislative basis on which your country has undertaken measures to implement Security Council resolution 661 (1990)?

    b)   Has there been any specific legislation enacted pursuant to Security Council resolution 661 (1990)?

    c)   What types of administrative orders, decrees etc., has your country passed pursuant to the relevant laws?

    Note: Copies of the relevant legislation would be highly appreciated.

2.   **Control of Imports or activities which would promote or are calculated to promote imports or transhipment of goods from Iraq and Kuwait**

    a)   Which authorities in your country are responsible for implementing the control of imports or activities as required by Security Council resolution 661 (1990)?

    b)   What specific measures has your country established to prevent breaches of Security Council resolution 661 (1990) by imports of items or activities covered by it?

3 - 2

0043

-2-

3. **Control of Exports or activities which would promote or are calculated to promote sales or supply of products and commodities to Iraq and Kuwait**

   a) Which authorities in your country are responsible for implementing the control of exports or activities as required by Security Council resolution 661 (1990)?

   b) What specific measures has your country established to prevent breaches of Security Council resolution 661 (1990) by exports of items or activities covered by it?

4. **Control of Financial or Economic Resources**

   a) What system of control exists in your country to prevent transfers of financial or economic resources covered by Security Council resolution 661 (1990)?

   b) What specific measures has your country taken so as to prevent unauthorized movements of funds in contravention of Security Council resolution 661 (1990?

5. **Enforcement**

   What types of enforcement (penalties, seizures, forfeitures, etc.) does your country apply so as to prevent breaches of Security Council resolution 661 (1990) by individuals and companies in your country?

6. **Other**

   a) What problems has your country confronted in ensuring full national implementation of Security Council resolution 661 (1990)?

   b) What legislative or other measures has your country taken so as to implement Security Council resolution 661 (1990) with regard to contracts entered into or licenses granted before the date of the resolution?

   c) What specific measures has your country taken to protect the assets of the legitimate Government of Kuwait and its agencies in accordance with paragraph 9 (a) of Security Council resolution 661 (1990)?

3-3

0044

외 무 부

UN

종 별 :

번 호 : UNW-2279   일 시 : 90 1016 1800

수 신 : 장 관 (국연,중근동,기정)

발 신 : 주 유엔 대사

제 목 : 이락사태 관련 안보리결의안 추진보도

　　1. 금 10.16 자 NYT 보도에 따르면 이락사태와 관련 영국은 이락의 쿠웨이트 침공으로 인하여 각국에 발생한 손실을 이락이 보상토록 요구하는 결의안을 준비중에 있으며, 이러한 내용의 새로운 결의안이 금주내 채택될 가능성이 있는 것으로 보도하였음.

　　2. 한편 미국은 동결의안 채택시 제3세계 국가들이 이스라엘에 대하여도 유사한요구를 제기할 우려가 있으므로 영국에 대하여 상기 결의안의 내용을 완화토록 촉구하고 있다함.끝

　　　(대사 현홍주-국장)

국기국　　1차보　　미주국　　중아국　　정문국　　안기부

90.10.17   08:16 FC

외신 1과 통제관

0045

외 무 부

종 별 :

번 호 : UNW-2307 일 시 : 90 1019 1200

수 신 : 장관(국연,중근동,기정)

발 신 : 주유엔대사

제 목 : 안보리 동향(이락사태)

1.10.19 현재 파악된바에 의하면 안보리 5개 상임이사국들은 이락사태와 관련한새로 운결의안 내용에 대하여 비공식협의, 대체로 합의한 것으로 알려짐.

미국정부는 동 결 의안을안보리에 공식 제기하는 문제를 현재검토중이라함.

2.동 내용은

1)각국 정부로 하여금 이락의 쿠웨이트점령 및 이락군대에 의한 인권침해로 인하여발생한 자국민의 대이락 배상청구 명세를작성, 제출토록 요청,

2)쿠웨이트에 잔류하고 있는4개국 대사관에 대한 식품공급, 급수등을 허용하도록이락정부에 촉구,

3)유엔 안보리의 각종결의의 테두리내에서 이락사태에 대한 외교적해결방안 강구노력을 계속토록유엔사무총장에게 촉구하는 내용임.

3.베이커 국무장관은 10.18 미 하원 외교분과위청문회에서 이락사태 관련 무력사용을 허용하는안보리 결의안 채택문제에 관하여 관련국과비공식 협의를 개시하였음을 밝히고 이러한내용의 결의안 채택에 대한 지지강도에놀랐다고 언급하였음.끝

(대사 현홍주-국장)

국기국 중아국 안기부

90.10.20 02:36 CT

외신 1과 통제관

0046

외 무 부

종 별 :

번 호 : UNW-2332

일 시 : 90 1023 1930

수 신 : 장 관(국연,중근동,기정)

발 신 : 주 유엔 대사

제 목 : 안보리(이락사태)

연: UNW-2307

1. 연호 언급한 안보리 5개 상임이사국간 합의된 이락사태 관련 새로운 안보리 결의안 초안을 별전 FAX 송부함.

2. 동 초안은 특히 제8항에서 쿠웨이트 침공 및 점령으로 쿠웨이트 및 제3국, 이들의 국민및 법인에 발생한 손해 배상에 대한 이락의 국가책임을 규정하고 있으며, 제9항에서 국가들에게 이락에 대한 상기 8항 배상청구에 관한 모든 정보를 수집할것을 요청하고 있음이 주목됨.

3. 안보리가 금주중 동 결의안을 채택할 것으로 예상되고 있음.

첨부:상기초안: UNW(F)-262 끝

(대사 현홍주-국장)

국기국   1차보   중아국   정문국   안기부

PAGE 1

90.10.24   09:06   WG

외신 1과   통제관

0047

-2332 의
점부물

UN IF7-262   01023 j≡°
(국연 . 중근동 . 기정)

충5매

WORKING PAPER BROADLY ACCEPTED BY THE FIVE

The Security Council,

A. __Reaffirming__ its resolutions 660 (1990), 661
(1990), 662 (1990), 664 (1990), 665 (1990), 666 (1990), 667
(1990) and 670 (1990),

B. __Reiterating__ its demand for the immediate and
unconditional withdrawal of all Iraqi forces from Kuwait, for
the restoration of Kuwait's sovereignty, independence and
territorial integrity, and of the authority of its legitimate
government,

C. __Condemning__ the actions by Iraq in flagrant
violation of the decisions of this Council, the Charter of the
United Nations and international humanitarian law to deport
Kuwaiti nationals, to take third state nationals hostage, to
murder, mistreat and oppress kuwaiti and third
state nationals, to destroy Kuwaiti demographic records, to
settle foreigners in Kuwait, to confiscate hospital supplies
and equipment and to carry out the unlawful and wanton
destruction and seizure of public and private property in
Kuwait as part of a general policy aimed at the destruction of
a nation,

D. __Reaffirming__ the expression of grave alarm in
its resolutions 662, 664, 667 and 670 over the situation of
nationals of third states in Kuwait and Iraq, including the
personnel of the diplomatic and consular missions of such
States,

5 —1

0048

2.

E. Recalling the efforts of the Secretary-General
and his special representative concerning the safety and well

F. Condemning these flagrant violations of
international law, and reaffirming the responsibility of Iraq
in respect of grave breaches of the fourth Geneva convention,
and of individuals who commit or order the commission of such
grave breaches,

G. Mindful of the economic cost to states, and in
particular developing countries, of carrying out their
obligations under the relevant resolutions of the Council,

H. Deeply concerned at the loss and suffering
caused to individuals,

Alarmed by the perils to international peace

I. Alarmed by the perils to international peace
and security caused by the Iraqi invasion and occupation of
Kuwait and affirming the Council's continued efforts to seek,
in accordance with relevant resolutions, a peaceful solution
to the crisis in the Gulf region caused by the Iraqi invasion
and occupation of Kuwait and to the restoration of peace,
stability and security,

J. Recalling also the important role that the
United Nations and its Secretary-general have played in the
peaceful solution of disputes and conflicts in conformity with
the United Nations Charter,

5 — 2

3.

K. **Acting** under chapter VII of the United Nations
Charter :

1. **Demands** that Iraq immediately cease and desist
from deporting Kuwaiti nationals, taking third state nationals
hostage, murdering, mistreating and oppressing Kuwaiti and
third state nationals, destroying Kuwaiti demographic records,
settling foreigners in Kuwait, confiscating hospital supplies
and equipment and carrying out unlawful and wanton destruction
and seizure of public and private property in Kuwait,

2. **Invites** States to collate information from any
source of grave breaches of the Geneva Conventions and other
relevant international obligations and to make this available
to the Council,

3. **Reaffirms** its demand that Iraq immediately
fulfill its international obligations to third state nationals
in Kuwait and Iraq, including the personnel of diplomatic and
consular missions, under the Charter, the Fourth Geneva
Convention, the Vienna Conventions on diplomatic and consular
relations, general principles of international law and the
relevant resolutions of the Council,

4. **Reaffirms** further its demand that Iraq permit
and facilitate the immediate departure from Kuwait and Iraq of
as many third state nationals, including diplomatic and
consular personnel, as wish to leave,

5. **Demands** that Iraq ensure the immediate
provision of food, water and basic services necessary to the
protection and well being of nationals of third states,
including the personnel of the diplomatic and consular
missions of such states,

5-3

0050

.4.

6. **Reaffirms** its demand that Iraq immediately
protect the safety and security of diplomatic and consular
personnel and premises in Kuwait and Iraq, rescind its order
for the closure of diplomatic and consular missions in Kuwait
and cease its violations of the immunity of their personnel,
and take no action to hinder the performance of the functions
of such missions in Kuwait and Iraq, including access to their
nationals and the protection of their person and interests,

7. **Requests** the Secretary-general and his special
representative to use their good offices to achieve the
objectives of the three previous paragraphs and in particular
the provision of food, water and basic services to the
diplomatic and consular missions in Kuwait and the evacuation
of third state nationals,

8. **Affirms** the liability of Iraq to make full
restitution or compensation for any loss, damage or injury
arising in regard to Kuwait and third states, and their
nationals and corporations, as a result of the illegal
invasion and occupation of Kuwait by Iraq,

9. **Invites** States to collect all relevant
information regarding their claims, and those of their
nationals and corporations, with a view to such arrangements
for the discharge by Iraq of its liability to make restitution
or compensation as may be established,

0051

10. _Encourages_ the Secretary-General to continue to make his good offices available for reaching a peaceful solution to the crisis in the Gulf region on the basis of resolutions 660 (1990), 662 (1990) and 664 (1990) and reestablishing peace, security and stability, and calls on all States to pursue their efforts to this end,

11. _Requests_ the Secretary-general to continue to report to the Security Council on the results of his efforts,

12. _Decides_ that, should Iraq not comply with the provisions of the present resolution and its previous resolutions, the Council will take further enforcement measures under the Charter,

13. _Decides_ to remain actively and permanently seized of the matter until the aggression has been suppressed and peace restored.

5-5

油價등락따라 各國 喜悲

걸프「高油價」…유엔報告書

3세계·東歐 2백億弗 부담
세계경제 침체가속…貧國 "富나누자" 요구도
英·蘇등 産油國 앉아서 橫財

외 무 부

종 별 :

번 호 : UNW-2373   일 시 : 90 1029 1730

수 신 : 장 관(국연,중근동,기정)

발 신 : 주 유엔 대사

제 목 : 안보리(이락 -쿠웨이트 사태)

　　　연: UNW-2332

　　1.10.29 표제건 협의를 위한 안보리가 속개됨.금일 안보리에서 연호 요지의 결의
안초안이 (카나다.핀란드.영국.미국.자이르.프랑스.소련.루마니아공동제안) 찬 13, 반
0, 기권 2 (큐바,예멘)로결의 674 (1990)로 채택됨.

　　2.금일 주요 발언요지는 아래와같음.

　　가.이락:

　　0.안보리는 국제재판소가 아니므로 손해배상등을 규정한 권한이 없음.

　　0.안보리는 분쟁 당사국인 이락과 협의할헌장상 의무를 준수하지 않았으며, 미국은
헌장51조, 52조를 위반하여 걸프만 지역에 군대를 파병하였음.

　　나.예멘,콜롬비아:

　　0.결의 674 PART B 에 규정된 유엔사무총장 평화중재 노력을 강조, 평화적인 방법
이외에는 다른 해결방법이 없음.

　　다.이디오피아, 자이르, 핀랜드, 루마니아:

　　0.이락에 의한 안보리 제반 결의의 조속한 이행촉구

　　라.영국:

　　0.이락이 안보리 결의를 계속 이행치 않을경우 안보리는 헌장 7장상의 조치를
취하지 않을수없음.

　　마.미국:

　　0.안보리 결의의 평화적인 이행을 달성시키는것이 미국의 목적임.모든 국가는 자국
국민을 보호할 의무가 있음.

　　바.중국:

　　0.이락에의한 결의안 준수를 기초로한 평화적해결 노력이 강화되어야함.

국기국　　2차보　　중아국　　정문국　　안기부　미주국 통상각 대책반 1차보

외신 1과 통제관

0054

0.금번 결의안에 유엔 사무총장의 평화적 중재노력에 관한 PART B 가 포함된 것을 평가함.

사.큐바:

0.안보리는 손해배상과 같은 법률적 문제를 다룰 권능이 없음.금번 결의안 내용중 평화중재 노력을 언급한 PARA 12 의 미약한 용어는 PARA 7 의 용어와 대조적으로 안보리가 평화적 수단의 사용을 주저함을 나타내는 것임.

3.결의 674 의 전문은 별전(FAX) 와 같음.

첨부: UNW(F)-267: 상기 결의안

끝

(대사 현홍주-국장)

UNW-2393 의
청부목

UN-HFI-267   이02P 1730
(국연.중근동.기정)

총 3 매

UNITED NATIONS
SECURITY
COUNCIL

PROVISIONAL*

S/21911
27 October 1990

ORIGINAL: ENGLISH

Canada, Finland, United Kingdom of Great Britain and
Northern Ireland, United States of America and Zaire:
            draft resolution   *France, USSR, Romania*

The Security Council,

Recalling its resolutions 660 (1990), 661 (1990), 662 (1990), 664 (1990), 665 (1990), 666 (1990), 667 (1990) and 670 (1990)

Stressing the urgent need for the immediate and unconditional withdrawal of all Iraqi forces from Kuwait, for the restoration of Kuwait's sovereignty, independence and territorial integrity, and of the authority of its legitimate government,

Condemning the actions by the Iraqi authorities and occupying forces to take third State nationals hostage and to mistreat and oppress Kuwaiti and third State nationals, and the other actions reported to the Council such as the destruction of Kuwaiti demographic records, forced departure of Kuwaitis, and relocation of population in Kuwait and the unlawful destruction and seizure of public and private property in Kuwait including hospital supplies and equipment, in violation of the decisions of this Council, the Charter of the United Nations, the Fourth Geneva Convention, the Vienna Conventions on Diplomatic and Consular Relations and international law,

Expressing grave alarm over the situation of nationals of third States in Kuwait and Iraq, including the personnel of the diplomatic and consular missions of such States,

Reaffirming that the Fourth Geneva Convention applies to Kuwait and that as a High Contracting Party to the Convention Iraq is bound to comply fully with all its terms and in particular is liable under the Convention in respect of the grave breaches committed by it, as are individuals who commit or order the commission of grave breaches,

Recalling the efforts of the Secretary-General concerning the safety and well being of third State nationals in Iraq and Kuwait,

Deeply concerned at the economic cost, and at the loss and suffering caused to individuals in Kuwait and Iraq as a result of the invasion and occupation of Kuwait by Iraq,

Acting under Chapter VII of the United Nations Charter,

* * *

2110E   3-1   /...

0056

S/21911
English
Page 2

Reaffirming the goal of the international community of maintaining international peace and security by seeking to resolve international disputes and conflicts through peaceful means,

Recalling also the important role that the United Nations and its Secretary-General have played in the peaceful solution of disputes and conflicts in conformity with the provisions of the United Nations Charter,

Alarmed by the dangers of the present crisis caused by the Iraqi invasion and occupation of Kuwait, directly threatening international peace and security, and seeking to avoid any further worsening of the situation,

Calling upon Iraq to comply with the relevant resolutions of the Security Council, in particular resolutions 660 (1990), 662 (1990) and 664 (1990),

Reaffirming its determination to ensure compliance by Iraq with the Security ...

 ... and diplomatic means,

A

1.   Demands that the Iraqi authorities and occupying forces immediately cease and desist from taking third State nationals hostage, and mistreating and oppressing Kuwaiti and third State nationals, and from any other actions such as those reported to the Council and described above, violating the decisions of this Council, the Charter of the United Nations, the Fourth Geneva Convention, the Vienna Conventions on Diplomatic and Consular Relations and international law;

2.   Invites States to collate substantiated information in their possession or submitted to them on the grave breaches by Iraq as per paragraph 1 above and to make this information available to the Council;

3.   Reaffirms its demand that Iraq immediately fulfil its obligations to third State nationals in Kuwait and Iraq, including the personnel of diplomatic and consular missions, under the Charter, the Fourth Geneva Convention, the Vienna Conventions on Diplomatic and Consular Relations, general principles of international law and the relevant resolutions of the Council;

4.   Reaffirms further its demand that Iraq permit and facilitate the immediate departure from Kuwait and Iraq of those third State nationals, including diplomatic and consular personnel, who wish to leave;

5.   Demands that Iraq ensure the immediate access to food, water and basic services necessary to the protection and well being of Kuwaiti nationals and of nationals of third States in Kuwait and Iraq, including the personnel of diplomatic and consular missions in Kuwait;

3 — 2

0057

6.   _Reaffirms_ its demand that Iraq immediately protect the safety and well
being of diplomatic and consular personnel and premises in Kuwait and in Iraq, take
no action to hinder these diplomatic and consular missions in the performance of
their functions, including access to their nationals and the protection of their
person and interests and rescind its orders for the closure of diplomatic and
consular missions in Kuwait and the withdrawal of the immunity of their personnel;

7.   _Requests_ the Secretary-General, in the context of the continued exercise
of his good offices concerning the safety and well being of third State nationals
in Iraq and Kuwait, to seek to achieve the objectives of paragraphs 4, 5 and 6 and
in particular the provision of food, water and basic services to Kuwaiti nationals
and to the diplomatic and consular missions in Kuwait and the evacuation of third
State nationals;

8.   _Reminds_ Iraq that under international law it is liable for any loss,
damage or injury arising in regard to Kuwait and third States, and their nationals
and corporations, as a result of the invasion and illegal occupation of Kuwait by
Iraq;

9.   _Invites_ States to collect relevant information regarding their claims,
and those of their nationals and corporations, for restitution or financial
compensation by Iraq with a view to such arrangements as may be established in
accordance with international law;

10.   _Requires_ that Iraq comply with the provisions of the present resolution
and its previous resolutions, failing which the Council will need to take further
measures under the Charter;

11.   _Decides_ to remain actively and permanently seized of the matter until
Kuwait has regained its independence and peace has been restored in conformity with
the relevant resolutions of the Security Council.

B

12.   _Reposes_ its trust in the Secretary-General to make available his good
offices and, as he considers appropriate, to pursue them and undertake diplomatic
efforts in order to reach a peaceful solution to the crisis caused by the Iraqi
invasion and occupation of Kuwait on the basis of Security Council resolutions
660 (1990), 662 (1990) and 664 (1990), and calls on all States, both those in the
region and others, to pursue on this basis their efforts to this end, in conformity
with the Charter, in order to improve the situation and restore peace, security and
stability;

13.   _Requests_ the Secretary-General to report to the Security Council on the
results of his good offices and diplomatic efforts.

3-3

0058

외 무 부

종 별 :

번 호 : UNW-2382   일 시 : 90 1030 1830

수 신 : 장 관(국연,중근동,기정)

발 신 : 주 유엔 대사

제 목 : 안보리(이락-쿠웨이트 사태)

1. 10.29 안보리내 군사위원회가 개최되었는바, 5개 안보리 상임위 대표로 구성된 동위원회에는 유엔사상 가장 고위급 군사장교들이 참석하였음. 동 위원회 소집자체가 유엔에 의한 대이락 무력사용 가능성을 시사하는 것으로 이는 대이락 압력제고가 그 목적인 것으로 관측되고 있음. 소련은 최근 수년간 동 군사위의 활성화를 주장해 왔으며 동 활성화를 위한 안보리 상임 이사국간 조속한 협의를 제의해 온바 있음.

2. 동 군사위 소집관련 발표문을 별전 FAX송부함.

첨부: UNW(F)-269: 동 발표문.끝

(대사 현홍주-국장)

국기국   1차보   중아국   정문국   안기부   통상국   미주국   그각선   대책반

PAGE 1   90.10.31   09:54 WG

외신 1과 통제관

0059

＃ UNW-2382 의 별첨

UNW(F)-269 01030 187~ 총 1매
(국연、 중근동、 기정)

<u>COMMUNIQUE</u>

On October 29, informal consultations of the members of the Military Staff Committee will be held, at a senior military level at the Mission of France, the current coordinator for the Five Permanent Members of the Security Council.

The objectives of their meeting will be to exchange views and information on :

1 - the situation in the Gulf Region;

2 - activities related to the implementation of the sanctions regime set out in Security Council resolutions 661, 665, 670;

The meeting will be held within the framework of the regular informal consultations among the Ambassadorial representatives of the Five Permanent Members. This informal consultative meeting will include among its participants the most senior military officers ever present at such a meeting. The military representatives will be :
- Vice-Admiral Alain COATANEA, Director of the Joint Staff (France),
- Major General Du KUANYI, Head of Delegation to the Military Staff Committee (China),
- Lieutenant-General Michael CARNS, Director of the Joint Staff (USA),
- Colonel General Bronislav A. OMELICHEV, First Deputy Chief of the General Staff (URSS),
- and Major-General BECKETT, Head of British Defence Staff in Washington (UK).

| ― |

0060

외 무 부

종 별 :

번 호 : UNW-2383   일 시 : 90 1030 1830

수 신 : 장 관(통일,국연,중근동)

발 신 : 주 유엔 대사

제 목 : 이락사태관련 유엔사무총장 서한

    연: UNW-2238

    1. 연호 10.8. 자 유엔사무총장 서한은 90.10.31.까지 아측의 회신을 요청하고
있는바, 연호 질문서에 대한 아측의 회신을 조속송부바람.

    2.연호 유엔 사무총장의 질문서에 대한 영국의 회신내용을 참고로 별전 FAX
송부함.

    첨부: UNW(F)-270: 영국의 회신서

    끝

    (대사 현홍주-국장)

통상국   2차보   중아국   국기국   정문국   안기부   미주국 1차보 대책반

PAGE 1   90.10.31   09:58 WG

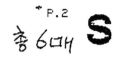

UNW(F)-270 01030 =0

(통일. 국련. 중근동)

총 6대 S

Security Council

Distr.
GENERAL

S/AC.25/1990/1
17 October 1990

ORIGINAL: ENGLISH

SECURITY COUNCIL COMMITTEE ESTABLISHED
BY RESOLUTION 661 (1990) CONCERNING
THE SITUATION BETWEEN IRAQ AND KUWAIT

Note verbale dated 12 October 1990 from the Permanent Representative of the United Kingdom of Great Britain and Northern Ireland to the United Nations addressed to the Secretary-General

The Permanent Representative of the United Kingdom of Great Britain and Northern Ireland to the United Nations presents his compliments to the Secretary-General of the United Nations and has the honour to attach a memorandum by the Government of the United Kingdom in response to the questionnaire circulated by the Secretary-General in his note SCPC/7/90 (3) of 8 October 1990. The Secretary-General is requested to circulate the memorandum as a document of the Security Council Committee established by resolution 661 (1990) concerning the situation between Iraq and Kuwait.

Also attached are copies of the legislation and other documents referred to in the memorandum.*

----

    *   Copies of the legislation and other documents may be consulted in room S-3520.

90-26591 2029b (E)

/...

6 - 1

0062

Annex

Memorandum

THE IMPLEMENTATION OF RESOLUTION 661 (1990): A QUESTIONNAIRE
CONCERNING NATIONAL MEASURES

UNITED KINGDOM RESPONSES

Question 1.

(a) New legislation has been created by the passage of Statutory Instruments
through Orders in Council to implement the provisions of Security Council
resolution 661 (1990).

(b) Legislation enacted since the adoption of resolution 661 (1990) is as
follows:

- The Hong Kong (Control of Gold, Securities, Payments and Credits: Kuwait
  and Republic of Iraq) Order 1990 (6 August).

- The Caribbean Territories (Control of Gold, Securities, Payments and
  Credits: Kuwait and Republic of Iraq) Order 1990: SI No. 1625
  (6 August).

- The Iraq and Kuwait (United Nations Sanctions) Order 1990: SI No. 1651
  (8 August).

- The Iraq and Kuwait (United Nations Sanctions) (Dependent Territories)
  Order 1990: SI No. 1652 (8 August).

- The Export of Goods (Control) (Iraq and Kuwait Sanctions) Order 1990:
  SI No. 1640 (8 August).

- The Iraq and Kuwait (United Nations Sanctions) (Amendment) Order 1990:
  SI No. 1768 (29 August).

- The Iraq and Kuwait (United Nations Sanctions) (Bermuda) Order 1990:
  SI No. 1769 (29 August).

- The Iraq and Kuwait (United Nations Sanctions) (Dependent Territories)
  (Amendment) Order 1990: SI No. 1770 (29 August).

- The Iraq and Kuwait (United Nations Sanctions) (Channel Islands)
  Order 1990: SI No. 1771 (29 August).

- The Iraq and Kuwait (United Nations Sanctions) (No. 2) Order 1990
  (5 October).

- The Iraq and Kuwait (United Nations Sanctions) (Dependent Territories)
  (No. 2) Order 1990 (5 October).

/...

6-2

(c) Separate legal directions were issued by HM Treasury on 2 and 4 August to freeze certain Iraqi and Kuwaiti assets:

-    The Control of Gold, Securities, Payments and Credits (Kuwait) Directions 1990: SI No. 1591 (2 August).

-    The Control of Gold, Securities, Payments and Credits (Republic of Iraq) Directions 1990: SI No. 1616 (4 August).

The Bank of England issued notices on 7 August:

    Emergency Laws (Re-enactments and Appeals) Act 1964: Kuwait.

    Emergency Laws (Re-enactments and Appeals) Act 1964: Iraq.

The Department of Trade and Industry has issued a number of licences under the Iraq and Kuwait (United Nations Sanctions) Order 1990 which authorize activities which would otherwise be prohibited as they involve trade with Iraq/Kuwait. These licences (which include general licences covering personal effects and mail) have been used as a means of protecting the interests of the legitimate Government of Kuwait. This was the purpose of an Open General Supply Licence which came into force on 10 September 1990 which authorizes the supply of goods to certain Kuwaiti corporations which have been clearly identified with the legitimate Government of Kuwait. A small number of import licences have also been issued for goods in transit before 7 August.

Question 2.

    (a) The Department of Trade and Industry and HM Customs and Excise are responsible for controlling imports. The latter is responsible for enforcing controls on the import into the United Kingdom of goods originating in Iraq or Kuwait.

    (b) Under an amendment to the Open General Import Licence of 4 December 1987 and the Iraq and Kuwait (United Nations Sanctions) Order 1990 the import of products originating in Iraq or Kuwait and activities which would promote or are calculated to promote imports or trans-shipment of goods from Iraq or Kuwait are prohibited except under the authority of a specific licence. The granting of licences falls to the Secretary of State for Trade and Industry. A small number of individual licences have been issued for the import of goods that were in transit before 7 August.

    HM Customs and Excise are responsible for ensuring that imports subject to control are not admitted without licences, and have adapted their entry processing system to identify suspect importations. Types of goods at risk and known importers have been identified. All ports and airports have been informed of the new legislation and the risks involved. Information will be collected and researched at a central intelligence point for dissemination to operational staff.

/...

6-3

0064

Question 3.

(a) Export controls are implemented by the Department of Trade and Industry
through a licensing system operated under the Iraq and Kuwait (United Nations
Sanctions) Order 1990 and the Export of Goods (Control) (Iraq and Kuwait Sanctions)
Order 1990. The implementation of controls is carried out in close consultation
with other interested government departments, notably the Foreign and Commonwealth
Office and HM Customs and Excise. HM Customs and Excise are responsible for
enforcing controls on the export of goods from the United Kingdom to Iraq or Kuwait
or to an Iraqi or Kuwaiti business.

(b) Ministers have ensured that there will be effective co-ordination of
information and action concerning potential and actual breaches of Security Council
resolution 661 (1990) by the rapid establishment of the Embargo Enforcement Unit.
Both the Department of Trade and Industry and Customs and Excise have undertaken
large-scale operations to ensure exporters are aware of the consequences of
breaching the embargo.

In addition, Customs and Excise staff at ports and airports in the United
Kingdom are keeping a constant look-out for potential offenders. HM Customs and
Excise have instructed senior managers responsible for ports and airports to
reorder their work to give a high priority to export controls. Staff at all levels
have been made aware of the risks associated with attempts to breach sanctions.
Steps have been taken to ensure that local management plans and operational unit
risk profiles reflect the dangers not only of direct traffic to Iraq but also the
risk of diversion via other countries. In addition, Customs have established a
central intelligence reference point to receive, process and disseminate
information throughout the Department; they are arranging for staff to visit known
exporters to Iraq and Kuwait to ensure they are aware of the sanctions provisions;
they are monitoring statistical data to identify any variation in patterns of
exports (and imports); and are generally ensuring a high level of awareness on the
subject within the Department.

Question 4.

(a) Although transfers may be made into the United Kingdom accounts of
persons resident in Iraq or Kuwait, all such accounts are blocked, and the
authorities exercise control on payments out of them.

(b) The powers given by the Treasury Directions effectively prevent
unauthorized movements of funds. HM Customs and Excise will carry through
investigation of potential import/export offences to cover financial aspects where
appropriate.

Question 5.

Customs and Excise have the powers to detain any item of equipment or person
they consider to be in breach of Security Council resolution 661 (1990).
Successful prosecution of offenders may lead to a maximum prison sentence of seven
years and/or unlimited fines, as detailed below.

/...

6-4   0065

Customs penalties for importing or exporting goods contrary to a prohibition or restriction are contained in the Customs and Excise Management Act 1979 (CEMA).

They are:

(a)   IMPORTS: (i) On conviction for minor offences based on untrue declaration (CEMA Section 167 (1)), there is a penalty of £1,000.

(ii)   On conviction for more serious untrue declaration offences, done knowingly or recklessly (CEMA Section 167 (1)) there is a penalty of an unlimited fine or imprisonment of up to two years, or both.

(iii)   On conviction for serious cases, where intent to evade is involved (CEMA Section 170), there is a penalty of an unlimited fine or imprisonment of up to seven years, or both.

(iv)   Whether the offence is under CEMA Section 167 or CEMA Section 170 the goods are liable to forfeiture.

(b)   EXPORTS: (i) On conviction for minor offence (CEMA Section 68 (1)) there is a penalty of £400 or three times the value of the goods, whichever is the greater.

(ii)   On conviction for serious offences, where intent is involved (CEMA Section 68 (2)), there is a penalty of an unlimited fine or imprisonment of up to seven years, or both.

(iii)   Whether the offence is under CEMA Section 68 (1) or 68 (2) the goods involved are liable to forfeiture.

The Act of Parliament under which financial sanctions are imposed makes no provisions for seizures or forfeitures, but there are penalties in the form of fines and/or imprisonment for contraventions.

Question 6.

(a)   No significant problems have been experienced on the trade side, although one area of slight difficulty has been uncertainty over the extent to which Security Council resolution 661 (1990) applies to services. There have been no problems in implementing the financial sanctions.

(b)   The legislation cited in reply to Question 1 applies equally in relation to contracts entered into before the date of Security Council resolution 661 (1990). [A small number of individual licences have, however, been issued by the Department of Trade and Industry for the import of goods in transit before 7 August.]

(c)   The Department of Trade and Industry has granted licences to corporations which are clearly identified with the legitimate Government of Kuwait. An Open General Supply Licence was issued on 10 September 1990 which allows any person to supply goods to such corporations.

/...

6 - 5

0066

S/AC.25/1990/1
English
Page 6

        The need to protect the assets of the legitimate Government of Kuwait, its
agencies and citizens, was an important consideration in determining whether or not
to grant the general permissions set out in the Bank of England's notices. Special
arrangements have also been put in place to ensure the continued smooth functioning
of such agencies as the Kuwait Investment Office, and of Kuwaiti-owned entities
such as the Kuwait Petroleum Corporation. The objective of all such measures is to
ensure that neither assets or liquid funds leave the control of the United Kingdom
except for legitimate purposes.

                                    -----

6 - 6

0067

관리번호 90-147ㅏ

재 무 부

외정 2224-214 　　　　(503-9262)　　　　1990. 11.1

수신 외무부장관

참조 통상국장

제목 대 이라크 경제제재

　　　　　　　　　　　　　　　　1991. 12.31 .에 예고문에
　　　　　　　　　　　　　　　　의거 일반문서로 재분류됨

1. 통일 2065-2525('90. 10.27)의 관련입니다.

2. 대 이라크 경제제재조치와 관련된 유엔의 질문서에 대한 답변내용을
별첨과 같이 송부합니다.

첨부 : 답변서 1부. 끝.

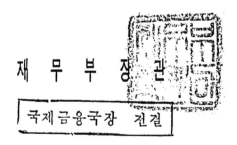

재 무 부 장 관

국제금융국장 전결

0068

U N 질 문	답 변 (안)
4. 금융·경제적 자원의 통제	
a) 안보리 결의 661호에 의거 규제된 금융·경제적자원의 이전을 막기 위한 귀국내 제도는?	- 외국환관리법에 의하여 외환 당국이 외국환은행의 업무처리에 대해 행정지도 가능
b) 안보리 결의 661호를 위반 하여 자본을 이동시키는 것을 막기 위해 귀국이 취한 구체적 조치는?	- 대이라크 경제제재조치에 관한 정부입장 발표내용을 모든 외국환은행에 통보 - 이라크 및 쿠웨이트와 관련된 업무처리시 유의해야 할 사항 으로서 거래중단 대상이 되는 금융기관명단 및 미국의 조치내용 등을 모든 외국환은행에 통보하고 업무처리에 대한 행정지도를 통해 유엔결의 내용이 준수되도록 조치

2-1   0069

U N 질 문	답 변 (안)·
6. 기 타 c) 합법적인 쿠웨이트 정부 및 　기관의 자산을 보호하기 위해 　귀국이 안보리 결의 661호 　9 (a) 항에 따라 취한 구체적 　조치내용은 무엇인가?	- 쿠웨이트 정부자산이 국내에는 　없음. - 그러나, 모든 외국환은행에 　대이라크 경제제재조치에 관한 　정부입장 발표 내용과 거래중단 　대상이 되는 금융기관 명단을 　통보하는 등 합법적인 쿠웨이트 　정부의 자산이 보호될 수 있도록 　조치

2-2

0070

대이라크 경제제재 관련 유엔질의서에 대한 회답(요지)

90. 11. 1
통 상 국
통 상 1과

1. 법률적 체제

a) 안보리결의 661호 이행을 위한 법률적 기반

　　ㅇ 대외무역법, 외환관리법, 해외건설촉진법, 해운업법등

b) 안보리결의 661호에 의거 제정한 법률 여부

　　ㅇ 기존의 법에 의거 조치 가능

c) 행정명령, 고시발표 여부

　　ㅇ 상품거래는 행정지침, 금융·건설·해운등은 행정지도를 통해 조치

2. 이라크로 부터의 수입통제

a) 담당부서

　　ㅇ 상공부 및 관세청

b) 구체적 조치내용

　　ㅇ IL 발급중단, 관세청에서 통관시 위반여부 확인

3. 이라크·쿠웨이트로의 수출통제

a) 담당부서

　　ㅇ 상공부, 관세청, 항만청

b) 구체적 조치내용

　　ㅇ EL 발급중단, 관세청에서 통관시 위반여부 확인

　　ㅇ 목적지가 이라크인 상품의 환적금지

0071

4. 금융·경제적 자원의 통제

a) 금융·경제적 자원 이전 통제제도

　　o 긴박한 국제적 상황 변화시, 외환관리법에 따라 통제 가능

b) 구체적 조치내용

　　o 외국환은행에 주의 환기

　　o 이라크에 대한 보험제공 금지

5. 강제집행

　o 관련법에 의거 처벌

　　- 상품거래 관련 위반시 5년이하 징역 또는 상품가격의 3배까지 벌금

6. 기 타

a) 안보리결의 수행상 문제점

　　o 여러기관에 의해 이행함에 따라 상설 대책반운영하고 있으며 안보리결의
　　　이행관련 문제점 없음.

b) 안보리결의 661호 채택이전에 체결된 계약에 대한 조치

　　o 건설의 경우 공사중단, 근로자 철수

c) 합법적인 쿠웨이트 정부자산 보호

　　o 아국내 동 재산 없는 것으로 확인

0072

발 신 전 보

번 호 : WUN-1803   901101 1655 DQ   종별 : 지급

수 신 : 주   유엔   대사. 총영사 ♣♣♣♣♣

발 신 : 장 관   (통일)

제 목 : 대이라크 제재조치 관련 질의서

　　　대 : UNW - 2238

　　　대호 유엔사무총장의 안보리결의 661호(대이라크 경제제재조치) 관련

질의서에 대한 아측 회신내용을 별전 fax 송부하니 귀직 명의 공한에 첨부,

유엔 사무국에 제출바람.　　　　끝.

　　　　　　　　　　　　　　　　　　(통상국장   김 삼 훈)

첨부: WUNA - 0070.

제1차관보 홍
제2차관보

대책반장
중동아국장 홍
국제기구조약국장

보 안	毕
통 제	

앙고재	90년11월1일	통상1과	기안자성명 안총기	과장 毕	국장	차관	장관 毕	외신과통제

0073

Memorandum

THE IMPLEMENTATION OF RESOLUTION 661 (1990) : QUESTIONNAIRE

CONCERNING NATIONAL MEASURES

RESPONSES OF THE REPUBLIC OF KOREA

1. Legislative Framework

Q. What is the legislative basis on which your country has undertaken
measures to implement Security Council resolution 661 (1990)?

A. The measures taken by the Government of the Republic of Korea to
implement Security Council resolution 661 are based on several laws
such as Foreign Trade Act, Foreign Exchange Control Act, Overseas
Construction Promotion Law, and Maritime Transportation Act. The
relevant provisions of these laws are attached.

Q. Has there been any specific legislation enacted pursuant to Security
Council resolution 661 (1990)?

A. There has been no specific legislation enacted pursuant to Security
Council resolution 661 (1990). Since the Government believes that
the Resolution can be effectively implemented by the application
of the existing laws mentioned above, it has not found it necessary
to legislate any new law.

- 1 -

0074

Q. What types of administrative orders, decrees etc., has your country
   passed pursuant to the relevant laws?

A. In the case of trade in goods, the Government issued a special
   administrative guideline in order to implement Security Council
   resolution 661. In the case of financial transactions, construction
   contract, and maritime transportation, appropriate administrative
   guidance was given by the Government to ensure compliance with
   resolution 661.

2. Control of imports or activities which would promote or are calculated to
   promote imports or transhipment of goods from Iraq and Kuwait.

   Q. Which authorities in your country are responsible for implementing
      the control of imports or activities as required by Security Council
      resolution 661 (1990)?

   A. The Ministry of Trade and Industry is mostly responsible for implement-
      ing the control of imports of all commodities and products originating
      in Iraq or Kuwait. The Office of Customs Administration is responsible
      for ensuring that all the imports without approval of the government
      are not admitted.

   Q. What specific measures has your country established to prevent
      breaches of Security Council resolution 661 (1990) by imports of items
      or activities covered by it?

   A. In the Republic of Korea, it is necessary to obtain government approval
      in the form of the IL(Import Licence) in order to import goods. The
      Government issued special administrative guideline to suspend issuance

- 2 -

0075

of the IL for all commodities and products originating in Iraq and Kuwait. Without the IL, the goods to be imported are not allowed to go through customs. The special guideline issued in accordance with the provisions of the Foreign Trade Act are specifically designed to prohibit the import of all goods, including crude oil, produced in or shipped from Iraq and Kuwait.

3. Control of exports or activities which would promote or are calculated to promote sales or supply of products and commodities to Iraq and Kuwait.

Q. Which authorities in your country are responsible for implementing the control of exports or activities as required by Security Council resolution 661 (1990)?

A. The Ministry of Trade and Industry is mostly responsible for implementing the control of exports. Also, the Office of Customs Administration is responsible for enforcing controls on the export goods. The Maritime and Port Administration is in charge of preventing any transhipment of goods to Iraq and Kuwait.

Q. What specific measures has your country established to prevent breaches of Security Council resolution 661 (1990) by exports of items or activities covered by it?

A. The Government announced, based on the Foreign Trade Act, special administrative guideline to suspend issuance of the EL (Export Licence) for the sale or supply by Korean nationals or Korean flag

- 3 -

0076

vessels of all commodities and products to any party in Iraq and Kuwait. As in the case of importation, any party who desires to export goods should obtain approval of the government through the application of the issuance of EL. Without the EL, the application for customs procedure cannot be submitted. The Government may approve issuance of the EL only for the export of items for medical and humanitarian purposes. The Government also prohibited transportation of goods to Iraq or Kuwait, or to the third port through which the goods can be transhipped to Iraq or Kuwait.

4. Control of Financial or Economic Resources.

Q. What system of control exists in your country to prevent transfers of financial or economic resources covered by Security Council resolution 661 (1990)?

A. In the Republic of Korea, foreign exchange is controlled by the Foreign Exchange Control Act. According to the Act, the Government may suspend foreign exchange transactions when emergency measures are deemed necessary in case of a radical change in the international or domestic situation.

Q. What specific measures has your country taken so as to prevent unauthorized movements of funds in contravention of Security Council resolution 661 (1990)?

A. The Government of the Republic of Korea, through administrative guidance, called upon all the Korean foreign exchange banks to pay special attention in their financial transactions with any financial

- 4 -

0077

institutions of Iraq and Kuwait so that the flow of financial
resources to Iraq and Kuwait should be prohibited. Korean insurance
companies were also called upon not to provide any insurance to
Iraqi vessels and aircraft.

5. Enforcement

Q. What types of enforcement (penalties, seizures, forfeitures, etc.)
   does your country apply so as to prevent breaches of Security Council
   resolution 661 (1990) by individuals and companies in your country?

A. Any violators of the special administrative guidelines set out above
   shall be subject to penalties according to the relevant provisions.
   For example, Article 67 of the Foreign Trade Act stipulates that any
   party found in contravention of the special measure shall be punished
   by imprisonment for not more than five years or a fine equivalent to
   three times or less of the price of goods to be exported or imported.

6. Others

Q. What problems has your country confronted in ensuring full national
   implementation of Security Council resolution 661 (1990)?

A. Since Security Council resolution 661 covers comprehensive range of
   measures, the Government of the Republic of Korea is implementing it
   through various agencies. The Government established the Special
   Inter-Ministerial Task Force to monitor implementation of the measures
   taken. Since its establishment on August 9, it has not found any
   violation of the special administrative guidelines by any person or

- 5 -

0078

body under the jurisdiction of the Government of the Republic of Korea. As such, no significant problems have yet been identified in ensuring full implementation of Security Council resolution 661.

Q. What legislative or other measures has your country taken so as to implement Security Council resolution 661 (1990) with regard to contracts entered into or licenses granted before the date of the resolution?

A. The construction contracts which were entered into before the Resolution were suspended, as the Korean employees withdrew to the Republic of Korea. The Government also gave appropriate administrative guidance so as to ensure the prohibition of the new procurement of construction contracts in Iraq and Kuwait.

Q. What specific measures has your country taken to protect the assets of the legitimate Government of Kuwait and its agencies in accordance with paragraph 9 (1) of Security Council resolution 661 (1990)?

A. It has been confirmed that there are no assets of the legitimate Government of Kuwait and its agencies in the Republic of Korea.

- 6 -

0079

(Attachment)

The relevant provisions

o Foreign Trade Act

Article 4 (Special Measures, such as Restriction on Trade, etc.) The
Minister of Trade and Industry may take special measures concerning restrictions on or prohibition of the export and import of goods in the following
cases :

1. Where a war, emergency, natural or terrestrial disaster occurs in the
    Republic of Korea or the counterpart country of the Republic of Korea
    in trade (herein-after referred to as "trade counterpart country") ;

Article 67 (Penal Provisions) Any person who falls under any of the
following Subparagraphs, shall be punished by imprisonment for not more
than five years or a fine equivalent to three times or less of the price
of goods to be exported or imported :

 1. A person who is in contravention of the special measure under
     Article 4 ;

o Foreign Exchange Control Act

Article 7 (Emergency Suspension of Transaction) The Minister of Finance
may, when emergency measures are deemed necessary in case of a radical
change in the international or domestic economic situation, may order
suspension of foreign exchange transactions, with an approval of the
President following a deliberation of the State Council.

0080

o Maritime Transportation Business Act

Article 30 (Orders to Improve Business) (1) If it is deemed necessary for strengthening international competitiveness, maintaining order in the navigational routes, or promoting the smooth transportation of cargo, the Administrator of the Korea Maritime and Port Administration may order the maritime cargo transportation businessmen of the following matters:

1. Changes of the business plan;

4. Measures necessary for protection of crew members;

6. Matters necessary for safe navigation of vessels, and

(2) When the maritime cargo transportation businessman violates an order issued under Paragraph (1) or does not perform as ordered, the Administrator of the Korea Maritime and Port Administration may limit various governmental aids.

0081

외 무 부

종 별 :

번 호 : UNW-2404   일 시 : 90 1101 1700

수 신 : 장 관 (통일,국연,중근동,기정)

발 신 : 주 유엔 대사

제 목 : 대 이락크 제재조치 관련 질의서

　　대: WUN-1803

　　대호 아측 회신을 금 11.1.자 유엔 사무총장앞 당관 구상서로 제출하였음.끝

　　(대사 현홍주-국장)

통상국　　1차보　　중아국　　국기국　　정문국　　안기부　　대책반

PAGE 1   90.11.02   07:15 FC

외신 1과 통제관

0082

외   무   부

종   별 :
번   호 : UNW-2443   일   시 : 90 1106 1830
수   신 : 장 관(통일,국연,중근동,기정)
발   신 : 주 유엔 대사
제   목 : 유엔 사무총장의 대 요르단 재정지원 요청

1. 유엔사무총장은 10.30 자 본직앞 서한 (화람서한)에서 안보리내 대이락 제제위의 요청에 따라 아국이 요르단에 대해 각종경제, 재정적 지원을 제공하여 줄것을 촉구하고 아울러 요르단의 안보리결의 661호 준수에 따른 동국의 경제적 곤궁을 덜어주기 위한 아국의 각종지원실적 금후지원예정 내역에 관한 정보를 제출해 줄것을 요청하여 왔음.

2. 상기서한에는 유엔 사무총장이 안보리내 제제위원회의 요청에 따라 요르단의 경제적 곤궁상태 평가와 동 구제방안 작성을 위해 요르단에 파견하였던 JEAN RIPERT 의 보고서 사본이 첨부되어 있음. 동 보고서 요지는 아래와 같음.

　　0. 안보리 결의 661 준수에 따른 요르단의 손실액은 금년중 7억3천만불, 내년중에는 매월 1억6천만불로 평가됨.

　　0. 요르단 경제의 규모로 보아 상기 손실은 국제사회의 긴급 재정지원을 요구하고 있음.

3. 사무총장 서한 및 상기보고서 (21페이지) 및 동보고서의 첨부물등은 파편송부함. 끝
　　(대사 현홍주=국장)

외 무 부

종 별 :

번 호 : UNW-2454

일 시 : 90 1107 1930

수 신 : 장 관(봉일,국연,중근동,기정)

발 신 : 주 유엔 대사

제 목 : 안보리 결의 661호 이행상태

대: WUN-1803

대호 유엔사무총장 질문서에 대한 아측의 답변을 수록한 각서가 11.1. 자 안보리 문서 (S/AC.25/1990/15) 로 배포되었음.동 문서는 파편보고함.끝

(대사 현홍주-국장)

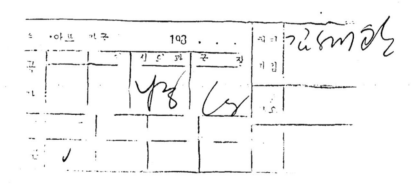

| 통상국 | 2차보 | 중아국 | 국기국 | 정문국 | 안기부 |

PAGE 1

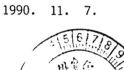

주 국 련 대 표 부

주국련 203132 -
　　　　　　864
수신 장관
참조 통상국장, 국제기구조약국장
제목 안보리 결의 661호 이행상태

1990. 11. 7.

　　　대 : WUN-1803

　　　유엔 사무총장의 질문서에 대한 아측의 답변을 수록한 대호 각서가
11.1차 안보리 문서로 배포되었는 바, 이를 별첨 송부합니다.

　　첨 부 : 상기 안보리 문서 2부.　　끝.

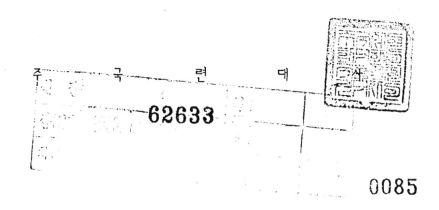

UNITED
NATIONS

Security Council

Distr.
GENERAL

S/AC.25/1990/15
1 November 1990

ORIGINAL: ENGLISH

SECURITY COUNCIL COMMITTEE ESTABLISHED
 BY RESOLUTION 661 (1990) CONCERNING
 THE SITUATION BETWEEN IRAQ AND
 KUWAIT

NOTE BY THE SECRETARY-GENERAL

The attached note verbale dated 1 November 1990 from the Permanent Observer of the Republic of Korea to the United Nations has been addressed to the Secretary-General.

90-29065 1920f (E)

/...

0086

<u>Annex</u>

<u>Note verbale dated 1 November 1990 from the Permanent Observer of the Republic of Korea to the United Nations addressed to the Secretary-General</u>

The Permanent Observer of the Republic of Korea to the United Nations presents his compliments to the Secretary-General of the United Nations and has the honour to forward a memorandum by the Government of the Republic of Korea in response to the questionnaire circulated by the Secretary-General in his note dated 8 October 1990.

It would be appreciated if the Secretary-General would circulate the memorandum as a document of the Security Council Committee established by resolution 661 (1990) concerning the situation between Iraq and Kuwait.

0087 /...

Enclosure I

Memorandum

Responses of the Republic of Korea concerning implementation of
resolution 661 (1990): questionnaire concerning national
measures

1. Legislative framework

Q. What is the legislative basis on which your country has undertaken measures to
implement Security Council resolution 661 (1990)?

A. The measures taken by the Government of the Republic of Korea to implement
Security Council resolution 661 (1990) are based on several laws such as the
Foreign Trade Act, the Foreign Exchange Control Act, the Overseas Construction
Promotion Law and the Maritime Transportation Act. The relevant provisions of
these laws are attached.*

Q. Has there been any specific legislation enacted pursuant to Security Council
resolution 661 (1990)?

A. There has been no specific legislation enacted pursuant to Security Council
resolution 661 (1990). Since the Government believes that the resolution can
be effectively implemented by the application of the existing laws mentioned
above, it has not found it necessary to legislate any new law.

Q. What types of administrative orders, decrees, etc., has your country passed
pursuant to the relevant laws?

A. In the case of trade in goods, the Government has issued a special
administrative guideline in order to implement Security Council resolution
661 (1990). In the case of financial transactions, construction contracts and
maritime transportation, appropriate administrative guidance has been given by
the Government to ensure compliance with resolution 661 (1990).

2. Control of imports or activities which would promote or are
calculated to promote imports or trans-shipment of goods
from Iraq and Kuwait

Q. Which authorities in your country are responsible for implementing the control
of imports or activities as required by Security Council resolution 661 (1990)?

---

* See enclosure II to the present document.

/...

0088

A. The Ministry of Trade and Industry is mostly responsible for implementing the control of imports of all commodities and products originating in Iraq and Kuwait. The Office of Customs Administration is responsible for ensuring that no imports are admitted without government approval.

Q. What specific measures has your country established to prevent breaches of Security Council resolution 661 (1990) by imports of items or activities covered by it?

A. In the Republic of Korea, it is necessary to obtain government approval in the form of an import licence in order to import goods. The Government has issued special administrative guidelines to suspend issuance of an import licence for all commodities and products originating in Iraq and Kuwait. Without an import licence, the goods to be imported are not allowed to go through Customs. The special guidelines issued in accordance with the provisions of the Foreign Trade Act are specifically designed to prohibit the import of all goods, including crude oil, produced in or shipped from Iraq and Kuwait.

> 3. Control of exports or activities which would promote or are calculated to promote sales or supply of products and commodities to Iraq and Kuwait

Q. Which authorities in your country are responsible for implementing the control of exports or activities as required by Security Council resolution 661 (1990)?

A. The Ministry of Trade and Industry is chiefly responsible for implementing and the Office of Customs Administration for enforcing controls on exports. The Maritime and Port Administration is in charge of preventing any trans-shipment of goods to Iraq and Kuwait.

Q. What specific measures has your country established to prevent breaches of Security Council resolution 661 (1990) by exports of items or activities covered by it?

A. The Government has established special administrative guidelines, based on the Foreign Trade Act, to suspend issuance of an export licence for the sale or supply by Korean nationals or Korean flag vessels of all commodities and products to any party in Iraq and Kuwait. As in the case of importation, any party who desires to export goods must obtain government approval by applying for an export licence. Without the export licence, the application for Customs procedure cannot be submitted. The Government may grant the export licence only for the export of items for medical and humanitarian purposes. The Government has also prohibited transportation of goods to Iraq and Kuwait, or to a third port through which the goods can be trans-shipped to Iraq and Kuwait.

0089 /...

4. Control of financial or economic resources

Q. What system of control exists in your country to prevent transfers of financial or economic resources covered by Security Council resolution 661 (1990)?

A. In the Republic of Korea, foreign exchange is controlled by the Foreign Exchange Control Act. According to the Act, the Government may suspend foreign exchange transactions when emergency measures are deemed necessary in case of a radical change in the international or domestic situation.

Q. What specific measures has your country taken so as to prevent unauthorized m vements of funds in contravention of Security Council resolution 661 (1990)?

A. The Government of the Republic of Korea, through administrative guidance, has called upon all Korean foreign exchange banks to pay special attention, in their financial transactions with any financial institutions of Iraq and Kuwait, to prohibiting the flow of financial resources to those countries. Korean insurance companies have also been called upon not to provide any insurance to Iraqi vessels and aircraft.

5. Enforcement

Q. What types of enforcement (penalties, seizures, forfeitures, etc.) does your country apply so as to prevent breaches of Security Council resolution 661 (1990) by individuals and companies in your country?

A. Any violators of the special administrative guidelines set out above shall be subject to penalties according to the relevant provisions. For example, article 67 of the Foreign Trade Act stipulates that any party found in contravention of a special measure shall be punished by imprisonment for not more than five years or a fine equivalent to three times or less of the price of goods to be exported or imported.

6. Other

Q. What problems has your country confronted in ensuring full national implementation of Security Council resolution 661 (1990)?

A. Since Security Council resolution 661 (1990) covers a comprehensive range of measures, the Government of the Republic of Korea is implementing it through various agencies. The Government has established the Special Inter-Ministerial Task Force to monitor implementation of the measures taken. Since its establishment on 9 August 1990, it has not found any violation of the special administrative guidelines by any person or body under the jurisdiction of the Government of the Republic of Korea. Consequently, no significant problems have yet been identified in ensuring full implementation of Security Council resolution 661 (1990).

/...

0090

Q. What legislative or other measures has your country taken so as to implement Security Council resolution 661 (1990) with regard to contracts entered into or licences granted before the date of the resolution?

A. As the Korean employees have returned to the Republic of Korea, the construction contracts which were entered into before the resolution have been suspended. The Government has also given appropriate administrative guidance so as to ensure the prohibition of the procurement of new construction contracts in Iraq and Kuwait.

Q. What specific measures has your country taken to protect the assets of the legitimate Government of Kuwait and its agencies in accordance with paragraph 9 (a) of Security Council resolution 661 (1990)?

A. It has been confirmed that there are no assets of the legitimate Government of Kuwait and its agencies in the Republic of Korea.

0091

/...

Enclosure II

The relevant provisions

Foreign Trade Act

"Article 4 (Special measures, such as restriction on trade etc.)

The Minister of Trade and Industry may take special measures concerning restrictions on or prohibition of the export and import of goods in the following cases:

"1. Where a war, an emergency or a natural or terrestrial disaster occurs in the Republic of Korea or the counterpart country of the Republic of Korea in trade (hereinafter referred to as 'trade counterpart country');"

"Article 67 (Penal provisions)

Any person who falls under any of the following subparagraphs shall be punished by imprisonment for not more than five years or a fine equivalent to three times or less of the price of goods to be exported or imported:

"1. A person who is in contravention of the special measure under article 4;"

Foreign Exchange Control Act

"Article 7 (Emergency suspension of transaction)

The Ministry of Finance may, when emergency measures are deemed necessary in case of a radical change in the international or domestic economic situation, order the suspension of foreign exchange transactions, with the approval of the President following a deliberation of the State Council."

Maritime Transportation Act

"Article 30 (Orders to improve business)

"1. If it is necessary for strengthening international competitiveness, maintaining order in the navigational routes or promoting the smooth transportation of cargo, the Administrator of the Korea Maritime and Port Administration may issue an order to the maritime cargo transportation businessmen on the following matters:

"(a) Changes of the business plan;

"(b) Measures necessary for protection of crew members;

"(c) Matters necessary for safe navigation of vessels;

0092 /...

"2. When the maritime cargo transportation businessmen violates an order issued under paragraph 1 or does not perform as ordered, the Administrator of the Korea Maritime and Port Administration may limit governmental assistance."

0093

원 본

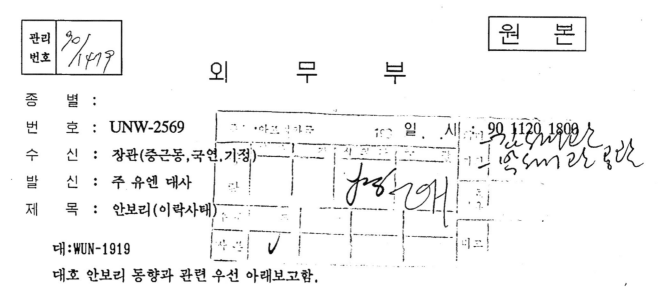

외 무 부

종 별 :

번 호 : UNW-2569

수 신 : 장관(중근동,국연,기정)

발 신 : 주 유엔 대사

제 목 : 안보리(이락사태)

대:WUN-1919

대호 안보리 동향과 관련 우선 아래보고함.

1. 표제 사태관련 무력사용 허용안보리 결의안 채택은 미국의 주도에의하여안보리 회원국대상 양자간 차원에서 추진되고 있으며 안보리 전체회원국간의 공식, 비공식협의는 11.20 현재까지 개최된바 없으며, 현재 예정된것도 아직은 없음.

2. 미국은 그간 양자간 협의를 통하여 무력사용 안보리 결의안 추진에대한 영, 불, 카나다, 자이레, 이디오피아, 코트디봐르, 핀랜드, 루마니아의 동의를 받았으며, 중국으로부터는 소련의 입장과 동일한 입장을 취할것임을 약속받은 것으로 알려지고있음. 한편 소련은 11.19 파리에서 개최된 미, 소 정상회담에서 현싯점에서의 동결의안 추진에 대해 명확한 동의를 표명치 않은것으로 알려짐.

3. 미국은 당초 베이커국무장관의 금주말 예멘방문등 큐바, 콜롬비아, 말레이지아등과도 양자간 협의를 계획하였다는바, 상기와같이 소련이 동건추진에 소극적인 태도를 보이고있음에 따라 금후 미국의 태도가 주목되고있음. 끝

(대사 현홍주-국장)

중아국   차관   1차보   국기국   정와대   안기부   대책반

PAGE 1

90.11.21   08:21

외신 2과 통제관 BT

0094

외 무 부

종 별 :

번 호 : UNW-2615

일 시 : 90 1126 1900

수 신 : 장 관(중근동,국연,기정)

발 신 : 주 유엔 대사

제 목 : 안보리동향(이락사태)

표제건 최근 동향을 아래보고함.

1. 미국은 안보리 의장국으로서 기한이 만료되는 금주말까지 대이락 무력사용을 허용하는 안보리결의안 채택을 목표로 현재 5개 상임이사국과 비공식 협의를 진행중에 있음. 중국.소련등 일부 국가의 입장을 감안, 결의안 문안에 '무력사용' 의 직접 언급대신 1991년 1월초 또는 1월말까지 이락이 쿠웨이트로 부터 철수치 않을경우 '모든 필요 한 수단' 을 사용토록 한다는 방향으로 협의가 진행되고 있는 것으로 알려짐.

2. 미국은 동건 토의를 위한 외무장관급 안보리를 11.29(목) 개최할것을 안보리 회원국에 게제의하였다함.끝

(대사 현홍주-국장)

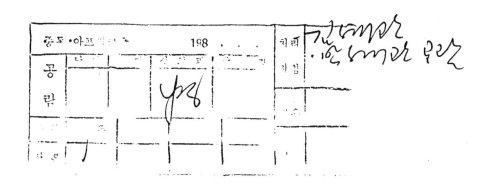

중아국   1차보   국기국   정문국   안기부

PAGE 1

90.11.27   09:34 WG

외신 1과 통제관

0095

외 무 부

종 별 :

번 호 : UNW-2618   일 시 : 90 1127 1830

수 신 : 장 관(국연)

발 신 : 주 유엔 대사

제 목 : 안보리(이락사태)

　　1. 쿠웨이트의 요청에 따라 금 11.27 표제건 토의를 위한 안보리가 개최되어 쿠웨이트 대표로 부터 이락군의 쿠웨이트내 잔학상에 대한 보고를 청취하였음.

　　2. 피점령 쿠웨이트에서 생활하다 최근 탈출한 5인의 쿠웨이트측 증인이 이들이 체험한 이락군의 잔학상에 대해 증언하고 쿠웨이트의 구출을 호소하였음.

　　3. 쿠웨이트대표는 쿠웨이트 인구 등록 자료를 유엔사무총장이 관리하여 줄것을 요청하는 별첨 결의안을 제출하였음.

　　4. 안보리 의장은 안보리 회원국간 비공식 협의를 통하여 동건 토의를 위한 추후회의 소집 일정을 결정할 것임을 선언하였음.

　　첨부:쿠웨이트 제출결의안(FAX):UNW(F)-299

　　끝

　　(대사 현홍주-국장)

국기국 미주국 중아국 1연보 2차보 강민국 대책반

PAGE 1   90.11.28   10:22 WG

외신1과 통제관

0096

UNITED NATIONS

Security Council

PROVISIONAL

S/21966
26 November 1990

ORIGINAL: ENGLISH

Kuwait: draft resolution

The Security Council,

Recalling resolutions 660 (1990) of 2 August 1990, 662 (1990) of 9 August 1990 and 674 (1990) of 29 October 1990,

Reiterating its concern for the suffering caused to individuals in Kuwait as a result of the invasion and occupation of Kuwait by Iraq,

Gravely concerned at the ongoing attempt by Iraq to alter the demographic composition of the population of Kuwait and to destroy the civil records maintained by the legitimate Government of Kuwait,

Acting under Chapter VII of the Charter of the United Nations,

1.   Condemns the attempts by Iraq to alter the demographic composition of the population of Kuwait and to destroy the civil records maintained by the legitimate Government of Kuwait;

2.   Mandates the Secretary-General to take custody of a copy of the population register of Kuwait the authenticity of which has been certified by the legitimate Government of Kuwait which covers the population registration up to 1 August 1990;

3.   Requests the Secretary-General to establish, in co-operation with the legitimate Government of Kuwait, an Order of Rules and Regulations governing access and use of the said copy of the population register.

——————

2269E

/ — /

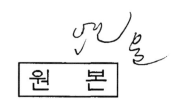

외 무 부

종 별 :

번 호 : UNW-2632   일 시 : 90 1128 1800

수 신 : 장 관(국연,중근동,기정)

발 신 : 주 유엔 대사

제 목 : 안보리(이락사태)

1. 안보리 5개 상임 이사국은 미국이 기초한 대이락 무력사용 승인 결의안 문안에 합의한 것으로 알려짐. 동 결의안은 명 11.29 외무장관급 안보리에서 채택될 것으로 알려진 바, 그 요지는 91.1.15 이전까지 이락이 쿠웨이트에서 철수하지 않을경우 쿠웨이트와 협력하고있는 회원국들이 '모든 필요한 수단' 을 사용할수 있는 권한을 부여하는 내용임.

2. 상기 초안은 별전(FAX) 과 같음.

첨부:상기 결의안 초안(FAX):UNW(F)-300

끝

(대사 현홍주-국장)

국기국   1차보   중아국   정문국   안기부   미주국 은상국 대책반 2과반

PAGE 1   90.11.29   09:55 WG

외신 1과 통제관

0098

THE SECURITY COUNCIL,

RECALLING AND REAFFIRMING its resolutions 660 (1990), 661 (1990), 662 (1990), 664 (1990), 665 (1990), 666 (1990), 667 (1990), 669 (1990), 670 (1990), 674 (1990).

NOTING that, despite all efforts by the United Nations, Iraq refuses to comply with its obligation to implement Resolution 660 (1990) and subsequent resolutions, in flagrant contempt of the Council,

MINDFUL of its duties and responsibilities under the Charter of the United Nations for the maintenance and preservation of international peace and security,

DETERMINED to secure full compliance with its decisions,

ACTING under Chapter VII of the Charter of the United Nations,

1. DEMANDS that Iraq comply fully with Resolution 660 (1990) and all subsequent relevant resolutions and decides, while maintaining all its decisions, to allow Iraq one final opportunity, as a pause of goodwill, to do so;

2. AUTHORIZES Member States cooperating with the Government of Kuwait, unless Iraq on or before January 15, 1991 fully implements, as set forth in Paragraph 1 above, the foregoing Resolutions, to use all necessary means to uphold and implement the Security Council Resolution 660 and all subsequent relevant Resolutions and to restore international peace and security in the area;

3. REQUESTS all States to provide appropriate support for the actions undertaken in pursuance of paragraph 2 of this resolution; and

4. REQUESTS the States concerned to keep the Council regularly informed on the progress of actions undertaken pursuant to paragraphs 2 and 3 of this Resolution.

/—/

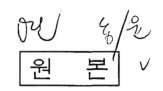

외 무 부

종 별 : 지 급

번 호 : UNW-2651
일 시 : 90 1129 2030

수 신 : 장 관(국연,중근동,기정)

발 신 : 주 유엔 대사

제 목 : 안보리(이락사태)

1.금 11.29 베이커 국무장관 주재하에 표제건 토의를 위한 안보리가 속개됨.금일 회의는 무력사용 권한 부여 결의안을 찬 12, 반2 (큐바,예멘), 기권 1 (중국) 의 표결로 채택 함. (결의 678 호)

2.금일 회의는 코트디브와르, 예멘을 제외한 13개 안보리회원국 외무장관 참석하에 개최되었음. 쿠웨이트 외무장관및 이락 주유엔대사도 토의에 참석함.

3.주요 발언요지

0.이락

- 무력사용 허가 결의는 유엔헌장 위반이며 미국에 의한 안보리의 패권주의적 지배결과임.냉전종료후 새로운 국제질서는 외교의 역할을 강조하는 것이어야함.

0.예멘

- 동 결의는 전쟁결의안으로서 광범위한 권한을 위임하는 것이며, 무력사용에 대한 유엔의 지휘통제가 없는점을 감안, 지지할수없음.

0.큐바

- 최후통첩, 전쟁선포와 다름없는 결의를 채택하는 것은 지지할수 없음.

0.중국

- 중국은 국제분쟁 해결에 있어 무력사용을 반대 하므로 동 결의안을 지지할수 없으며, 반면 동 결의안이 중국의 입장을 반영하는 쿠웨이트에서의 이락철수등 기존 안보리결의 이행을 촉구하는 내용을 포함하고 있어 거부권을 행사하지는 않고자함.

0.프랑스, 영국, 소련, 미국

- 91.1.15.까지 대 이락추가제재등 새로운 결의안 추진을 지지하지않을 것이며, 이락이 평화를 선택할 시간적 여유를 주고자함.단, 이락이 억류 중인 인질에게 해를 끼칠시에는 대응책을 취할 권리를 유보하며 제네바 인권규약, 전시법등을 위반할시

국기국   1차보   중아국   정문국   안기부

PAGE 1
90.11.30   11:02 WG

외신 1과   통제관

0100

개인책임을 추궁할것임을 밝힘.

　　0.카나다, 소련

　　- 안보리의 단합이 아랍-이스라엘간 항구적 평화모색을 위한 기회가 되기를 희망

　　0.핀란드, 콜롬비아

　　- 유엔사무총장의 중재노력을 기대함.

　　0.데뀨야르 유엔사무총장

　　- 91.1.15까지 45일간의 기간이 평화를 위해 건설적으로 사용될수 있기를 희망

　　4.평가

　　0.금일 채택된 결의는 유엔역사상 회원국들에게 무력사용 권한을 부여한 최초의 결의안 (한국동란의 경우 안보리는 회원국들에게 침략을 격퇴하기 위한 필요한 지원을 한국에 제공토록 권고하였음.) 이나, 동결의안이 헌장 제7조상 몇조에 근거한 것인지, 명시하지 않은것이 주목됨.

　　0.영,불 소련, 미국등은 91.1.15 까지는 인질에 대한 위해등 특별한 사태 악화가 발생하지않는한 안보리에서의 추가적 조치를 추진하거나 지원하지 않을것임을 밝혔는 바, 당분간 이락의 대응을 지켜보겠다는 뜻을 강조한 것으로보임.

　　0.유엔사무총장은 이락이 희망시 중재노력을 할용의가 있음을 직접 적극 표명하였고, 다수 안보리회원국이 동 중재노력을 강조하였는바, 이는 이락에 대해 외교적 노력을 모색할수 있는 경로와 기회를 상기시킨 것으로 평가됨.

　　첨부:동 결의전문(FAX):UNW(F)-303

　　끝

　　(대사 현홍주-국장)

PAGE 2

0101

#UNW-2651의 ~~첨부됨~~   UNW(F)-303 0112P 2030
(주인.중근동.기정)   총(매)

UNITED NATIONS

Security Council

Distr.
GENERAL

S/21969
28 November 1990

678호

ORIGINAL: ENGLISH

Canada, Union of Soviet Socialist Republics, United Kingdom
of Great Britain and Northern Ireland and United States of
America: draft resolution

The Security Council,

Recalling and reaffirming its resolutions 660 (1990), 661 (1990), 662 (1990),
664 (1990), 665 (1990), 666 (1990), 667 (1990), 669 (1990), 670 (1990), 674 (1990)
and 677 (1990),

Noting that, despite all efforts by the United Nations, Iraq refuses to comply
with its obligation to implement resolution 660 (1990) and the above subsequent
relevant resolutions, in flagrant contempt of the Council,

Mindful of its duties and responsibilities under the Charter of the United
Nations for the maintenance and preservation of international peace and security,

Determined to secure full compliance with its decisions,

Acting under Chapter VII of the Charter of the United Nations,

1. Demands that Iraq comply fully with resolution 660 (1990) and all
subsequent relevant resolutions and decides, while maintaining all its decisions,
to allow Iraq one final opportunity, as a pause of goodwill, to do so;

2. Authorizes Member States co-operating with the Government of Kuwait,
unless Iraq on or before 15 January 1991 fully implements, as set forth in
paragraph 1 above, the foregoing resolutions, to use all necessary means to uphold
and implement Security Council resolution 660 (1990) and all subsequent relevant
resolutions and to restore international peace and security in the area;

3. Requests all States to provide appropriate support for the actions
undertaken in pursuance of paragraph 2 of this resolution;

4. Requests the States concerned to keep the Council regularly informed on
the progress of actions undertaken pursuant to paragraphs 2 and 3 of this
resolution;

5. Decides to remain seized of the matter.

90-33056 2317E

/ —/

0102

↑ WOIMUBU K24651...

0103

↓ 0

↑ WOIMUBU K24651

↓ GE02 6979229A001 (7726/   )

FROM: A1UNITNA

56247-11
     I HAVE THE HONOUR TO TRANSMIT HEREWITH THE TEXT OF
RESOLUTION 678 (1990) ADOPTED BY THE SECURITY COUNCIL
AT ITS 2963RD MEETING ON 29 NOVEMBER 1990.
QUOTE
THE SECURITY COUNCIL,

     RECALLING AND REAFFIRMING ITS RESOLUTIONS 660 (1990), 661
(1990), 662 (1990), 664 (1990), 665 (1990), 666 (1990), 667 (1990),
669 (1990), 670 (1990), 674 (1990) AND 677 (1990),

     NOTING THAT, DESPITE ALL EFFORTS BY THE UNITED NATIONS, IRAQ
REFUSES TO COMPLY WITH ITS OBLIGATION TO IMPLEMENT RESOLUTION 660
(1990) AND THE ABOVE SUBSEQUENT RELEVANT RESOLUTIONS, IN FLAGRANT
CONTEMPT OF THE COUNCIL,

     MINDFUL OF ITS DUTIES AND RESPONSIBILITIES UNDER THE CHARTER OF
THE UNITED NATIONS FOR THE MAINTENANCE AND PRESERVATION OF THE
INTERNATIONAL PEACE AND SECURITY,

     DETERMINED TO SECURE FULL COMPLIANCE WITH ITS DECISIONS,

     ACTING UNDER CHAPTER VII OF THE CHARTER OF THE UNITED NATIONS,

     1. DEMANDS THAT IRAQ COMPLY FULLY WITH RESOLUTION 660 (1990)
AND ALL SUBSEQUENT RELEVANT RESOLUTIONS AND DECIDES, WHILE
MAINTAINING ALL ITS DECISIONS, TO ALLOW IRAQ ONE FINAL OPPORTUNITY,
AS A PAUSE OF GOODWILL, TO DO SO SEMICOLON

     2. AUTHORIZES MEMBER STATES CO-OPERATING WITH THE GOVERNMENT OF
KUWAIT, UNLESS IRAQ ON OR BEFORE 15 JANUARY 1991 FULLY IMPLEMENTS, AS
SET FORTH IN PARAGRAPH 1 ABOVE, THE FOREGOING RESOLUTIONS, TO USE ALL
NECESSARY MEANS TO UPHOLD AND IMPLEMENT SECURITY COUNCIL RESOLUTION
660 (1990) AND ALL SUBSEQUENT RELEVANT RESOLUTIONS AND TO RESTORE
INTERNATIONAL PEACE AND SECURITY IN THE AREA SEMICOLON

     3. REQUESTS ALL STATES TO PROVIDE APPROPRIATE SUPPORT FOR THE
ACTIONS UNDERTAKEN IN PURSUANCE OF PARAGRAPH 2 OF THIS RESOLUTION
SEMICOLON

     4. REQUESTS THE STATES CONCERNED TO KEEP THE COUNCIL REGULARLY
INFORMED ON THE PROGRESS OF ACTIONS UNDERTAKEN PURSUANT TO PARAGRAPHS

DETERMINED TO SECURE FULL COMPLIANCE WITH ITS DECISIONS,

ACTING UNDER CHAPTER VII OF THE CHARTER OF THE UNITED NATIONS,

1. DEMANDS THAT IRAQ COMPLY FULLY WITH RESOLUTION 660 (1990)
AND ALL SUBSEQUENT RELEVANT RESOLUTIONS AND DECIDES, WHILE
MAINTAINING ALL ITS DECISIONS, TO ALLOW IRAQ ONE FINAL OPPORTUNITY,
AS A PAUSE OF GOODWILL, TO DO SO SEMICOLON

2. AUTHORIZES MEMBER STATES CO-OPERATING WITH THE GOVERNMENT OF
KUWAIT, UNLESS IRAQ ON OR BEFORE 15 JANUARY 1991 FULLY IMPLEMENTS, AS
SET FORTH IN PARAGRAPH 1 ABOVE, THE FOREGOING RESOLUTIONS, TO USE ALL
NECESSARY MEANS TO UPHOLD AND IMPLEMENT SECURITY COUNCIL RESOLUTION
660 (1990) AND ALL SUBSEQUENT RELEVANT RESOLUTIONS AND TO RESTORE
INTERNATIONAL PEACE AND SECURITY IN THE AREA SEMICOLON

3. REQUESTS ALL STATES TO PROVIDE APPROPRIATE SUPPORT FOR THE
ACTIONS UNDERTAKEN IN PURSUANCE OF PARAGRAPH 2 OF THIS RESOLUTION
SEMICOLON

4. REQUESTS THE STATES CONCERNED TO KEEP THE COUNCIL REGULARLY
INFORMED ON THE PROGRESS OF ACTIONS UNDERTAKEN PURSUANT TO PARAGRAPHS
2 AND 3 OF THIS RESOLUTION SEMICOLON

5. DECIDES TO REMAIN SEIZED OF THE MATTER.
UNQUOTE
HIGHEST CONSIDERATION.

JAVIER PEREZ DE CUELLAR
SECRETARY-GENERAL
UNATIONS NEW YORK
COL CKD M4825
G.SCHLITTLER 3520A   SMI

=1130900219GMT

0104

NN-NN

0
↑ WOIMUBU K24651

GLGL
EXR0482 2 /AFP-BM32
IRAQ-U.N.-VOTE LEAD-1
    URGENT'''

    NEW YORK. UNITED NATIONS. NOV 29 (AFP) - THE U.N. SECURITY
COUNCIL THURSDAY AUTHORIZED THE USE OF MILITARY FORCE TO LIBERATE
KUWAIT IF IRAQ DOES NOT WITHDRAW FROM THE TINY EMIRATE BY JANUARY
15.
    - THE 15-MEMBER COUNCIL. MEETING EXTRAORDINARILY AT THE FOREIGN
MINISTERS LEVEL. ADOPTED THE USE-OF-FORCE RESOLUTION BY A VOTE OF
12 TO TWO. CUBA AND YEMEN VOTED AGAINST AND CHINA ABSTAINED.
    IT WAS ONLY THE SECOND TIME IN THE UNITED NATION'S 45-YEAR
HISTORY THAT THE WORLD BODY HAS ENDORSED MILITARY ACTION AGAINST A
MEMBER NATION. IN 1950 THE SECURITY COUNCIL AUTHORIZED THE USE OF
FORCE TO COUNTER NORTH KOREA'S INVASION OF SOUTH KOREA.
    PRIOR TO THE VOTE, U.S. SECRETARY OF STATE JAMES BAKER. WHO
PRESIDED OVER THE MEETING, LED THE DRIVE FOR THE TOUGH ANTI-IRAQ
MEASURE. ''WE MUST PUT THE CHOICE TO (IRAQI PRESIDENT) SADDAM
HUSSEIN IN UNMISTAKABLE TERMS,'' HE SAID.
    MORE
    AFP 292231 GMT NOV 90
AFP   292235 GMT NOV 90

GLGL
EXR0483 2 /AFP-BM33
IRAQ-U.N.-VOTE LEAD-2
    (NEW YORK)

    KUWAITI FOREIGN MINISTER SHEIKH SABAH AL-AHMAD AL-JABER ALSO
APPEALED FOR U.N. ACTION. ASSAILING THE IRAQIS AS ''WILD BEASTS''
WHO WERE DESTROYING HIS COUNTRY.
    BUT IN A STATEMENT EARLIER THURSDAY IN BAGHDAD, MR. HUSSEIN HAD
ALREADY REJECTED THE U.N. ULTIMATUM -- THE CULMINATION OF A GLOBAL
LOBBYING CAMPAIGN BY U.S. PRESIDENT GEORGE BUSH AND MR. BAKER.
    ''IRAQ WILL NOT BEND BEFORE THE STORM.'' MR. HUSSEIN SAID. ''IF
WAR WERE IMPOSED ON IRAQ. THE IRAQIS WILL FIGHT IN A WAY THAT WILL
HONOR ARABS AND MOSLEMS.''
    IRAQI AMBASSADOR ABDUL AMIR AL-ANBARI. ADDRESSING THE COUNCIL
BEFORE THE VOTE, SAID. ''THIS WOULD BE THE MOST DANGEROUS
RESOLUTION EVER PASSED BY THE SECURITY COUNCIL AND A VIOLATION OF
THE U.N. CHARTER.''
    THURSDAY'S RESOLUTION -- SPONSORED BY THE UNITED STATES, THE
SOVIET UNION. CANADA. FRANCE. BRITAIN AND ROMANIA -- DEMANDED THAT
BAGHDAD COMPLY FULLY WITH 11 EARLIER COUNCIL RESOLUTIONS CALLING
FOR IRAQ'S UNCONDITIONAL WITHDRAWAL FROM KUWAIT, WHICH IT INVADED
AUGUST 2 AND SUBSEQUENTLY ANNEXED. AND IMPOSING A STRICT TRADE
EMBARGO ON IRAQ.
    THE NEW MEASURE SAID THE COUNCIL HAD DECIDED ''TO ALLOW IRAQ
ONE FINAL OPPORTUNITY, AS A PAUSE OF GOODWILL.'' TO COMPLY WITH THE
RESOLUTIONS. SETTING A DEADLINE OF JANUARY 15 FOR WITHDRAWAL FROM
KUWAIT.
    UNLESS IRAQ COMPLIES BY THAT DATE. THE RESOLUTION AUTHORIZES
U.N. MEMBERS STATES ''TO USE ALL NECESSARY MEANS TO UPHOLD AND
IMPLEMENT SECURITY COUNCIL RESOLUTION 660 AND ALL SUBSEQUENT
RELEVANT RESOLUTIONS AND TO RESTORE INTERNATIONAL PEACE AND
SECURITY IN THE AREA.''
    MORE

0105

GLGL
EXR0486 3 /AFP-BM36
IRAQ-U.N.-TEXT
TEXT OF RESOLUTION AUTHORIZING THE USE OF FORCE IN GULF CRISIS

NEW YORK, UNITED NATIONS, NOV 29 (AFP) - HERE IS THE TEXT OF
SECURITY COUNCIL RESOLUTION 678 GIVING IRAQ UNTIL JANUARY 15 TO
WITHDRAW FROM KUWAIT OR FACE MILITARY ATTACK FROM U.N. MEMBERS:
THE SECURITY COUNCIL,
RECALLING AND REAFFIRMING ITS RESOLUTIONS 660 (1990), 661
(1990), 662 (1990), 664 (1990), 665 (1990), 666 (1990), 667 (1990),
669 (1990), 670 (1990), 674 (1990) AND 677 (1990),
NOTING THAT, DESPITE ALL EFFORTS BY THE UNITED NATIONS, IRAQ
REFUSES TO COMPLY WITH ITS OBLIGATION TO IMPLEMENT RESOLUTION 660
AND THE ABOVE SUBSEQUENT RELEVANT RESOLUTIONS, IN FLAGRANT CONTEMPT
OF THE COUNCIL,
MINDFUL OF ITS DUTIES AND RESPONSIBILITIES UNDER THE CHARTER OF
THE UNITED NATIONS FOR THE MAINTENANCE AND PRESERVATION OF
INTERNATIONAL PEACE AND SECURITY,
DETERMINED TO SECURE FULL COMPLIANCE WITH ITS DECISIONS,
ACTING UNDER CHAPTER VII OF THE CHARTER OF THE UNITED NATIONS,
1. DEMANDS THAT IRAQ COMPLY FULLY WITH RESOLUTION 660 AND ALL
SUBSEQUENT RELEVANT RESOLUTIONS AND DECIDES, WHILE MAINTAINING ALL
ITS DECISIONS, TO ALLOW IRAQ ONE FINAL OPPORTUNITY, AS A PAUSE OF
GOODWILL, TO DO SO.
2. AUTHORIZES MEMBERS STATES COOPERATING WITH THE GOVERNMENT OF
KUWAIT, UNLESS IRAQ ON OR BEFORE 15 JANUARY 1991 FULLY IMPLEMENTS,
AS SET FORTH IN PARAGRAPH ONE ABOVE, THE FOREGOING RESOLUTIONS, TO
USE ALL NECESSARY MEANS TO UPHOLD AND IMPLEMENT SECURITY COUNCIL
RESOLUTION 660 AND ALL SUBSEQUENT RELEVANT RESOLUTIONS AND TO
RESTORE INTERNATIONAL PEACE AND SECURITY IN THE AREA.
3. REQUESTS ALL STATES TO PROVIDE APPROPRIATE SUPPORT FOR THE
ACTIONS UNDERTAKEN IN PURSUANCE OF PARAGRAPH TWO OF THIS RESOLUTION.
4. REQUESTS THE STATES CONCERNED TO KEEP THE COUNCIL REGULARLY
INFORMED ON THE PROGRESS OF ACTIONS UNDERTAKEN PURSUANT TO
PARAGRAPHS TWO AND THREE OF THIS RESOLUTION.
5. DECIDES TO REMAIN SEIZED ON THE MATTER.
AFP
AFP 292238 GMT NOV 90
AFP 292244 GMT NOV 90

걸프사태정세 〈110〉

(11.30. 16:00 현재)

중동아프리카국
중 근 동 과

1. U.N 안보리, 對 이라크 武力制裁 決議案 採擇

> U.N 안보리는 11.29(현지시간) 전체회의를 열고, 다국적군의 對
> 이라크 무력사용 承認등 5개 항목의 決議案(678호)을 15개 이사국중
> 12개국 贊成(반대 2 : 예멘, 쿠바, 기권 1 : 중국)으로 採擇함.

○ 결의안 주요내용

- 이라크에게 마지막 기회를 부여하기 위해, 660호등 기채택된
  11개 U.N 결의안을 이행토록 이라크에게 촉구
- 91.1.15.까지 이라크가 쿠웨이트로부터 완전철수치 않을 경우,
  회원국에게 필요한 모든 수단 사용을 허용
- 모든국가에게 동 결의안 이행을 위해 필요한 지원제공 촉구등

○ 사담 후세인 이라크 대통령, 동 결의안을 거부하고, 전쟁도 불사
할것임을 표명

- 만일 전쟁이 일어난다면 아랍인과 회교도의 명예를 걸고 싸울것임.

2. 다국적군, 경계態勢 돌입

> U.N. 의 對 이라크 무력사용 許容 決議案 채택에 대한 이라크의 奇襲
> 報復 가능성에 대비하여, 걸프만에 駐屯해 있는 다국적군이 경계태세
> 에 돌입함.

○ 이라크군의 이동 조치에 따라, 영국군 황색경계, 사우디 1급 경계
태세에 돌입

3. 僑民撤收 現況

○ 이라크 총 723명, 철수인원 588, 잔류 135명   0107
- 철수인원, 집입과 돕입

長官報告事項

1990. 11. 30.
國際機構條約局
國際聯合課(75)

題 目 : 페만事態 관련 유엔安保理 決議 (第678號)

90.11.29. 유엔安保理는 이락이 91.1.15限 쿠웨이트로부터 撤收치 않을
경우 유엔會員國이 必要한 모든 措置를 취할수 있도록 許容하는 決議를 採擇한
바, 同 內容을 아래 報告드립니다.

---

1. 決議 678號 提案 및 採擇

○ 提案國 : 美國, 蘇聯, 카나다, 불란서, 英國, 루마니아

○ 票決結果 : 贊成 12, 反對 2(쿠바, 예멘), 棄權 1(中國)로 採擇됨.

2. 決議 678號 內容

○ 쿠웨이트에서 이락軍의 撤收등을 要求하는 페만事態 관련 決議를
이락이 91.1.15限 履行치 않을 경우 유엔會員國은 "必要한 모든措置
(all necessary means)"를 취할수 있음.

○ 同 決議 履行을 위하여 취해지는 措置에 대하여 各國이 支援할 것을
促求함.

0108

3. 決議 678號의 特徵

o 91.1.15限 이락이 쿠웨이트로부터 撤收치 않을 경우 武力을 包含한
  모든措置를 취할 權利를 美國등 유엔會員國에게 許容함으로써 이락에
  대한 最後 通牒的 性格의 決議

o 1950年 韓國戰時 유엔軍派兵決議 以後 유엔歷史上 侵略國에 대한 두번째
  武力使用 許容

o 유엔創設 以後 安保理 理事國 外務長官이 代表로서 參席한 네번째
  安保理會議 開催 (同 決議案의 比重을 높이기 위한 美國의 考慮)

4. 이락의 反應

o 決議 678號 採擇以前(11.28) 후세인 大統領은 最後 通牒的 性格의 同
  유엔決議 관련, "페만에서 戰爭 勃發時 아랍圈의 영광을 위하여 鬪爭할
  것임"을 밝힌바 있음.

添附 : 1. 安保理 決議 678號

      2. 페만事態 관련 安保理 決議 目錄 1부.   끝.

0109

안보리결의 678호

90. 11. 29.

The Security Council,

Recalling and reaffirming its resolutions 660 (1990),
661(1990), 662(1990), 664(1990), 665(1990), 666(1990), 667(1990),
669(1990), 670(1990), 674(1990) and 677(1990),

Noting that, despite all efforts by the United Nations,
Iraq refuses to comply with its obligation to implement
resolution 660 and the above subsequent relevant resolutions,
in flagrant contempt of the council,

Mindful of its duties and responsibilities under the
Charter of the United Nations for the maintenance and preservation
of international peace and security,

Determined to secure full compliance with its decisions,

Acting under Chapter VII of the Charter of the United

0110

1. <u>Demands</u> that Iraq comply fully with resolution 660 and all subsequent relevant resolutions and <u>decides</u>, while maintaining all its decisions, to allow Iraq one final opportunity, as a pause of goodwill, to do so.

2. <u>Authorizes</u> Members States cooperating with the Government of Kuwait, unless Iraq on or before 15 January 1991 fully implements, as set forth in paragraph one above, the foregoing resolutions, <u>to use all necessary means to uphold and implement</u> Security Council resolution 660 and all subsequent relevant resolutions and to restore international peace and security in the area.

3. <u>Requests</u> all States to provide appropriate support for the actions undertaken in pursuance of paragraph two of this resolution.

4. <u>Requests</u> the States concerned to keep the council regularly infomed on the progress of actions undertaken pursuant to paragraphs two and three of this resolution.

5. <u>Decides</u> to remain seized on the matter.

페만사태 관련 안보리 결의

결의안 표결일자	결의주요내용	부표결과 (찬:반:기권)	결의번호
90.8.2.	○ 이락의 쿠웨이트 침공 규탄 및 이락군의 무조건 철수 촉구	14:0:0	660 (1990)
8.6.	○ 이락에 대한 광범위한 경제제재 조치 결정 - 안보이사회내에 제재위원회 설치 - 유엔비회원국 포함 모든국가의 661호 이행 촉구	13:0:2 (쿠바,예멘)	661
8.9.	○ 이락의 쿠웨이트 합병 무효 간주 ○ 쿠웨이트 신정부 승인 금지	15:0:0	662
8.18.	○ 이락,쿠웨이트내 제3국민들의 즉각 출국허용 요구 ○ 외국 공관폐쇄 철회 요구	15:0:0	664
8.25.	○ 결의 661호 위반 선박에 대한 조치 권한 부여	13:0:2	665
9.13.	○ 인도적 목적의 대이락 식품 수출 제한적 승인	13:0:2	665
9.16.	○ 쿠웨이트주재 외국공관 침입 비난 ○ 외국공관원 즉시 석방 및 보호 요구	15:0:0	667
9.24.	○ 대이락 제재조치에 따른 피해국 지원	15:0:0	669
9.25.	○ 모든국가의 이락 및 쿠웨이트내 공항 이착륙 및 영공통과 불허 (인도적 식품 및 의약품운송 제외) ○ 모든국가에 의한 이락 국적선박 억류 허용	14:1:0 (쿠바)	670
10.29.	○ 이락의 쿠웨이트 침공으로 인한 전쟁피해 및 재정적 손실에 대한 이락의 책임 규정 및 추궁	13:0:2 (쿠바,예멘)	674
11.28.	○ 이락에 의한 쿠웨이트국민의 국적 말소기도 비난 ○ 쿠웨이트 인구센서스 기록의 유엔내 보존	미확인	677
11.29.	○ 이락이 91.1.15한 상기 안보리 제결의를 이행치 않을 경우, 유엔 회원국에게 필요한 모든조치를 취할 수 있도록 허용	12:2:1 (쿠바,예멘) (중국)	678

0112

걸프사태 관련 안보리 결의

결의호수	일 자	내 용	비 고
660	8. 2	- 이라크의 쿠웨이트 침공 비난 - 철군 촉구	
661	8. 6	- 경제 재재 - 교역, 경제지원 전면 금지	
662	8. 9	- 쿠웨이트 합병 무효 - 쿠웨이트 신정부 승인 금지	
664	8.18	- 억류 외국인 출국 촉구 - 쿠웨이트 공관 폐쇄 명령 철회 촉구	
665	8.25	- 경제봉쇄 위한 제한적 무력사용 승인	
666	9.13	- 인도적 목적의 대 이라크 식품등 수출 기본지침 규정	
667	9.16	- 이라크 군대의 쿠웨이트 일부 외국공관 침범 규탄	
669	9.24	- 전선국가 경제 원조	
670	9.25	- 대 이라크 공중 봉쇄	
674	10.29	- 대 이라크 피해 보상 책임 요구	
677	11.28	- 쿠웨이트 인구센서스자료 유엔 보존 결의	
678	11.30	- 대이라크 무력 사용 승인 결의 "모든 필요한 조치"	

0113

長 官 報 告 事 項

1990. 11. 30.
國際機構條約局
國際聯合課(75)

題 目 : 페만事態 관련 유엔安保理 決議 (第678號)

90.11.29. 유엔安保理는 이락이 91.1.15限 쿠웨이트로부터 撤收치 않을 경우 유엔會員國이 必要한 모든 措置를 취할수 있도록 許容하는 決議를 採擇한 바, 同 內容을 아래 報告드립니다.

---

1. 決議 678號 提案 및 採擇

ㅇ 提案國 : 美國, 蘇聯, 카나다, 불란서, 英國, 루마니아

ㅇ 票決結果 : 贊成 12, 反對 2(쿠바, 예멘), 棄權 1(中國)로 採擇됨.

2. 決議 678號 內容

ㅇ 쿠웨이트¨에서 이락軍의 撤收등을 要求하는 페만事態 관련 決議를 이락이 91.1.15限 履行치 않을 경우 유엔會員國은 "必要한 모든 措置 (all necessary means)"를 취할수 있음.

ㅇ 同 決議 履行을 위하여 취해지는 措置에 대하여 各國이 支援할 것을 促求함.

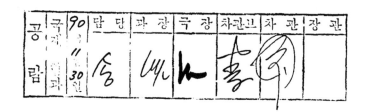

0114

3. 決議 678號의 特徵

o 91.1.15限 이락이 쿠웨이트로부터 撤收치 않을 경우 武力을 包含한
  모든 措置를 취할 權利를 美國등 유엔會員國에게 許容함으로써 이락에
  대한 最後 通牒的 性格의 決議

o 1950年 韓國戰時 유엔軍派兵決議 以後 유엔歷史上 侵略國에 대한 두번째
  武力使用 許容

o 유엔創設 以後 安保理 理事國 外務長官이 代表로서 參席한 네번째
  安保理會議 開催 (同 決議案의 比重을 높이기 위한 美國의 考慮)

4. 이락의 反應

o 決議 678號 採擇以前(11.28) 후세인 大統領은 最後 通牒的 性格의 同
  유엔決議 관련, "페만에서 戰爭 勃發時 아랍圈의 영광을 위하여 鬪爭할
  것임"을 밝힌바 있음.

    1. 안보리 결의 678호
添 附 : 2.페만事態 관련 安保理 決議 目錄 1부.   끝.

0115

(첨부 1)

안보리결의 678호

90. 11. 29.

<u>The Security Council,</u>

<u>Recalling and reaffirming</u> its resolutions 660 (1990),
661(1990), 662(1990), 664(1990), 665(1990), 666(1990), 667(1990),
669(1990), 670(1990), 674(1990) and 677(1990),

<u>Noting</u> that despite all efforts by the United Nations,
Iraq refuses to comply with its obligation to implement
resolution 660 and the above subsequent relevant resolutions,
in flagrant contempt of the council,

<u>Mindful</u> of its duties and responsibilities under the
Charter of the United Nations for the maintenance and preservation
of international peace and security,

<u>Determined</u> to secure full compliance with its decisions,

<u>Acting</u> under Chapter VII of the Charter of the United

0116

1. Demands that Iraq comply fully with resolution 660 and all subsequent relevant resolutions and decides, while maintaining all its decisions, to allow Iraq one final opportunity, as a pause of goodwill, to do so.

2. Authorizes Members States cooperating with the Government of Kuwait, unless Iraq on or before 15 January 1991 fully implements, as set forth in paragraph one above, the foregoing resolutions, to use all necessary means to uphold and implement Security Council resolution 660 and all subsequent relevant resolutions and to restore international peace and security in the area.

3. Requests all States to provide appropriate support for the actions undertaken in pursuance of paragraph two of this resolution.

4. Requests the States concerned to keep the council regularly infomed on the progress of actions undertaken pursuant to paragraphs two and three of this resolution.

5. Decides to remain seized on the matter.

폐만사태 관련 안보리 결의

결의안 표결일자	결 의 주 요 내 용	투표결과 (찬:반:기권)	결의번호
90.8.2.	ㅇ 이락의 쿠웨이트 침공 규탄 및 이락군의 무조건 철수 촉구	14:0:0	660 (1990)
8.6.	ㅇ 이락에 대한 광범위한 경제제재 조치 결정 - 안보이사회내에 제재위원회 설치 - 유엔비회원국 포함 모든국가의 661호 이행 촉구	13:0:2 (쿠바,예멘)	661
8.9.	ㅇ 이락의 쿠웨이트 합병 무효 간주 ㅇ 쿠웨이트 신정부 승인 금지	15:0:0	662
8.18.	ㅇ 이락, 쿠웨이트내 제3국민들의 즉각 출국허용 요구 ㅇ 외국 공관폐쇄 철회 요구	15:0:0	664
8.25.	ㅇ 결의 661호 위반 선박에 대한 조치 권한 부여	13:0:2 (쿠바,예멘)	665
9.13.	ㅇ 인도적 목적의 대이락 식품 수출 제한적 승인	13:0:2 (쿠바,예멘)	666
9.16.	ㅇ 쿠웨이트주재 외국공관 침입 비난 ㅇ 외국공관원 즉시 석방 및 보호 요구	15:0:0	667
9.24.	ㅇ 대이락 제재조치에 따른 피해국 지원	15:0:0	669
9.25.	ㅇ 모든국가의 이락 및 쿠웨이트내 공항 이착륙 및 영공통과 불허 (인도적 식품 및 의약품운송 제외) ㅇ 모든국가에 의한 이락 국적선박 억류 허용	14:1:0 (쿠바)	670
10.29.	ㅇ 이락의 쿠웨이트 침공으로 인한 전쟁피해 및 재정적 손실에 대한 이락의 책임 규정 및 추궁	13:0:2 (쿠바,예멘)	674
11.28.	ㅇ 이락에 의한 쿠웨이트국민의 국적 말소기도 비난 ㅇ 쿠웨이트 인구센서스 기록의 유엔내 보존	15:0:0 미확인	677
11.29.	ㅇ 이락이 91.1.15한 상기 안보리 제결의를 이행치 않을 경우, 유엔 회원국에게 필요한 모든조치를 취할 수 있도록 허용	12:2:1 (쿠바,예멘) (중국)	678

0118

걸 프 사 태 정 세 <116>

(12.7. 15:00 현재)

중동아프리카국

1. 이라크, 모든 抑留 人質 釋放 豫定 (이라크 INA 통신 보도)

> 후세인 이라크 大統領은 12.6. 이라크와 쿠웨이트에 抑留돼 있는 모든 外國人 人質들을 釋放 할것 이라고 하면서, 抑留된 外國人들은 크리스마스와 새해에 맞춰 自由롭게 歸國할 수 있도록 許容될 것이라 함.

- o 후세인, 다국적군의 공격 저지를 위해 억류 인질의 여행 제한 중단을 의회에 요청
  - 억류인질 개개인이 겪은 부당한 처사에 사과 표명
- o 미.영.소.일등 주요 국가들, 동 조치가 걸프사태의 일대 전환점이 될지 모른다며 환영의 뜻을 표시
  - 미국 : 희망적 신호이며, 후세인이 그의 위치를 깨달았음을 보여주고 있다고 시사
  - 영국 : 크게 환영하며, 그러나 이라크가 유엔이 결의한 나머지 조건도 충족해야 한다고 논평
  - 소련 : 환영을 표시하고, 이 조치는 이라크가 쿠웨이트에서 철수할 것이라는 신호임을 논평
  - 일본 : 이번 조치가 유엔 결의안에 따른 걸프사태의 평화적 해결을 향한 첫번째 진전임을 시사

2. 유엔 安保理 5個 理事國, 中東平和 問題 關聯 國際會議 開催 合議

(AP, UPI 연합 보도)

> 美.英.蘇.中.프랑스등 5個 理事國은 걸프事態 解決을 위해 이라크측이 提起한 要求事項中 하나인 中東平和 問題에 관한 國際會議를 適切한 時期에 開催 한다는 決議案 文案을 原則的으로 承認 하였다고 함.

- o 중동평화 회담에 반대해온 미국은 동 문제를 신중히 다룰것을 제의

3. 主要 關聯 動向

<미 국>

- o 대이라크 전격전 가능성에 대비, NATO 회원국에 걸프만 다국적 군사력 증강을 위한 추가 지원 요청 예정

※ <유가동향>

- o 런던 유가, 배럴당 2$ 하락으로 25.60$ (내년 1월분 인도)
  - 후세인 이라크 대통령의 억류인질 전원 석방 발표에 기인

4. 僑民 撤收 動向

- o 이라크 총723명중 철수인원 594명, 잔류 129명
  - 철수인원, 전일과 동일

0119

외 무 부

종 별 :

번 호 : UNW-2744   일 시 : 90 1212 1420

수 신 : 장 관(통일,중근동,국연,기정)

발 신 : 주 유엔 대사

제 목 : 쿠웨이트 외무장관 서한

　　1.당지 쿠웨이트 대사는 12.6.자 본직앞 서한으로 최호중 외무장관 앞 쿠웨이트
부총리겸 외무장관의 별첨서한을 송부하여 왔음.

　　2.동 서한은 안보리 결의 674 호상 이락의 대쿠웨이트 침공및 점령에 따라 제3국이
입은 각종손실에 대한 이락의 국제법상 책임에 관한 조항에대해 언급하면서,
쿠웨이트도 제3국인 및 법인에 대한 도덕적, 법적 책임을 느끼고있다고 강조하고
안보리를 통하여 외국인들의 권익을 보호하는데 기여하고자 한다고 밝히고
있음.동서한은 또한 아측의 협력이 안보리가 이러한 목적의 달성을 위해 적절한
메카니즘을 수립하는데 기여할것임을 강조하였음.

　　첨부:상기 서한(아랍어 원본 및 영어번역본)(FAX):UNW(F)-317

　　끝

　　(대사 현홍주-국장)

통상국　　1차보　　중아국　　국기국　　안기부

PAGE 1   90.12.13   09:30

　　　　　　　　　　　　　　　　　　　　외신 1과 통제관

　　　　　　　　　　　　　　　　　　　　　　　　　　0120

PERMANENT MISSION
OF THE STATE OF KUWAIT
TO THE UNITED NATIONS
NEW YORK

وفد دولة الكويت الدائم
لدى الأمم المتحدة
نيويورك

334/90

December 6, 1990

Excellency,

I have the honour to forward a letter by H.E.
Sheikh Sabah Al Ahmed Al Sabah, Deputy Prime Minister and
Minister of Foreign Affairs of the State of Kuwait, to
H.E. Mr. Ho-Joong Choi, Minister of Foreign Affairs of
Republic of Korea.

It would be appreciated if this letter could be
transmitted to its high destination.

Accept, Excellency, the assurances of my highest
consideration.

Sincerely,

MOHAMMAD A. ABULHASAN
Permanent Representative

H.E. MR. HONG-CHOO HYUN
Permanent Observer of the Republic
of Korea to the United Nations
866 United Nations Plaza, Suite 300
New York, N.Y. 10017

5-1

SABAH AL-AHMED AL JABER AL SABAH

Deputy Prime Minister Minister of Foreign Affairs

معالي الوزير الصديق هو جونج شوي   الموقر

تحية طيبة وبعد ،

لا شك أن السكرتير العام للأمم المتحدة قد أبلغ معاليكم بنص قرار
مجلس الأمن رقم ٦٧٤ (١٩٩٠) والصادر بتاريخ ٢٩ أكتوبر ١٩٩٠ .

وفي هذا الصدد أود أن أشير الى منطوق الفقرتين التنفيذيتين
الثامنة والتاسعة من هذا القرار واللتين نصهما كما يلي :

الفقرة : ٨ يذكر العراق بمسؤوليته ، بموجب القانون الدولي ، عن أي خسائر
أو أضرار أو اصابات تنشأ فيما يتعلق بالكويت والدول الأخرى
ورعاياها وشركاتها ، نتيجة لغزو العراق واحتلاله غير المشروع
للكويت .

الفقرة : ٩ يدعو الدول الى جمع المعلومات ذات الصلة المتعلقة بمطالباتها
ومطالبات رعاياها وشركاتها للعراق لجبر الضرر أو التعويض المالي
بغية وضع ما قد يتقرر من ترتيبات وفقا للقانون الدولي .

ان هاتين الفقرتين ، وكما هو واضح ، ترتبان مسؤولية قانونية على
حكومة العراق تجاه الأفراد ، والشركات العاملة في الكويت والتي تعرضت
مصالحها للضرر والخسارة .

وان حكومة الكويت في سعيها لتحديد معالم هذه المسؤولية وفرضها على
العراق من خلال مجلس الأمن ، انما تريد تأكيد ادراكها لمسؤولياتها الأدبية
والقانونية تجاه أولئك الأفراد والشركات الذين ساهموا بكل جد واخلاص في
برامج التنمية الاقتصادية والاجتماعية في الكويت وكانوا عنصر خير ومشاركة
في مسيرة الكويت ، كما أنها حريصة كل الحرص على أن تساهم بقدر ما تستطيع
في حفظ حقوق أولئك الأفراد والشركات من خلال القنوات المتاحة وعلى رأسها
مجلس الأمن .

5-2

0122

SABAH AL-AHMED AL JABER AL SABAH

Deputy Prime Minister, Minister of Foreign Affairs

بسم الله الرحمن الرحيم

صباح الأحمد الجابر الصباح
نائب رئيس مجلس الوزراء وزير الخارجية

- ۲ -

ان قرار مجلس الأمن ٦٧٤ (۱۹۹۰) يفتح الباب لتحقيق الحصول على التعويض
من العراق عن الخسائر والأضرار التي لحقت بمواطنيكم وشركاتكم العاملة في
الكويت وذلك بدءا بتجميع المعلومات ذات الصلة بالمطالبات .

وإنني يا معالي الصديق على ثقة بأن من شأن تعاوننا أن يساعد مجلس
الأمن الدولي على وضع الآلية المناسبة للحصول على التعويضات من الحكومة
العراقية ، بما يحفظ حقوق المتضررين نتيجة للعدوان العراقي الغادر على
دولة الكويت .

وتفضلوا بقبول فائق التقدير والاحترام ،،،

صباح الأحمد الجابر الصباح

٤ ديسمبر ۱۹۹۰م

٥-٣

0123

Excellency,

No doubt the United Nations Secretary-General has
informed Your Excellency of the text of Security Council
Resolution 674 (1990) of 29 October 1990.

In this regard, I should like to refer back to
the text of the two operative paragraphs (8) and (9) of
this Resolution, which read as follows:

> Paragraph 8: Reminds Iraq that under
> international law, it is liable for any loss,
> damage or injury arising in regard to Kuwait
> and third States, and their nationals and
> corporations, as a result of the invasion and
> illegal occupation of Kuwait by Iraq;

> Paragraph 9: Invites States to collect
> relevant information regarding their claims
> and those of their nationals and corporations,
> for restitution or financial compensation by
> Iraq with a view to such arrangements as may
> be established in accordance with international
> law;

It is evident that these two paragraphs place
legal responsibility on the Government of Iraq toward
individuals and corporations operating in Kuwait and whose
interests have been subjected to damage or loss.

In its endeavor to define the elements of that
responsibility in order to enforce it on Iraq through the
....II, II .... of Kuwait wishes to
emphasize its awareness of its moral and legal
responsibilities toward those individuals and corporations
who have contributed with all diligence and loyalty to the
economic and social development programs in Kuwait. They
were an attribute of true virtue and participation in the
development of Kuwait. Kuwait is extremely keen to
contribute, as much as it can, in preserving the rights of
those individuals and corporations through the available
channels, most notably the Security Council.

Security Council Resolution 674 (1990) opens the
door to obtaining compensation from Iraq for the losses

5-4

0124

and damages sustained by your nationals and corporations
operating in Kuwait starting with collecting the relevant
information regarding the claims.

     I am confident, Your Excellency, that our
cooperation will help the United Nations Security Council
set the appropriate mechanism for obtaining the
reparations from the Iraqi Government to ensure the
preservation of the rights of those affected due to the
perfiduous Iraqi aggression against the State of Kuwait.

     Accept, Excellency, the assurances of my highest
consideration.

                        SHEIKH SABAH AL AHMED AL SABAH
                        Deputy Prime Minister and
                        Minister of Foreign Affairs

5-5

0125

걸 프 사 태 정 세 〈125〉
(12.19. 15:00 현재)

중동아프리카국
중 근 동 과

1. 이라크, 美서 유엔 決議案 계속 强要時 協商 拒否 豫定

> 후세인 이라크 大統領은 美國이 이라크가 拒否하고 있는 유엔 決議案을 계속
> 固執하려 든다면 美國과의 直接 平和 協商을 拒否할 것이라고 함.

- ○ 후세인, 자신들은 미국의 지시를 받기 위해 미국에 가지 않을것이라고 언급
  (터어키 TV 방송 인터뷰시)
- ○ 부쉬 미 대통령, 이라크와 어떠한 타협도 하지 않겠다는 미국 정부의 기본
  입장을 재천명

2. EC, 이라크의 別途 協商 提議 拒否

> EC는 이라크가 걸프事態와 關聯하여 別途 協商을 갖자고 提議한데 대해,
> 이라크가 美國과의 會談을 갖기 전에는 協商을 하지 않겠다고 함.

- ○ EC, 미측과 공동 보조 예정
- ○ 부쉬 미 대통령, EC가 독자적으로 이라크와 접촉치 않고 미국과의 공동
  보조를 취하기로 결정한데 대해 찬사 표명

3. 主要 關聯 動向

〈이 라 크〉

- ○ 이라크, 체류중인 소련인 출국 허용

  (바그다드 주재 소련 대사관 대변인 말 인용 AFP 보도)

  - 현재 2,565만명의 소련인 체류중

〈일   본〉

- ○ 걸프 주둔 미군에 3억불 상당의 컴퓨터 의료기기 제공 예정

〈아 랍 권〉

- ○ 시리아, 이라크의 완전 철수 없이는 걸프사태에 대한 협상의 여지가
  없음을 경고

4. 僑民 撤收 動向

- ○ 이라크 총723명중 철수인원 603명, 잔류 120명
  - 철수인원 전일과 동일

0126

분류번호	보존기간

발 신 전 보

WUN-1919   901120 1534 FK

번   호 : _____   종별 : _____

WUS -3831

수   신 : 주 수신처 참조 ~~///대사.~~ 총영사

발   신 : 장 관 (중근동)

제   목 : 걸프사태

1. 걸프 사태와 관련, 미국은 이라크의 쿠웨이트 철수가 없는한 이라크에 대한 가일층의 압력 수단으로서~~를~~ 또는 실제 군사행동을 위한 ~~대비~~ ^{사전} 조치로서 유엔 안보리의 무력 사용 결의를 확보하려고 할것임.

2. 따라서 안보리의 동 결의 채택 시기는 미국의 ~~무력 사용 전쟁가 글개~~ 선택을 예측하는데 있어서와 ~~활동~~ 시기를 예측하는데 주요한 참고 요소가 될것이므로, 이와 관련한 미국과 유엔 안보리의 동향을 계속 보고 바람. 끝.

군사적 방안을 선택할 경우 그

(중동아국장   이 해 순)

예 고 : 91.6.30. 일반

수신처 : 주 유엔, 미 대사

1991. 6.3ㄱ. 애 예고문에 의거 일반문서로 재 분류됨.

미주국장
 국제기구국장

앙 고 재	80 년 11 월 일 중근동 과	기안자 성명 박창오	과 장	심의관	국장 전기료	차 관	장 관	보 안 통 제

외신과통제

0127

외 무 부

종 별 :

번 호 : UNW-2618   일 시 : 90 1127 1830

수 신 : 장 관(국연)

발 신 : 주 유엔 대사

제 목 : 안보리(이락사태)

　　1.쿠웨이트의 요청에 따라 금 11.27 표제건 토의를 위한 안보리가 개최되어
쿠웨이트 대표로 부터 이락군의 쿠웨이트내 잔학상에 대한 보고를 청취하였음.

　　2.피점령 쿠웨이트에서 생활하다 최근 탈출한 5인의 쿠웨이트측 증인이 이들이
체험한 이락군의 잔학상에 대해 증언하고 쿠웨이트의 구출을 호소하였음.

　　3.쿠웨이트대표는 쿠웨이트 인구 등록 자료를 유엔사무총장이 관리하여 줄것을
요청하는 별첨 결의안을 제출하였음.

　　4.안보리 의장은 안보리 회원국간 비공식 협의를 통하여 동건 토의를 위한
추후회의 소집 일정을 결정할 것임을 선언하였음.

　　첨부:쿠웨이트 제출결의안(FAX):UNW(F)-299

　　끝

　　(대사 현홍주-국장)

국기국　이규직　중아국　김문직　1차보　2차보　대책반

PAGE 1   90.11.28   10:22 WG

외신 1과 통제관

0128

UNITED
NATIONS

S

Security Council

PROVISIONAL

S/21966
26 November 1990

ORIGINAL: ENGLISH

Kuwait: draft resolution

The Security Council,

Recalling resolutions 660 (1990) of 2 August 1990, 662 (1990) of 9 August 1990 and 674 (1990) of 29 October 1990,

Reiterating its concern for the suffering caused to individuals in Kuwait as a result of the invasion and occupation of Kuwait by Iraq,

Gravely concerned at the ongoing attempt by Iraq to alter the demographic composition of the population of Kuwait and to destroy the civil records maintained by the legitimate Government of Kuwait,

Acting under Chapter VII of the Charter of the United Nations,

1.   Condemns the attempts by Iraq to alter the demographic composition of the population of Kuwait and to destroy the civil records maintained by the legitimate Government of Kuwait;

2.   Mandates the Secretary-General to take custody of a copy of the population register of Kuwait the authenticity of which has been certified by the legitimate Government of Kuwait which covers the population registration up to 1 August 1990;

3.   Requests the Secretary-General to establish, in co-operation with the legitimate Government of Kuwait, an Order of Rules and Regulations governing access and use of the said copy of the population register.

2269E

/ - /

외　무　부

종　별 : 지 급

번　호 : UNW-2651　　　　　　　　　일　시 : 90 1129 2030

수　신 : 장 관(국연,중근동,기정)

발　신 : 주 유엔 대사

제　목 : 안보리(이락사태)

　　1.금 11.29 베이커 국무장관 주재하에 표제건 토의를 위한 안보리가 속개됨.금일 회의는 무력사용 권한 부여 결의안을 찬 12, 반2 (큐바,예멘), 기권 1 (중국) 의 표결로 채택 함.(결의 678 호)

　　2.금일 회의는 코트디브와르, 예멘을 제외한 13개 안보리회원국 외무장관 참석하에 개최되었음. 쿠웨이트 외무장관및 이락 주유엔대사도 토의에 참석함.

　　3.주요 발언요지

　　0.이락

　　- 무력사용 허가 결의는 유엔헌장 위반이며 미국에 의한 안보리의 패권주의적 지배결과임.냉전종료후 새로운 국제질서는 외교의 역할을 강조하는 것이어야함.

　　0.예멘

　　- 동 결의는 전쟁결의안으로서 광범위한 권한을 위임하는 것이며, 무력사용에 대한 유엔의 지휘통제가 없는점을 감안, 지지할수없음.

　　0.큐바

　　- 최후통첩, 전쟁선포와 다름없는 결의를 채택하는 것은 지지할수 없음.

　　0.중국

　　- 중국은 국제분쟁 해결에 있어 무력사용을 반대 하므로 동 결의안을 지지할수 없으며, 반면 동 결의안이 중국의 입장을 반영하는 쿠웨이트에서의 이락철수등 기존 안보리결의 이행을 촉구하는 내용을 포함하고 있어 거부권을 행사하지는 않고자함.

　　0.프랑스, 영국, 소련, 미국

　　- 91.1.15.까지 대 이락추가제재등 새로운 결의안 추진을 지지하지않을 것이며, 이락이 평화를 선택할 시간적 여유를 주고자함.단, 이락이 억류 중인 인질에게 해를 끼칠시에는 대응책을 취할 권리를 유보하며 제네바 인권규약, 전시법등을 위반할시

국기국　　1차보　　중아국　　정문국　　안기부

개인책임을 추궁할것임을 밝힘.

    0.카나다, 소련
    - 안보리의 단합이 아랍-이스라엘간 항구적 평화모색을 위한 기회가 되기를 희망
    0.핀란드, 콜롬비아
    - 유엔사무총장의 중재노력을 기대함.
    0.데뀨야르 유엔사무총장
    - 91.1.15까지 45일간의 기간이 평화를 위해 건설적으로 사용될수 있기를 희망
    4.평가

    0.금일 채택된 결의는 유엔역사상 회원국들에게 무력사용 권한을 부여한 최초의
결의안 (한국동란의 경우 안보리는 회원국들에게 침략을 격퇴하기 위한 필요한 지원을
한국에 제공토록 권고하였음.) 이나, 동결의안이 헌장 제7조상 몇조에 근거한 것인지,
명시하지 않은것이 주목됨.

    0.영,불 소련, 미국등은 91.1.15 까지는 인질에 대한 위해등 특별한 사태 악화가
발생하지않는한 안보리에서의 추가적 조치를 추진하거나 지원하지 않을것임을 밝혔는
바, 당분간 이락의 대응을 지켜보겠다는 뜻을 강조한 것으로보임.

    0.유엔사무총장은 이락이 희망시 중재노력을 활용의가 있음을 직접 적극
표명하였고, 다수 안보리회원국이 동 중재노력을 강조하였는바, 이는 이락에 대해
외교적 노력을 모색할수 있는 경로와 기회를 상기시킨 것으로 평가됨.

    첨부:동 결의전문(FAX):UNW(F)-303
    끝

    (대사 현홍주-국장)

**UNITED
NATIONS**

Security Council

Distr.
GENERAL

S/21969
28 November 1990

ORIGINAL: ENGLISH

<u>Canada, Union of Soviet Socialist Republics, United Kingdom
of Great Britain and Northern Ireland and United States of
America: draft resolution</u>

<u>The Security Council</u>,

<u>Recalling and reaffirming</u> its resolutions 660 (1990), 661 (1990), 662 (1990), 664 (1990), 665 (1990), 666 (1990), 667 (1990), 669 (1990), 670 (1990), 674 (1990) and 677 (1990),

<u>Noting that</u>, despite all efforts by the United Nations, Iraq refuses to comply with its obligation to implement resolution 660 (1990) and the above subsequent relevant resolutions, in flagrant contempt of the Council,

<u>Mindful</u> of its duties and responsibilities under the Charter of the United Nations for the maintenance and preservation of international peace and security,

<u>Determined</u> to secure full compliance with its decisions,

<u>Acting</u> under Chapter VII of the Charter of the United Nations,

1.   <u>Demands</u> that Iraq comply fully with resolution 660 (1990) and all subsequent relevant resolutions and decides, while maintaining all its decisions, to allow Iraq one final opportunity, as a pause of goodwill, to do so;

2.   <u>Authorizes</u> Member States co-operating with the Government of Kuwait, unless Iraq on or before 15 January 1991 fully implements, as set forth in paragraph 1 above, the foregoing resolutions, to use all necessary means to uphold and implement Security Council resolution 660 (1990) and all subsequent relevant resolutions and to restore international peace and security in the area;

3.   <u>Requests</u> all States to provide appropriate support for the actions undertaken in pursuance of paragraph 2 of this resolution;

4.   <u>Requests</u> the States concerned to keep the Council regularly informed on the progress of actions undertaken pursuant to paragraphs 2 and 3 of this resolution;

5.   <u>Decides</u> to remain seized of the matter.

90-33056   2317E

/---/ (handwritten)

0132

유연과 보편적 집단안전보장체제

(페르샤만 사태와 관련하여)

1. 이라크의 쿠웨이트 침공과 유엔 안보이사회 결의

1990년 8월 2일 주권독립국인 쿠웨이트에 대한 이라크의 무력침공은 중동지역은 물론 전세계에 커다란 충격과 경종을 가하였다. 이로 인하여 유연에서는 쿠웨이트와 미국의 공동 요청으로 안보이사회의 긴급회의가 소집되어 페르샤만 위기가 토의되었다. 안보이사회는 이라크의 쿠웨이트 침공이 국제평화와 안전에 대한 침해라고 규정한 후 이라크 규탄, 모든 이라크군의 즉각 무조건 철수, 이라크와 쿠웨이트간의 즉각 협상 촉구등을 내용으로 한 결의 (660호)를 만장일치(14:0:0)로 가결하였다. (예면대표는 본국정부 훈령 미접이유로 투표에 불참)

동 회의에서 쿠웨이트대표는 이라크의 침공이 유연헌장 위반이고, 안보이사회가 쿠웨이트의 주권과 영토를 보호할 책임이 있으며, 이라크군의 즉각 무조건 철수를 요구해야 한다고 역설하였다. 한편 이라크 대표는 금번 사태가 이라크의 국내문제이므로 안보이사회가 관여할 바가 아니며, 쿠웨이트의 신정부가 국내질서 회복을 위하여 이라크의 지원을 요청하였다고 주장하였다. 미국대표는 이라크의 쿠웨이트 침공이 사전 모의된 것이며, 이라크군의 즉각 무조건 철수를 강조하고 미국은 쿠웨이트를 원조할 것임을 밝혔다. 소련대표는 안보이사회가 신속하고 단호한 대처를 취할 것을 촉구하였고, 중국대표는 이라크군이 철수되어야 한다고 발언하였다. 여타 이사국대표들도 대체로 이라크의 침공을 유연헌장과 국제법 위반이라고 비난하고 이라크군의 철수를 촉구하였다.

0133

이라크는 안보이사회 결의 660호를 수락하지도 않고 이행도 하지
않았을 뿐만 아니라 8월 8일에는 쿠웨이트의 이라크 합병을 공표하였다.
이라크는 이어 쿠웨이트 거주 제3국 국민들의 이라크에의 강제이송 및
인질화, 쿠웨이트 주재 외국공관 포위, 침입 및 폐쇄등을 강행하였으며
쿠웨이트 점령을 계속하였다. 8월말 암만에서 이루어진 유연사무총장과
이라크 외무장관간의 회담에서도 이라크측은 강경입장을 고수하였다.
이와 같은 상황에 대처하여 안보이사회는 이라크의 쿠웨이트 침공직후
상기 결의 660호외에 주로 이라크를 겨냥하여 9개의 결의(11월중순 현재)를
가결하였는 바, 각 결의의 주요내용은 아래와 같다.

결의안 표결일자	결의 주요 내용	투표결과 (찬:반:기권)	결의번호
1990. 8.6.	○ 이라크에 대하여 광범위한 경제제재 　　조치 결정 　- 안보이사회내에 제재위원회 설치 　- 유엔비회원국 포함 모든국가의 661호 　　이행 촉구	13:0:2 (쿠바, 예멘)	661 (1990)
8.9.	○ 이라크의 쿠웨이트 합병 무효 간주 ○ 쿠웨이트 신정부 승인 금지	15:0:0	662
8.18.	○ 제3국민들의 즉각 출국허용 요구 ○ 외국 공관폐쇄 철회 요구	15:0:0	664
8.25.	○ 결의 661호 위반 선박에 대한 필요 　조치 권한 부여	13:0:2 (쿠바, 예멘)	665
9.13.	○ 인도적 목적의 대이라크 식품 수출허용	13:0:2 (쿠바, 예멘)	666

0134

결 의 안 표결일자	결 의 주 요 내 용	투표결과 (찬:반:기권)	결의번호
9.16.	○ 쿠웨이트 주재 외국공관 침입 비난 ○ 외국공관원 즉시 석방 및 보호 요구	15:0:0	667
9.24.	○ 대이라크 제재조치에 따른 피해국 지원	15:0:0	669
9.25.	○ 모든국가의 이라크 및 쿠웨이트내 공항 　이착륙 및 영공통과 불허(인도적 식품 　및 의약품 운송 제외) ○ 모든국가에 의한 이라크 국적선박 　억류 허용	14:1:0 (쿠바)	670
10.29.	○ 이라크의 쿠웨이트 침공으로 인한 전쟁 　피해 및 재정적 손실에 대한 이라크의 　책임 규정 및 추궁	13:0:2 (쿠바,예멘)	674

2. 안보이사회 조치의 특징

　　이라크의 쿠웨이트 침공, 합병과 강점 및 제3국 국민의 인질화등에
대응한 안보이사회에서의 토의과정과 이사회가 가결한 일련의 결의 조치에는
특기할만한 측면이 있다.

　　첫째, 안보이사회는 페르샤만 사태의 평화적 해결을 추구하고 있다.
(11월중순 현재) 이라크군이 쿠웨이트로부터의 철수를 거부함에 따라 안보
이사회는 1968년이래 유엔으로서는 처음으로 가장 강력하고 광범위한 경제
제재를 이라크에 가할 것을 결의하였고,주1) 이라크로 통하는 모든 육로,
해로와 항공로를 봉쇄하였다.　그러나 한편 안보이사회는 이라크의 계속

0135

집요한 입장에 직면하여 헌장 제 6장이 규정한 평화적 해결 수단의 한계를 인식하면서도 소련등 주요국의 대이라크 외교적 교섭의 기회는 봉쇄하지 않고 있다.

둘째, 미국은 안보이사회에서 이라크와 긴밀한 군사 협력관계를 유지 하여온 소련의 협력을 시종일관 확보하였다. 소련은 페르샤만 사태와 관련한 상기 10개 결의안에 모두 찬성 투표하였을 뿐만 아니라 결의안 666호, 670호 및 674호에는 미국과 함께 공동제안까지 하였다. 이를 가능케 한 배경으로는 1988년 미.소 양국 수뇌가 유엔총회 연설을 통하여 유엔 중시 정책을 천명한 사실, 1989년 제 44차 유엔총회때는 유엔역사상 처음으로 미.소 양국이 국제평화.안보.협력을 위한 결의안을 공동 제안하여 통과 시킨 사실등을 들 수 있다. 유엔에서의 미.소 공동보조가 여타 이사국 대표의 입장에 긍정적인 영향을 미친 것은 확실하다.

셋째, 안보이사회가 페르샤만 위기에 대처하여 주요 결의안을 상정 함에 있어서 유엔헌장 제 7장의 일부 강제규정을 발동하고 만장일치로 가결 함으로써 안보이사회의 집단적 결의를 단호하게 표명하였다. 안보이사회는 또한 40년간 사실상 유명무실하였던 유엔 군사참모위원회로 하여금 페르샤만 사태를 논의케 하여 동 위원회의 기능을 활성화 하였다. 안보이사회는 헌장 제 24조의 규정에 따라 국제평화와 안전의 유지라는 유엔의 제일차적 책임을 유엔회원국 전체를 대신하여 그 임무를 수행하고 있는 것이다.

위와 같이 페르샤만 위기와 관련한 안보이사회의 조치는 유엔의 권능을 강화하고 유엔에 대한 전세계의 보편적 기대를 새롭게 증대시키는데 크게 기여하고 있다고 평가되는 바, 그 기대속에는 유엔헌장 기초자들이 의도하였던 집단 안전보장 체제발전 가능성이 포함 되어 있다고 본다. 그렇다면 집단안보체제가 왜 확립되지 못하였는가? 유엔은 그 대안으로 무엇을 창출하였는가? 탈냉전시대에 유엔집단안보 체제의 확립 가능성은 있는가?

0136

3. 안보이사회의 권능

　　1945년 4월 유연창설을 위한 헌장제정 목적으로 샌프란시스코에 모인
50개국의 대표들은 전후세대의 국제평화 유지를 위해서는 "국제연맹"보다
권능이 강화된 "국제연합"의 필요에 대하여 인식을 같이 하였다.　이러한
인식을 기초로 이들은 헌장 제 1조에 국제평화와 안전의 유지를 유연의
제 1차적 목적으로 명시하고 이 목적 달성을 위하여는 집단적 조치를 취할
것을 분명히 하였다.　대표들은 또한 국제평화와 안전 유지에 관한 중요한
책임을 안보이사회에 부과하고 유연회원국 전체를 대신하여 그 임무를 수행
토록 규정하였다.　이어 이들은 헌장 제 6장에서 분쟁의 평화적 해결을 위한
제반 수단의 원용을 강조한후, 제 7장에서는 평화의 위협, 침해 및 침략
행위에 대하여 첫단계로서 잠정조치(제 40조), 다음 단계에서는 제재(제 41조),
최종단계에서는 군사적 행동(제 42조)에 관하여 규정하였다.　회원국은
이러한 군사적 행동에 필요한 병력과 원조와 편의를 제공할 의무(제 43조)를
지도록 하였다.　이와 같은 강제조치를 규정한 제 7장은 유연헌장의 심장
이라고 말할 수 있다.

　　유연헌장제정 대표들은 제 2차 대전을 승리로 이끈 연합국의 전시
협력이 전후에도 안보이사회의 5개 상임강대국간에 국제평화를 위한 협조와
공동노력으로 연결될 것으로 상정하였다.　그러나 이들의 상정은 일찍부터
장애에 봉착하였다.　1946년 1월 10일 런던에서 제 1차 유연총회가 마치
세계연방수립도 가능할 듯한 밝은 희망과 크나큰 기대속에 개막된지 10일도
안되어 이란은 소련 주둔군이 자국으로 부터 철수하지 않고 내정에 간섭하고
있다고 주장, 이 문제를 안보이사회에 제기하였다.　이에 대하여 소련은

0137

이란의 배후에 미국과 영국의 조종이 있다고 단정하여 영국군의 그리스 내정간섭 문제를 안보이사회에 상정함으로써 미국과 영국에 응수하였다. 같은 해에 시리아와 레바논이 영국과 프랑스의 군대 주둔은 각각 주권의 침해라고 지적, 이를 안보이사회에 제기하였을때 미국은 외국군대의 조속한 철수 교섭을 촉구하는 결의안을 상정 하였다. 소련은 동 결의안 내용이 불충분하다는 이유로 반대투표 하였는 바, 이는 안보이사회에서 최초의 거부권 행사였다.

이와 같이 강대국간에 싹트기 시작한 상호 불신과 대립은 1948년 소련의 베를린 봉쇄가 감행되었을때 일촉 즉발의 위기가 조성되어 급기야는 미.소 양대국을 각각 주축으로 한 동.서 진영간의 소위 냉전으로 진전하는데 그 주요 요인이 되기도 하였다. 그후 40년동안 계속된 국제적 긴장과 대립 상황은 유엔에 큰 영향을 미쳤으며, 연례적으로 상정되었던 "한국문제"에 대하여 1975년에는 총회에서 상반된 결의안이 채택된 사실로써도 동.서간 대립의 심각상을 예증할 수 있었다.

냉전의 영향을 가장 직접적으로 받은 유엔의 주요기관은 안보이사회 였다. 이로 인하여 이사회의 기능은 4차에 걸친 중동전쟁(1948, 1956, 1967, 1973), 3차에 걸친 인도.파키스탄 전쟁(1947-48, 1965, 1971), 이란. 이라크전쟁 (1980-88)등으로 중대한 시련을 겪었다.주3) 이사회는 또한 레바논 내전(1958), 콩고문제(1960), 쿠바위기(1962), 사이프러스 내전 (1963)등에서도 그 권능의 한계를 노정하였다. 강대국이 당사자가 된 스에즈운하 위기(1956), 소련의 대형가리 무력개입(1956), 월남전쟁(1965-1975), 소련의 아프가니스탄 침공(1979), 미국의 그레나다 및 파나마 침공 (1983, 1989)등에 직면하여 안보이사회는 거의 무력증마저 나타냈다.

0138

4. "평화 단결" 결의와 "평화유지군"

위와 같은 상황에 직면한 주요 회원국 대표들은 국제평화 유지를 위한 효과적인 대안을 강구하게 되었는 바, 그 주요 산물로는 "평화단결" 결의와 "평화유지군"의 창출을 들 수 있을 것이다.

1950년 6월 북한의 무력남침에 대처하여 안보이사회의 신속한 결의 로써 유엔으로서는 처음으로 침략자에 대한 군사적 행동을 취할 수 있었다. 이러한 군사적 조치가 가능하였던 것은 소련이 자유중국의 대표권에 항의 하여 안보이사회 회의에 불참한데 따른 것임은 주지의 사실이다. 그러나 1950년 8월 소련대표가 안보이사회 회의에 복귀한 후로는 냉전적 성격의 안건 처리가 어렵게 되자 미국은 평화유지에 관한 안보이사회의 기능을 총회가 대신하여 다룰 수 있는 내용의 결의안을 총회에 상정하여 소련권의 반대를 극복하여 통과시켰다. 동 결의(377호 : 1950)는 (1) 안보이사회가 국제평화와 안전의 유지에 대하여 그 주요책임을 수행하지 못할 경우 총회가 평화의 침해 또는 침략행위에 대하여 무력사용을 포함한 집단적 조치 권고, (2) 평화감시위 설치, (3) 회원국 군대 일부의 유엔 제공, (4) 24시간내 긴급특별총회 소집등을 내용으로 하고 있었다. 이 개혁적인 결의에 따라 1956년 스에즈 운하위기때부터 1967년 중동전쟁시까지 수회에 걸쳐 긴급특별 총회가 소집된 바 있었으나, 동 결의가 안보이사회의 권한을 침해하였다는 비난을 면치 못하였다.

헌장 제 43조에서 규정된 유엔상비군 설치를 위한 안보이사회 상임 이사국간의 협의가 상호 이해대립으로 인하여 정체되고 있던중 1948년 제1차 중동전쟁(이스라엘 대 아랍국)이 발발하였다. 그후 성립된 휴전을 감시하기 위하여 유엔 휴전감시기구가 설치되었는 바, 이는 유엔평화유지군 활동의 효시가 되었다. 유엔의 본격적인 평화유지군 활동은 1956년 제 2차 중동전쟁

0139

(이스라엘 대 이집트)때였다. 함마숄드 유엔사무총장은 피어슨 카나다 외무장관의 제의를 수락하여 10개국 총 6,000명의 병력으로 편성된 군대를 중동지역에 파견하여 정전과 철수를 성공적으로 수행케 함으로써 평가를 받았다. 유엔은 지난 40여년간 18개 분쟁지역에서 평화유지 활동을 수행하여 왔고, 50여개국으로부터 연 50여만명이 참여한 국제평화 증진 실적을 인정받아 1988년에는 노벨 평화상을 받았다. 평화유지군은 현재도 8개 지역에서 활동을 계속하고 있다. 주3)

유엔헌장 제정시 예견하지 못하였던 평화유지군의 활동도 안보이사회 강대국간 대립의 지속을 극복하기 위한 임기응변적 조치이기는 하였으나 당시의 국제정세에 적응하는 실제적인 대책이었다고 인정되었다. 그러나 다년간의 경험을 고찰하였을때 평화유지군의 활동은 안보이사회의 승인으로 부터 실제 파병에 이르기까지의 매번 번거롭고 시일이 많이 소요되는 절차 과정, 기본적으로 임시방편적인 성격, 급변하는 사태 대처에 실기할 가능성과 일단 파견된 평화유지군의 주둔 대체로 장기화됨으로써 야기되는 재정적 부담 증가등은 평화유지군의 단점으로 지적되고 있다.

5. 보편적 집단 안보체제

유엔헌장은 상기한 바와 같이 제 1조에서 국제평화에 대한 위협과 침략행위에 대하여 집단적 조치를 취할 것등과 제 2조에서는 모든 회원국이 국제관계에 있어서 무력의 위협 또는 사용을 자제할 것등을 규정하고 있다. 또한 제 24군 규정에 따라 회원국은 안보이사회의 결정을 수락하고 이행할 의무를 진다. 이와 같이 유엔회원국 전체가 분쟁의 방지, 억압 및 상호 안전 조치에 동참하는 보편적 집단 안보체제는 "평화는 불가분하다"는 개념에 입각하여 있으며, NATO 또는 Warsaw Pact 같은 선별적, 지역적 군사 동맹체제와는 구별된다. 주4)

0140

유연현장 규정에도 불구하고 보편적 집단 안보체제가 아직 확립되지
못한 주요 원인으로는 헌장이 규정한 유연 상비군이 설치되지 못한 미비점,
다수의 지역분쟁에 효과적으로 대응하지못한 실정, 한국전쟁외에는 실제로
집단 군사적 행동을 실행하지 못한 사실등을 들 수 있다. 무엇보다도 5개
상임이사국간의 이해 상충으로 주요분쟁 해결에 공동보조를 취할 수 없었던
것이 가장 큰 원인이라고 할 수 있다.

그러나 1988년부터 국제환경은 긴장이 완화되고 화해와 협력이 증진
되는 추세를 보여 왔다. 1988년 9월 안보이사회 상임 5개국 외무장관들은
성명을 통하여 지역분쟁 해결을 위한 유연의 적극적인 관여를 환영하였다.
또한 미.소 양국은 상기와 같이 1989년에 이어 1990년 제 45차 유연총회
에서도 협력자세를 더욱 명백히 하는 조치로 "변화된 세계에서의 평화와
안전을 위한 책임 "이라는 공동성명을 발표하였다. 이 성명에서 양국 외무
장관은 국제평화와 안전을 증진하기 위한 유연의 역할이 강화되도록 모든
회원국과의 협력을 다짐하였다. 냉전의 종식이 새로운 국제질서를 예고하고
있다. 더우기 금번 페르샤만 위기는 냉전종식후 강대국간의 협력의지에
대한 첫시험이 되고 있는 바, 현재 (11월 중순)까지는 이 위기에 대처함에
있어서 안보이사회는 강력한 결집력을 과시하였다. 위기 극복에 강대국간의
수평적 협력 지속이 관건이다. 이와 같이 호전된 유연환경과 강대국간의
협조관계를 감안할때 이라크의 쿠웨이트 침공, 합병은 유연의 보편성 집단
안보체제의 확립에 기여할 수 있는 중요한 계기를 제공하고 있다고 하겠다.
이러한 계기를 활용함이 바람직하다. 이를 위해 안보이사회가 취할 수 있는
조치로 다음과 같은 내용의 결의안을 검토할 수 있을 것이다.

0141

첫째, 사우디아라비아에 파견된 다국적군에 유연기 사용권을 부여한다. 이는 한국전쟁때 선례가 있으며, 다국적군에게 "유연연합군"으로서 파견의 합법성과 정통성을 부여할 것이다. 이와 같은 결의는 이라크에 대한 가중된 압력으로 작용할 수 있을 것이다.

둘째, 안보이사회 결의 660호 이행을 목적으로 유연기를 사용하는 다국적군에게 무력사용을 한정적으로 엄격한 조건하에 승인한다. 이는 최후의 선택인 바 신중을 기해야 할 것이고, 소련, 프랑스, 중국등의 협조 확보와 아울러 미국군의 파견 목적과의 조정 및 합의가 긴요할 것이다.주5)

셋째, 헌장 제 43조가 규정한 유연상비군 결성을 위한 협정체결을 촉구한다. 유연 상비군 조직은 군사 참모위원회의 기능을 재활하는데도 기여할 것이다. 냉전의 종식 결과로 강대국의 유연상비군용 병력과 장비 제공 가능성이 증대할 것이다.

넷째, 유연사무총장의 권한을 강화한다. 헌장 제 99조에 따라 사무총장은 국제평화와 안전의 유지를 위협하는 사태에 대하여 안보이사회의 주의를 환기할 수 있는 바, 사무총장의 이와 같은 활동결과로 사태 악화를 예방할 수 있다. 사무총장은 이러한 예방 외교를 위하여 유연의 신속한 정보수집 및 분석 능력 강화의 필요를 강조해 오고 있다. 주6) 유연은 분쟁의 평화적 해결을 위한 사무총장의 영향력 있는 중재를 포함하여 노력을 조장할 수 있어야 한다.

페르샤만 사태의 평화적 해결을 계속 거부하는 이라크에 대한 다국적군의 군사적 행동은 다수의 인명피해와 막대한 재산의 손실은 물론 유가의 폭등 으로 인한 세계 경제의 혼란, 전후 중동지역 정세의 계속 불안 및 세계평화 위협 가능성등을 초래할 중대한 위협이 예견된다. 그러므로 페르샤만 위기가 유연을 통하여 평화적 방법으로 극복되도록 다각적 노력을 경주하여야 할 것이며, 유연사무총장은 사우디 및 인근해역에 포진하고 있는 다국적군이 이라크에 대하여 안보이사회의 승인을 받지 않은 독자적인 군사행동을 개시 하지 못하도록 다국적군측과 고섭하여야 할 것이다.

0142

　　　　상기 첫째 및 둘째의 조치 방안도 사태를 가급적 조기에 해결할 목적
으로 최후 통첩격인 압력수단으로 활용할 수 있을 것이다. 유엔이 안보
이사회에서의 강대국간 협력을 통하여 페르샤만 사태를 수습하게 된다면,
인접한 주권 독립국가에 대한 무력침공과 같은 평화 파괴행위 재발을 억지
하는데 공헌하게 될 것이고, 나아가서 유엔의 보편적 집단안전보장체제의
확립을위한 토대를 구축할 수 있을 것으로 본다.　　　　　　끝.

외교문서 비밀해제: 걸프 사태 18

걸프 사태 유엔안전보장이사회 동향 1

초판인쇄 2024년 03월 15일
초판발행 2024년 03월 15일

지은이 한국학술정보(주)
펴낸이 채종준
펴낸곳 한국학술정보(주)
주 소 경기도 파주시 회동길 230(문발동)
전 화 031-908-3181(대표)
팩 스 031-908-3189
홈페이지 http://ebook.kstudy.com
E-mail 출판사업부 publish@kstudy.com
등 록 제일산-115호(2000. 6. 19)

ISBN 979-11-6983-978-5 94340
      979-11-6983-960-0 94340 (set)